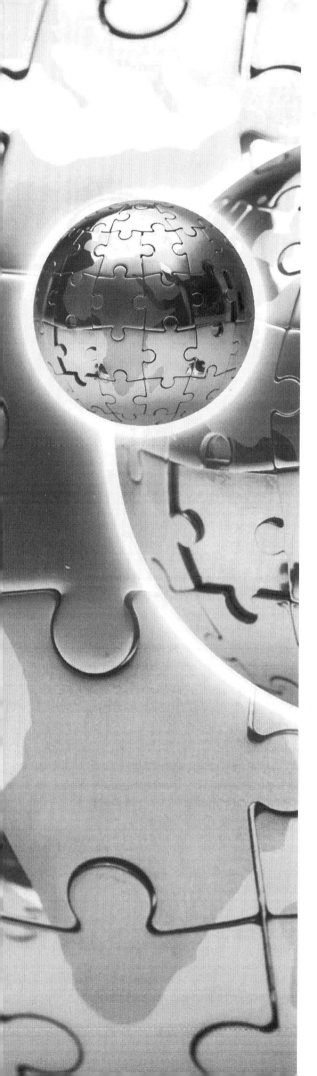

GW00792249

Investment Operations Certificate

Managing
Cyber-Security

Edition 3, October 2018

This learning manual relates to syllabus
version 3.0 and will cover exams from
11 January 2019 to 10 January 2021

APPROVED WORKBOOK

Welcome to the Chartered Institute for Securities & Investment's Managing Cyber-Security study material.

This workbook has been written to prepare you for the Chartered Institute for Securities & Investment's Managing Cyber-Security examination.

Published by:
Chartered Institute for Securities & Investment
© Chartered Institute for Securities & Investment 2018
20 Fenchurch Street
London
EC3M 3BY
Tel: +44 20 7645 0600
Fax: +44 20 7645 0601

Email: customersupport@cisi.org
www.cisi.org/qualifications

Author:
Mark Johnson

Reviewers:
Michael Imeson
Irwin Spilka

This is an educational workbook only and the Chartered Institute for Securities & Investment accepts no responsibility for persons undertaking trading or investments in whatever form.

While every effort has been made to ensure its accuracy, no responsibility for loss occasioned to any person acting or refraining from action as a result of any material in this publication can be accepted by the publisher or authors.

A learning map, which contains the full syllabus, appears at the end of this workbook. The syllabus can also be viewed on cisi.org and is also available by contacting the Customer Support Centre on +44 20 7645 0777. Please note that the examination is based upon the syllabus. Candidates are reminded to check the Candidate Update area details (cisi.org/candidateupdate) on a regular basis for updates as a result of industry change(s) that could affect their examination.

The questions contained in this workbook are designed as an aid to revision of different areas of the syllabus and to help you consolidate your learning chapter by chapter.

Learning workbook version: 3.1 (October 2018)

Learning and Professional Development with the CISI

The Chartered Institute for Securities & Investment is the leading professional body for those who work in, or aspire to work in, the investment sector, and we are passionately committed to enhancing knowledge, skills and integrity – the three pillars of professionalism at the heart of our Chartered body.

CISI examinations are used extensively by firms to meet the requirements of government regulators. Besides the regulators in the UK, where the CISI head office is based, CISI examinations are recognised by a wide range of governments and their regulators, from Singapore to Dubai and the US. Around 50,000 examinations are taken each year, and it is compulsory for candidates to use CISI learning workbooks to prepare for CISI examinations so that they have the best chance of success. Our learning workbooks are normally revised every year by experts who themselves work in the industry and also by our Accredited Training Partners, who offer training and elearning to help prepare candidates for the examinations. Information for candidates is also posted on a special area of our website: cisi.org/candidateupdate.

This learning workbook not only provides a thorough preparation for the examination it refers to, it is also a valuable desktop reference for practitioners, and studying from it counts towards your Continuing Professional Development (CPD). Mock examination papers, for most of our titles, will be made available on our website, as an additional revision tool.

CISI examination candidates are automatically registered, without additional charge, as student members for one year (should they not be members of the CISI already), and this enables you to use a vast range of online resources, including CISI TV, free of any additional charge. The CISI has more than 40,000 members, and nearly half of them have already completed relevant qualifications and transferred to a core membership grade. You will find more information about the next steps for this at the end of this workbook.

The Background and Nature of Information Security and Cybercrime . .   1   **1**

The Legislative Environment   81   **2**

The Public-Private Interface in Combating Cybercrime.   109   **3**

Cybercrime and the Financial Services Industry   141   **4**

Combating Cybercrime   173   **5**

Trends in Economic Crime Compliance   225   **6**

Glossary   243

Multiple Choice Questions.   253

Syllabus Learning Map.   273

It is estimated that this manual will require approximately 80 hours of study time.

What next?
See the back of this book for details of CISI membership.

Need more support to pass your exam?
See our section on Accredited Training Partners.

Want to leave feedback?
Please email your comments to learningresources@cisi.org

Before you open Chapter 1

It's free

We love a book! ...but don't forget you have been sent a link to an ebook, which gives you a range of tools to help you study for this qualification

Depending on the individual subject being studied and your device, your ebook may include features such as:

Watch video clips related to your syllabus

Read aloud function*

Adjustable text size allows you to read comfortably on any device*

Pop-up definitions

Highlight, bookmark and make annotations digitally*

Images, tables and animated graphs

Links to relevant websites

End of chapter questions and interactive multiple choice questions

* These features are device dependent. Please consult your manufacturers guidelines for compatibility

CISI
CHARTERED INSTITUTE FOR SECURITIES & INVESTMENT

Find out more at cisi.org/ebooks

The use of online videos and voice functions allowed me to study at home and on the go, which helped me make more use of my time. I would recommend this as a study aid as it accommodates a variety of learning styles.

Billy Snowdon, Team Leader, Brewin Dolphin

Chapter One

The Background and Nature of Information Security and Cybercrime

1.	Definitions	3
2.	Distinctions	21
3.	Fundamental Issues	27
4.	Technical Cybercrime Attacks	33
5.	The Human Firewall	66

This syllabus area will provide approximately 12 of the 50 examination questions

The only truly secure system is one that is powered off, cast in a block of concrete and sealed in a lead-lined room with armed guards. Dr. Eugene Spafford, Professor in Computer Science, Purdue University

1. Definitions

Not only are the new threats to information security more diverse, but they are increasing in complexity and many are launched in a co-ordinated fashion by attackers numbering in the thousands. Social media, exploit kits and free online training tools are all being used to construct an advanced, diffuse attack model, sometimes with political or environmental drivers that can target major concerns at will. Attacks in mid-2016 on the SWIFT banking network and earlier attacks on the US financial services sector in 2012 illustrate this new reality, leading the then US President, Barrack Obama, and other senior figures to speak publicly about a cyber-security threat to the global economic system, or of a *Cyber Pearl Harbor*, as Leon Panetta, then US Secretary of Defence, put it at the time of the 2012 attacks.

1.1   The Internet and the World Wide Web (WWW)

Learning Objective

1.1.1   Know the difference between the internet and the World Wide Web

There is often confusion about what the **internet** is and how it relates to the **World Wide Web (WWW)**. Many of us use these terms interchangeably, but they are in fact two completely different technologies.

1.1.1   The Internet

The internet is a network of networks; a system of interconnected computer networks that span the globe. All of these networks use a standard set of rules called protocols. These protocols allow the linking of billions of devices worldwide.

The internet is home to millions of networks, including private, public, academic, business and government networks of local and even global scope. The physical connections are provided by a wide range of technologies: satellite, wireless, copper wire and optical fibre cables.

1.1.2   The World Wide Web (WWW)

The network of networks known as the internet supports, in turn, a very wide range of resources and services. Perhaps the best-known is the web of interlinked hypertext documents and applications that make up the WWW. In addition, the internet supports the infrastructure to offer email services and peer-to-peer networking for file sharing and telephony.

1.1.3 Governance of the Internet

The internet operates without centralised governance, both in terms of its technology and limitations and in terms of the policies governing its access and usage. Each of the internet's constituent networks sets its own policies.

Key exceptions to this general lack of centralisation are the mechanisms for defining names on the internet, specifically the internet protocol (IP) address space and the **domain name system (DNS)**. These are directed by a maintainer organisation, the Internet Corporation for Assigned Names and Numbers (ICANN).

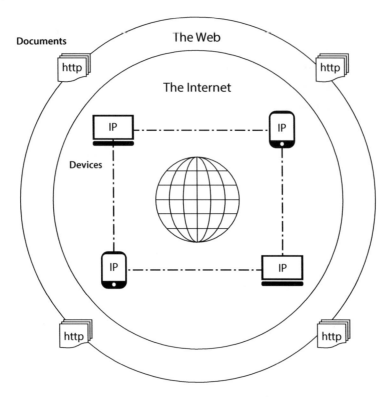

Figure 1: The Internet and the World Wide Web

The technical specification and standardisation of the core internet protocols is carried out by the Internet Engineering Task Force (IETF), a not-for-profit organisation made up of international participants. Anyone may associate with the IETF by providing technical expertise.

1.2   The Deep Web and the Darknet

Learning Objective

1.1.2   Know the meaning of: the Deep Web; the Darknet

The phrases 'Deep Web' and 'Darknet' refer to two little understood but important aspects of the internet and the WWW. While the WWW comprises interlinked hypertext documents and pages that are capable of being indexed by conventional search engines (eg, Google), most data held online does not sit in that surface web. About 90% of all online data sits in what is known as the Deep Web, and a small proportion is hidden away in the Darknet which is home to a variety of unpleasant characters.

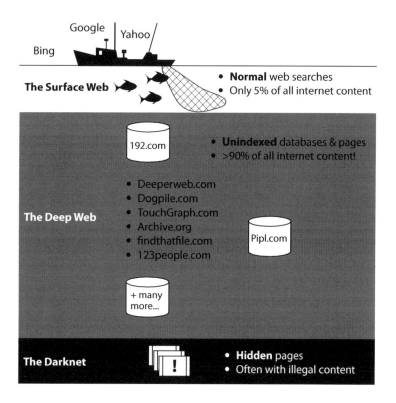

Figure 2: The Deep Web and the Darknet

1.2.1   The Deep Web

The **Deep Web** is the portion of online content that is not indexed by standard search engines, generally because it sits in large databases that search engines cannot easily reach. The data may be public but registration, username and password access may be required.

Examples of important Deep Web resources include numerous academic resources, government databases such as criminal records, registers of births and deaths, motor vehicle registrations, and Companies House records.

About 96% of all data stored online is believed to reside in the Deep Web, more than eight Zettabytes in total. The surface web itself (just under 4% of online content) comprises six billion separate web pages, so the size of the Deep Web is truly enormous.

A number of Deep Web search engine services have developed over the last few years. One of the most popular of these is 192.com and another is Pipl.com, which is more US focused.

Mike Bergman, founder of BrightPlanet, who is often credited with coining the phrase 'Deep Web', is reported as saying that searching on the internet today can be compared to dragging a net across the surface of the ocean; a great deal may be caught in the net but there is a wealth of information that lies much deeper and is therefore missed. The level of use of personal virtual private network (VPN) services is unclear but one solution provider, Hotspot Shield (www.hsselite.com), claims to have delivered its tool via download 250 million times. Some commentators have expressed the opinion that such a large number of downloads can only be indicative of illicit or illegal use, but this remains conjecture.

1.2.2   The Darknet

The **Darknet** or **Dark Web** is effectively a subsection of the Deep Web. It consists of an estimated 10,000 proxy servers that support anonymous, encrypted communications. Special software called The Onion Router (TOR) Project is needed in order to access this portion of the web. In these dark spaces, people who wish to avoid detection or surveillance, such as journalists or bloggers living in hostile regimes, and users who are engaged in criminal activities, such as trafficking, offences against children, illegal pornography, narcotics and arms dealing, conduct their business with seeming impunity.

Estimates vary, but it seems likely that about 50% of all Darknet activities are illegal. The preferred financial instrument in the Darknet is Bitcoin, an anonymous crypto-currency.

1.2.3   Silk Road and Other Darknet Markets

One of the most infamous examples of a Darknet site was **Silk Road**, an online black market, best known as a platform for selling illegal drugs. It was operated as a hidden service through the use of the free application called TOR, which provided anonymity on the internet.

The site was launched early in 2011 and ran until 2013 when it was shut down by the US Federal Bureau of Investigations (FBI). The FBI arrested Ross William Ulbricht and charged him with being the founder of the site. Ulbricht operated under the pseudonym Dread Pirate Roberts. Ulbricht has since been convicted of related offences.

By March 2013, Silk Road was offering 10,000 separate products for sale by vendors. Of these, 70% were illegal narcotics grouped under various headings, including stimulants, psychedelics, prescription, precursors, other, opioids, ecstasy, cannabis and steroids. The site's terms of service prohibited the sale of certain items, such as child pornography, stolen credit cards, assassination services and weapons of any type.

AlphaBay Market was another popular Darknet market that operated for several years until July 2017, when it was shut down by international law-enforcement action. This action was one aspect of 'Operation Bayonet', a coordinated law-enforcement response to the most harmful aspects of the Darknet, led by agencies in countries including the United States, Canada and Thailand. Other Darknet services shut down in the same operation included the Hansa Market.

The alleged founder of AlphaBay Market, Alexandre Cazes, a Canadian citizen, was found dead in his cell in Thailand several days after his arrest, after a suspected suicide.

The Armory, a Black Market sister site, offered weapons for sale during 2012 but was shut down due to a lack of consumer demand, but other sites offering narcotics, weapons, counterfeit currency and documents, and even hacking services, abound.

1.2.4 Statistics

For reasons that should be obvious to most, arriving at authoritative cybercrime statistics is not an exact science. Many major cyber incidents, and possibly most, go unreported. Where reports are made, many organisations minimise the impact of events in order to similarly minimise brand damage or the impact on share prices.

As a necessary consequence most of the figures supplied in this workbook are best estimates. These are based on a combination of the statistics provided in published reports and industry surveys and the author's three decades' experience in managing and investigating high-tech crime incidents.

In the main, therefore, the CISI has avoided posing exam questions based on these statistics and has instead focused on candidates' underlying grasp of the related causes, controls and other effects.

1.3 Cloud Computing

Learning Objective

1.1.3 Know the meaning of the term 'cloud computing'

The cloud is another widely used term that many people have heard of but few fully grasp. What is it?

The cloud is nothing more than computing technology and infrastructure hosted on the internet. For example, if you put pictures into **iCloud** or **Dropbox**, you are using the cloud. If you upload videos to YouTube, you are using the cloud. If you post status updates on Facebook to be read by your friends, you are using the cloud.

When you use the cloud, you are substituting the storage technology available at your fingertips, either on your computer or on backup drives, with storage technology located somewhere on the internet. You are putting your data online and potentially using online applications to process that data instead of using applications that you hold locally.

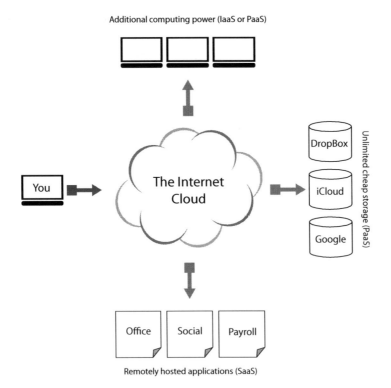

Additional computing power (IaaS or PaaS)

Unlimited cheap storage (PaaS)

Remotely hosted applications (SaaS)

Figure 3: The Cloud

The huge advantage of cloud services is that the providers are able to achieve tremendous economies of scale by offering centralised shared resources. If every one of us opted to purchase our own additional storage we would be charged the premium rate for each device, but when we allow an online service provider to acquire that storage for us collectively, the prices fall substantially because of the volume of the purchase.

These economies of scale allow cloud service providers to offer their corporate and consumer clients cost-effective solutions very rapidly. It is this cost effectiveness that has made **cloud computing** so popular.

However, the practice of sending corporate data and personal data to the cloud, as well as storing and processing it there, introduces three potential risks:

- You may not be able to access your cloud data should internet services go down.
- Others may be able to access your data in the cloud because of security failures on the part of service providers.
- As it passes across a network between the user and the cloud, the security of data may constitute the primary risk.

1.4   Software as a Service (SaaS), Platform as a Service (PaaS) and Infrastructure as a Service (IaaS)

Learning Objective

1.1.4   Understand the meaning of: Software as a Service (SaaS); Platform as a Service (PaaS); Infrastructure as a Service (IaaS)

There are three classes of cloud service:

1. **Software as a Service (SaaS)** – software applications are supplied remotely by the cloud service provider. Users login across the internet and make use of the third-party application without having to own a licence, although fees for these services may still be payable.
2. **Platform as a Service (PaaS)** – users rent space on remote computing platforms, either to store data or to run applications or both. Some of these services are provided free of charge to the end user (as is the case with Dropbox) but the platform is provided in an operational state with the operating system installed and running.
3. **Infrastructure as a Service (IaaS)** – infrastructure such as computing platforms is provided remotely and in a centralised fashion but the user installs and manages the operating system and applications remotely.

The US National Institute of Standards and Technology (NIST) lists five essential characteristics of cloud computing:

1. **On-demand self-service** – a consumer can automatically and unilaterally obtain computing capabilities as required, such as server time and network storage, without the need for human interaction with each service provider.
2. **Broad network access** – capabilities are available over the network and accessed through standard mechanisms that promote use by heterogeneous thin or thick client platforms (eg, mobile phones, tablets, laptops and workstations).
3. **Resource pooling** – the provider's computing resources are pooled to serve multiple consumers using a multi-tenant model, with different physical and virtual resources, dynamically assigned and reassigned according to consumer demand.
4. **Rapid elasticity** – capabilities can be elastically provisioned and released, in some cases automatically, to scale rapidly outward and inward, commensurate with demand. To the consumer/ end user, the capabilities available for provisioning often appear unlimited and can be appropriated in any quantity at any time.
5. **Measured service** – cloud systems automatically control and optimise resource use by leveraging a metering capability at some level of abstraction appropriate to the type of service (eg, storage, processing, bandwidth and active user accounts). Resource usage can be monitored, controlled and reported, providing transparency for both the provider and consumer of the utilised service.

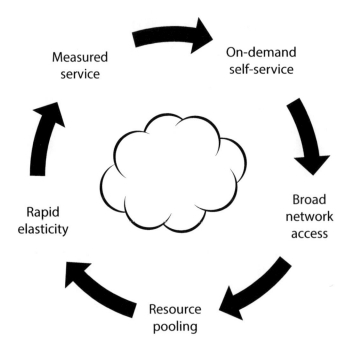

Figure 4: Essential Cloud Characteristics

1.4.1   Deployment Models

In addition to the three cloud models described above, there are a range of service deployment options and you will no doubt have heard some of these phrases used in the course of business conversations.

The main categories are:

- **private cloud**
- **public cloud**
- **hybrid cloud**
- **community cloud**.

Private Cloud

Private cloud is cloud infrastructure operated exclusively for a single organisation, whether managed locally or by a third party, and is situated either internally or externally.

Public Cloud

In a public cloud the services are delivered over a network that is open for public use. Public cloud services are often free.

Hybrid Cloud

Hybrid cloud is a combination of two or more cloud services (which may be private, community or public). The services remain distinct but operate in conjunction with each other.

Community Cloud

A community cloud shares infrastructure and services between several organisations from a specific community with common concerns, eg, security, compliance, jurisdiction.

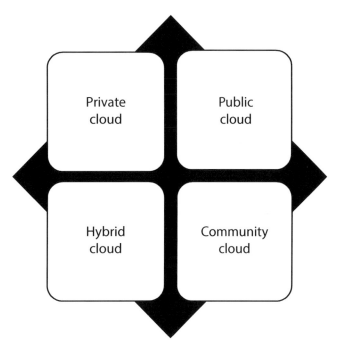

Figure 5: Primary Cloud Deployment Models

1.4.2   Security Concerns

As suggested in section 1.3, the cloud computing model introduces a number of security concerns and these should be addressed by cloud service providers, as well as being audited and confirmed by organisations with responsibility for securing the data that is going online.

Conceptually at least, cloud service providers can access data that is stored on their sites, unless such data is encrypted or otherwise secured. The service provider could accidentally or deliberately alter information, insert new information or even delete information. In such an event, unless the client organisation has up-to-date backups, there could be serious business continuity risks.

In the era of the war on terror, any data hosted in another jurisdiction may well be subject to inspection by foreign governments and law enforcement. If the data in question is subject to data protection regulation in the home country, data custodians may find themselves being held liable for data breaches. Therefore, establishing exactly what data is being stored, as well as where and under what conditions, is an essential first step in establishing secure cloud services deployment.

According to the Cloud Security Alliance, the top three threats faced by organisations with deployments in the cloud are:

1. insecure interfaces and **application programme interfaces** (APIs) (29% of cases)
2. data loss and leakage (25% of cases)
3. hardware failure (10% of cases).

Additional risks arise when different cloud service users share the same cloud platform; for example, there is a potential for one user to penetrate the services and data of another user, again raising issues in terms of privacy and data protection, not to mention corporate security and market abuse.

Hackers are reportedly spending significant time and effort penetrating the cloud. If a hacker could penetrate a large shared cloud platform, he or she could potentially access or take control of thousands of customers' accounts and/or data, causing huge issues for both the service provider and its clients.

In general, physical control of the computer equipment (ie, private cloud) is regarded as a more secure approach than public cloud. Companies which put sensitive data into Dropbox folders, for example, may be exposing themselves to significant levels of risk although they also face lower costs. Ironically, this realisation has led public cloud suppliers to invest more in security, so it is difficult to predict what the future of the cloud will look like.

1.5   Other Important Concepts

Learning Objective

1.1.5   Know the meaning of: database structure; internet protocol (IP) addressing versions 4 and 6; domain name servers; routers and gateways; data packets

1.5.1   Database Structure

A **database** is normally a collection of structured data. Unstructured data is information that is relatively difficult to classify, for example the content of emails, tweets or Facebook posts. While such data is also stored, its elements cannot be organised and linked without advanced processing having taken place, such as deriving sentiment from keywords in an unstructured string of data.

Database users manage databases through the use of a database management system (DBMS), ie, software applications that sit between the user and the database and also link into other applications or data sources.

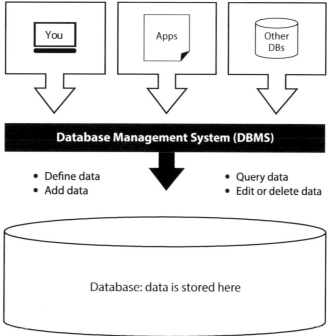

People, applications and other databases may all need to add or read (query) information stored in a database

Figure 6: Database Management

A DBMS supports the definition of the database itself and its creation, as well as the querying of the database's content by users or third-party applications, the updating of the database and general administration of the database. Popular DBMS systems include MySQL, PostgreSQL, Microsoft SQL Server, Oracle, Sybase and IBM DB2.

Each database is unique because databases are designed to reflect the information they will hold and the business processes they will support. Database designers start by examining the business in detail, determining the various data sources and formats, as well as the data volumes and defining the primary needs of users in order to build a structure that supports the business.

Normalisation

A key part of database design is known as **normalisation**. This is the task of ensuring that each data element appears only once within a database and is not duplicated in different locations. By normalising the data, database administrators ensure that any changes (insertions, updates and deletions) to a particular value only occur once in one location. This avoids given data elements having different values across the database and thus causing problems for the business. It also keeps the database as small as possible by eliminating duplication.

Relational Databases

The **relational database** model is the most popular in use in many organisations and is represented by the structured query language (SQL).

Relational databases are arranged in an organised fashion, typically as a collection of tables. This allows every field in the data to be assigned a particular property or type. The most common example of such tables are the Excel tables with which most readers will be very familiar. Data is arranged in columns and rows and while the properties of each cell might differ, the classification of each cell is clear.

The particular management system that governs the operation of a relational database is often known as a relational database management system (RDBMS).

Because many databases hold large volume of sensitive personal and financial data, they are often a target of hackers and internal fraudsters. Database security is therefore a key part of any cyber-security management programme.

1.5.2 Internet Protocol (IP) Addressing Versions 4 and 6

In section 1.1.1, we touched on the role of the transmission control protocol/internet protocol (TCP/IP) in providing a standardised framework for communications across the globalised network of networks that is the internet. There are in fact two types of internet protocol addressing (IP address) currently in use around the world.

IP Version 4 (IPv4)

IP version 4 was the earliest operational form of internet addressing. Its principal function is to allow data packets to travel across network boundaries and successfully arrive at a given network address at some distant point. Without such addressing, the internet would not function, in the same way that traditional postal systems would not function in the absence of house numbers, street names and postal codes.

However, because of the format of IP v4 addresses and the huge growth in internet usage, available IP v4 address ranges began to run out several years ago.

IP Version 6 (IPv6)

IP version 6 addresses were introduced primarily in order to increase the number of available addresses on the network. While IPv4 uses a 32-bit format, IPv6 addresses are 128-bits in length.

While IPv4 supported approximately 4.3 billion addresses, IPv6 supports 7.9 x 1028 times as many addresses as its predecessor. This is a vast increase in the number of available addresses and it seems unlikely that we will ever exhaust this new supply.

Features of IPv6 also improve the efficiency of routing and other facets of the internet's operations – the details of these features are beyond the scope of this workbook.

1.5.3 Data Packets

Imagine that you wanted to send the text of a book you have written to a publisher but the postal system would not allow you to send more than two or three pages in any one envelope. How would you send the manuscript?

You would probably start by breaking your manuscript down into two- or three-page segments. You could put each of these in a separate envelope and post it to the publisher's address. What additional issues might you need to consider in this scenario?

Firstly, you would want to be sure that the publisher reassembled the manuscript in the correct order, regardless of the order in which they opened the envelopes. So, you might choose to mark each envelope with a serial number or sequence number to indicate where it fits within the stream of envelopes you are posting.

You would also want to be sure that all your envelopes arrive on the same desk and are dealt with by the same person so that you do not have chapter 1 sitting in one part of the publisher's organisation and chapter 2 in another. So, when you address the envelope, you might choose to address it to a particular person within the publisher's organisation, rather than just to the publisher's domain.

Even with these precautions it might cross your mind that other authors will be doing exactly the same thing as you and that the person to whom you are addressing your envelopes could be receiving dozens of envelopes from other writers. Therefore, you would want to clearly mark your communication as coming from you.

The next thought you might have is that you need to be sure that the publisher knows that they have received all the envelopes and that they have received the final envelope and can now proceed to read the manuscript without waiting for a further delivery. You could achieve this by informing them about how many envelopes they should expect and you could confirm the identity of the final envelope by marking it clearly with the word 'final'.

Once the publisher has reassembled and read the manuscript, you would hope that they would get back in touch with you, so you would no doubt include the return address in the correspondence.

When data is passed across a network, similar challenges and issues arise. Most networks are shared by numerous devices and the volume of data passing through them can be very large. If one device could dominate the network and use all of its capacity in order to send a large document or file as a continuous stream of bits, none of the other devices on the network would be able to send or receive information until that dominant device had finished its session. In general, this would not be an efficient way to provide network services.

For devices to share the finite capacity of any network, the data they send is broken down into much smaller packets, like digital envelopes, and these packets stream across the network separately, each one sitting between packets going from other devices to different destinations.

Each of these network packets includes a header that contains all the information necessary for the receiving device to do exactly what your publisher was doing to reassemble any message or file and present it to a user or application in its complete format.

This type of communication using data 'packets' is referred to as packet data and it is the method of communication used by the internet and most other modern networks.

1.5.4   Routers and Gateways

Routers

The internet and its component networks are physically massive, while the number of packets being passed through its networks is mind-boggling. If we were to attempt to simply connect every computer to the network without any sort of interposed management system, there would be chaos.

Just like traffic lights at road junctions, which manage the flow of traffic across the road grid, special devices are needed to manage the flows of data across these networks. The most important of these devices are the network routers.

Routers provide a service that is exactly as it sounds – they route **data packets** between computers on a network. Routers do this by reading the details of the desired address which the sender has placed within the packet header and then looking up the location of that address by referring to an external database. Once they know where the packet is supposed to go, they send it via an appropriate route, based on routing tables and defined policies.

You can think of routers as postmen. They collect packets from senders and deliver packets to receivers.

Gateways

We saw in section 1.1.1, the internet is a network of networks rather than a single, homogenous network. To illustrate this, imagine that you have just moved into a new house and you want to connect four laptops belonging to each of your family members, a games console and your private cloud storage box to the internet via a single Wi-Fi route that has been given to you by your telecoms provider.

The Wi-Fi network that now exists within your home, to which all of your devices are connected, is a network in its own right. Even without an internet connection you can access your local private cloud storage and share files between the devices on your home network. When you want to connect to the internet your router acts as a gateway between your home network and the outside network, which in turn passes through at least one more gateway in your telecom service provider's network before it reaches the global internet.

Therefore, gateways can either be dedicated devices fulfilling just that function, or they can be other devices such as routers that have an additional gateway function. In fact, any PC or server can also act as a gateway.

In a corporate setting, gateway servers frequently power **firewall** and other functions that manage the flow of data and protect the enterprise security from external attacks.

1.5.5   Domain Name Servers (DNSs)

If routers are our internet postmen, domain name servers (DNSs) are our post offices. As you will recall, packets are delivered on the internet to IP addresses. But IP addresses are numeric values and very few human beings could hope to walk around with a list of IP addresses in their heads.

We use text names, such as www.cisi.org, to identify the domains we wish to visit on the internet. Likewise, we generally use text-based email addresses for the same reason; our brains can accommodate a fairly long list of such addresses and even where we have forgotten them we can instantly recognise them at a glance and then type them on our keyboards, which is certainly not the case with an IP address.

So, if we enter a text-based name as the address for an email or website, our internet postmen (the routers) need to ask someone or something to translate that name into an IP address. This is the primary function of the domain name servers; they serve up IP addresses in exchange for domain names and then help to execute the necessary routing.

1.5.6 Handshakes

In section 1.1.1 you read about the principle of using a set of protocols, or universally agreed rules, to manage the way in which the internet and other IP networks function. In daily life, at least in most Western societies, it is customary for two people to shake hands when they first meet and possibly when they say goodbye. This is an example of a protocol. Failure to shake hands and say 'good morning', 'good afternoon' or 'nice to meet you', is considered rude and seen as a breach of protocol.

In a similar fashion, devices connected to a network need to shake hands before they can communicate with each other. The handshake tells each device something about the other one and the rules that will govern their communication. Once the handshake is complete, the devices can exchange data across the network.

Certificates and Encryption

Security on the internet depends, to a great extent, on the use of secure encrypted communication links between devices and, for example in the case of databases holding sensitive **information**, encryption of the data held on those devices. This is because the internet is a shared resource. All of those packets being sent across the internet share the physical infrastructure with packets coming and going from billions of other devices situated in every country and in the hands of half of the world's population. If a legitimate packet has a route into a computer system, then malicious packets can potentially follow the same path.

It would be unworkable for all of this information, much of it highly sensitive, to be sent without any security, because anyone on the internet could potentially sniff or read other people's communications and expose their secrets or defraud them.

Encrypted communications are achieved through a system of algorithms and **encryption** and decryption keys, some of which are public and others private. To ensure that the user of a given key is legitimate, **digital certificates** are issued by a certificate authority (CA). Parties involved in an online exchange automatically check the relevant certificates to validate the other party's identity. Your browser software, for example, holds lists of valid certificates for many popular websites.

1.6 Electronic Money

Electronic money is not new, but its uses are increasingly diverse and it is taking new forms, some of which are difficult to comprehend. FCA guidance on electronic money (e-money) generally refers to the European Commission's Electronic Money Directive (EMD) and defines electronic money in the following terms:

*   stored electronically, including magnetically
*   issued upon receipt of funds
*   used for the purposes of making payment transactions (as defined in Regulation 2 of the Payment Services Regulations)
*   accepted as a means of payment by persons other than the issuer, and
*   is not otherwise excluded by the Electronic Money Regulations.

More recently, new digital currencies, including the cryptocurrency Bitcoin, have become increasingly popular. For example, the Silk Road website (mentioned in section 1.2.3) dealt in transactions that almost exclusively used Bitcoin. The growth and evolution of increasingly complex and unregulated electronic forms of payment suggests that control and supervision, particularly with regard to compliance, will also become more complex.

1.6.1   Cryptocurrencies

Cryptocurrencies, such as Bitcoin, allow electronic money systems to be decentralised. Examples include:

*   **Bitcoin** – a peer-to-peer electronic monetary system based on cryptography.
*   **Litecoin** – originally based on the Bitcoin protocol, but intended to improve upon its reported inefficiencies.
*   **Dogecoin** – a Litecoin-based system, intended to reach a broader audience.
*   **Ripple monetary system** – a system based on a trust network.

Because these systems have no central bank backing, they are often criticised for the level of consumer risk they might generate. The price of many cryptocurrencies can fluctuate wildly – sometimes by as much as 50% – because they are arguably less currencies and more a medium for speculation. Some will disagree with this analysis; however, as a quick visit to Darknet sites selling illegal goods and services will demonstrate, there is strong evidence that these forms of payment are widely used by criminals. Transaction monitoring is non-existent in many cases and tracing the movement of funds is extremely difficult.

Other services, such as webmoney.com, use regular credit card payments as the basis for transactions but use a network of peers to transfer value across borders without regulatory oversight. All of these services and currencies are products of the internet, which supports globalisation and commercial freedom, but also accentuates risks.

1.7 Cyber-Security and Information Security

Learning Objective

1.1.7   Understand the definition of information security

1.2.1   Know how cyber security is distinct from information security

Some commentators take the view that cyber-security is merely a trendy term that has no real meaning; instead, it is argued that the correct terminology is information security. There are, however, important differences between information security and cyber-security, as will be explained in the following section.

Information security (or InfoSec) refers to the systems and processes used to protect information from unauthorised access, use, disclosure, disruption, modification, perusal, inspection, recording or destruction.

Cherdantseva and Hilton (2013) define information security in the following terms:

Information security is a multidisciplinary area of study and professional activity which is concerned with the development and implementation of security mechanisms of all available types (technical, organisational, human-oriented and legal) in order to keep information in all its locations (within and outside the organisation's perimeter) and, consequently, information systems, where information is created, processed, stored, transmitted and destroyed, free from threats.

Threats to information and information systems may be categorised and a corresponding security goal may be defined for each category of threats. A set of security goals, identified as a result of a threat analysis, should be revised periodically to ensure its adequacy and conformance with the evolving environment. The currently relevant set of security goals may include: confidentiality, integrity, availability, privacy, authenticity and trustworthiness, non-repudiation, accountability and auditability.

While cyber-security refers to attacks coming via a network such as the internet, **InfoSec** is a general term that is used for information or data in any form. For example, if you were to print out a confidential memo and then leave it behind on the train, it would be an information security breach but not a cyber-security breach.

On the other hand, if you were to flood your organisation's web-facing server with data packets in order to prevent it from functioning, that would constitute a cyber-attack but not an information security breach.

- **InfoSec breaches** – the theft of data in any format.
- **Cyber-security breaches** – any type of attack conducted via a network, including some types of information security breach.

1.7.1 Key Concepts in InfoSec

At the heart of information security is the triangle of confidentiality, integrity and availability.

- **Confidentiality** – information is classified according to its sensitivity and importance; sensitive data is stored in such a way that its confidentiality is assured, ie only those with a need and a right to know are able to view, edit or delete that data.
- **Integrity** – the accuracy and consistency of data is assured over its entire lifecycle; data cannot be modified in an unauthorised or undetected manner.
- **Availability** – information is available when and where it is needed, at the time it is needed. Business processes, computing processes and security controls do not prevent the data from being accessible to authorised users.

Other concepts in information security include:

- **Authenticity** – the data are genuine and have not been interfered with in an unauthorised way.
- **Non-repudiation** – no party to a communication can dishonestly deny having sent or received given data elements.

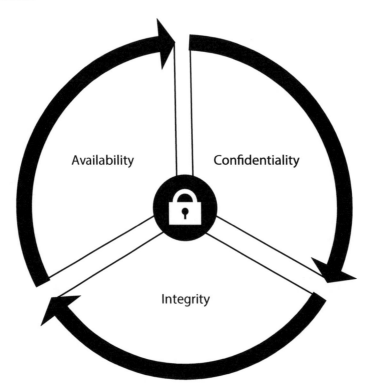

Figure 7: The Information Security Triangle

2. Distinctions

2.1 Cybercrime and Cyber-Enabled Crime

Learning Objective

1.2.2   Understand the distinction between cybercrime and cyber-enabled crime

Cybercrime refers to attacks conducted via a network, regardless of the goal or target. Typical targets include data, systems and the supporting network itself. The phrase '**cyber-enabled crime**' is not precisely defined, but is generally used to describe traditional crimes, for example drug trafficking and money laundering, that have a cyber-component. This might arise when a traditional organised criminal hires hackers to gather intelligence on their next target; a subsequent assassination could be described as having been cyber-enabled.

Just imagine what your world would be like if the internet were disabled in some way. Could your business operate? What about your journey to and from work – how would you make it if there was chaos on the train lines or if the traffic light systems were no longer working? How would food be delivered to your local supermarket? For how long would power and water supplies last? What about communications services? Let's not even think about entertainment and news!

Such a scenario may seem far-fetched, but in reality there are actual threats to the availability and quality of internet services and one of the key threats is cybercrime. Starting on 18 March 2013, Dutch anti-spam company, Spamhaus, began to experience what has since been described as the largest ever recorded **distributed denial of service (DDoS)** attack. A DDoS attack typically floods an organisation's servers with messages or other data, with the result that the organisation loses its ability to communicate online.

The Spamhaus attack was so large that the European Network and Information Security Agency (ENISA) (since renamed the European Union Agency for Network and Information Security) implied in a report on the incident that, had the level of flooding been much greater, it would have had the potential to seriously degrade or even block internet services across the whole of Europe.

Incidents such as this serve to remind us about the extent to which modern society depends on the internet. Cybercrime threatens us all, whether we are its immediate victims or merely affected by the wider collateral damage. We all have a stake in and, therefore, a common duty to come to grips with this topic, to ensure that as individuals and organisations we are creating secure operational frameworks and enforcing safe cyber-practices at all levels, both within business and the home.

The cyber-security landscape changes daily. This is largely due to the fact that there is no single group of threat actors, just as there is no well-defined group of victims. A disparate assembly of actors with varying levels of skill, access to funding and motives, is targeting an equally diverse and fragmented set of targets, ranging from individual consumers (even children) all the way up to the largest global conglomerates, government bodies and nation states. In some instances, pure cybercrimes are committed; in others, the focus is on cyber-enabled crimes. For example, in its *Internet Security*

Threat Report Volume 20 for 2014, internet security firm Symantec reported an increase in so-called **ransomware** (described in section 4.8.6 of this chapter) up 113% over the previous year, and stated that corporate defences are falling behind as cybercriminals continue to find weak links in security. Today, the firm reports, the weakest link in the chain is not technological; it is us, the users.

Targeting users in order to execute social engineering scams has become one of the most dominant themes in the cyber-enabled crime domain. The clear shift away from purely technical cybercrime hacking attacks towards the exploitation of user ignorance, laziness or naivety, for the purpose of committing cyber-enabled crimes, is significant because the modern user, particularly when bringing their own device to work (BYOD) is now acting not merely as a user, but also as a system administrator, procurement manager and security officer.

Raising the awareness of users at all levels is, therefore, one job for cyber-security managers. The modern security team is no longer a small group of highly skilled technicians sitting in a back office – the modern security team is all of us.

2.1.1 Dependency

The past 100 years have seen an accelerating set of advancements in the field of communications. Both telecommunications and internet services are evolving at an astounding rate, but as they undergo this continuous process of transformation, new risks are continually emerging.

This CISI course is designed specifically for the non-technical student and provides an extensive but relatively jargon-free description of both the evolving technologies and the emerging threats, primarily in the context of contemporary financial services.

The scope of the new services and the attendant risks spans the full spectrum of modern technology, from computing hardware and software to data and users. The increasing availability of lower cost, smaller, more powerful devices has put electronic data processing within the reach of small businesses and home users. At the same time, the interconnection of these devices via the internet serves to link not only like-minded individuals and organisations, but also criminals and their victims.

Our absolute dependence on information and communication technologies (ICT) has given rise to a need for greatly enhanced methods for protecting these devices and the information they store, process and transmit. New academic disciplines of computer security and information assurance have emerged along with the common goals of ensuring the security, availability and reliability of information systems.

2.1.2 Main Risk Areas

According to Symantec, 2017 was a year in which 'cryptojacking' overtook phishing, ransomware, data breaches and denial of service attacks to become the main online threat. The report states that:

> *A meteoric crypto currency market triggered a gold rush for cyber criminals. Detections of coin miners on endpoint computers increased by 8,500 percent in 2017, with Symantec logging 1.7 million in December alone.*

With only a couple lines of code, or delivered via browser, cyber criminals harness stolen processing power and cloud CPU usage to mine crypto currency. Coin mining slows devices and overheats batteries. For enterprises, coin miners put corporate networks at risk of shutdown and inflate cloud CPU usage, adding cost.

Data breaches and other more traditional forms of attack have not gone away and they continue to affect both governmental and private sector organisations. Cyber-attacks are not restricted to Western Europe or the US; virtually every nation, every economy, indeed every internet user worldwide is a target for the combined attack tools of phishing, malware, hacking and other techniques that you will read about later in this workbook.

Six other areas of risks are commonly identified:

1. mobile devices and the 'internet of things'
2. web threats
3. social media and social engineering scams targeting the 'human firewall'
4. targeted attacks against specific individuals
5. data breaches
6. eCrime and malware, such as ransomware and spyware.

A key finding is the contrast between the speed and agility demonstrated by attackers and the relatively slow response of victims. One example cited is the 'Heartbleed' vulnerability which affected encrypted links that exist between computers on the internet. Within a few hours of this vulnerability being reported, hackers were exploiting it in large numbers, while victims and solution providers took days (at best) to correct the issue.

It is this period between the discovery and exploitation of a new vulnerability and the development and information of countermeasures that is referred to as the '**zero day**' period. The vulnerabilities themselves are, not surprisingly, known as zero day vulnerabilities, or ZDVs.

In 2014, operating system developers took 204 days, 53 days and 22 days respectively, to develop patches for the top three zero day vulnerabilities reported. As a consequence of this lag, hackers were able to exploit the top five ZDVs for a total of 295 days before fixes (**patches**) were made available.

During the investigation into the 2016 'Panama papers' data breach, security experts were able to ascertain that the Panamanian law firm from which the files had been stolen had not updated some of its web-facing and email platforms in several years. It is precisely this kind of failure that creates opportunities hackers will exploit, although exactly how the Panama papers were exposed has not yet been confirmed.

2.1.3 Targeted Attacks

Most readers will be familiar with the concept of phishing. In its most common form this comprises unsolicited emails sent at random which try to entice the reader to respond by clicking on a link that takes them to a web page where personal data is collected by the attacker. Similar ploys involve the use of social media services, text messages or other messaging technologies, such as WhatsApp. Typically, this personal data will be used to commit financial crimes, or as a basis for developing email lists to which marketing **spam** email can then be sent, or which will be sold online, often in the Darknet.

One excellent example of the effectiveness of this type of attack occurred in 2012 when hackers sent phishing emails to employees in the control room at the port of Antwerp. The emails contained links to malicious web pages and when some employees clicked those links, malware was downloaded and the port's systems were then accessed remotely by the hackers. The end result was that the attackers, who worked for an organised drug trafficking gang, were able to control the movements of the cargo containers that held their illegally shipped narcotics.

Spear phishing is the targeted version of phishing. As the name suggests, spear phishing takes place when an attacker focuses on specific victims, who will often have been identified and studied online, using sites like LinkedIn. The spear phishing attack will often have a social engineering component, in the sense that the attacker will use his knowledge of the victim's profile to develop an approach which is more likely to entice that particular individual. For example, if I wish to spear phish you, I might research you online, discover facts about your employment and your family status, your likes and interests, and then send you a phishing email containing your name and sufficient information to entice you to respond.

Targeted spear phishing can elicit a better response for the attacker than sending random spam. Although the collection of details related to potential victims requires greater effort and sophistication, the return on investment can be higher.

Another form of targeted attack involves the use of so-called Trojan software directed at software applications known or suspected to be used by a potential victim. The term 'Trojan' refers to the fact that, as with the Trojan horse, the malicious software is hidden inside an innocent looking package, such as a software update or add-on that the user can download. When such an update is downloaded, the hidden malware also executes and installs itself on the victim's device.

A particular target of this kind of Trojan malware during 2014 involved malicious device driver updates from devices included in the internet of things. We will examine this concept in more detail in chapter 6, but for now the internet of things refers to the myriad of interconnected devices that are now available and which range from computers and mobile phones to robotic vehicles.

A key point to note is the extent to which attackers have started to employ sophisticated levels of surveillance and intrusion into organisations in order to gather the necessary background information for this kind of attack. In addition to conducting online searches, attackers have identified details of their victims' suppliers, conducted physical surveillance on their victims in a traditional manner and have even gone as far as to insert employees into their target organisation.

Looking at how this area of criminal activity is evolving, it seems that cyber-space is rapidly becoming a war zone in which highly advanced attacks are increasingly commonplace, while victims are struggling to comprehend the nature and sophistication of the threat. In fact, it was reported that 60% of all targeted attacks observed struck small- and medium-sized companies which lacked the resources to invest in security and the skills required to implement basic best practices. It is this imbalance that we hope to address through the delivery of this training material.

2.1.4 The Rise of Malware

The volume of new malware samples appearing on a daily basis has now risen from what was already a torrent to a virtual tsunami. During 2015, almost 320,000,000 new pieces of malware were created worldwide – equivalent to almost 1,000,000 new threats each day.

Things really came to a head with the WannaCry ransomware attacks of May 2017. This was a worldwide cyber-attack that targeted computers running the Microsoft Windows operating system. The '**worm**' encrypted data and demanded ransom payments in the Bitcoin cryptocurrency. It propagated through EternalBlue, an exploit in older Windows systems released by The Shadow Brokers a few months prior to the attack.

While Microsoft had released patches previously to close the exploit, much of WannaCry's spread occurred in organisations like the UK's National Health Service (NHS) that had not applied these updates, or that were using older Windows systems no longer supported by Microsoft.

This highlights two key issues:

- Patching or updating of operating systems, applications, anti-malware solutions, browsers and plug-ins is an essential security measure.
- The practice of software and system vendors unilaterally choosing to terminate their support for older systems, particularly their security patching support, needs to be reviewed. Large organisations that invest in hundreds of thousands of machines should never find themselves compromised in this fashion. Carefully thought-through and mutually-agreed migration paths to the latest versions of software are vitally important.

The attack was stopped within a few days of its discovery due to emergency patches released by Microsoft, and the discovery of a 'kill switch' that prevented infected computers from spreading WannaCry further. The attack is reported to have affected more than 200,000 computers across 150 countries.

The volume of malware is now so huge that it is practically impossible to deal with it all. Depending on anti-malware solutions is no longer sufficient. We need to give a lot more thought to what the attackers' targets are, particularly with regard to sensitive data and consider where such data should be stored and in what format. The assumption should now be that an attacker will eventually break through and, therefore, the focus must be to ensure that, when that happens, the impact is not catastrophic.

This is underscored by the observation that the most prevalent form of malware in 2015 was so-called crypto-extortion malware. This trend has continued during 2016, with Crypto-locker featuring as one of the most popular malicious applications. Once this kind of infection invades the victim's system, it encrypts or encodes critical data, for example photographs, client data and other files, so that the victim can no longer access them. In order to recover these encrypted files, the victim is required to make a payment to the malware developer, often in Bitcoin, is a virtually untraceable and unregulated electronic currency. Once this Bitcoin payment has been made, the victim is sent a digital decryption key by the attacker.

2.1.5 Key Risks of Social Media and Mobile Devices

Cybercriminals make frequent use of social media, both as a means of collecting intelligence on their targets and making contact with their victims. Social media users' low levels of risk awareness, and their habit of posting confidential personal data online in public view, have made sites such as Facebook, Twitter and Periscope a favoured resource for attackers. LinkedIn is also extensively used to target corporations and their employees.

Furthermore, mobile devices and the apps (applications) they run, including social media apps, are also a prime target, as they serve as a mechanism for extracting personal data and **geolocation** information. A majority of users have little or no security on their smartphones and it was reported that in 2015 a staggering 17% of Android apps (totalling one million) contained malware. It should be noted that these tainted apps were not posted on the Google Play store; instead they were sold or delivered free via third-party sites.

App developers are heavily involved in what is known as the big data market. They offer free apps to users who, in return, are required to share personal information such as their geographic location for inclusion in the developer's contact lists. Most users are unaware that this information is sold on to large corporate data brokers who develop marketing intelligence using these consolidated data sets which are in turn sold on to corporations and governments. The primary use of big data is marketing and sales, but it is clear that it could be extensively used by criminals and others with malicious intent.

Some apps collect even more sensitive data. Health apps on wearable devices monitor a range of health indicators for users, but 52% of such apps on the market in 2015 did not even have a privacy policy in place. Of these apps, 20% sent personal information as well as login and password information across the mobile network in an unencrypted and therefore insecure format.

Even the introduction of the European Union's General Data Protection Regulation (GDPR), enforced from 25 May 2018, has had a limited effect because many apps come from small developers based outside the EU, and because some app developers have carefully rephrased their terms and conditions rather than rewriting their software. One prominent dating app has added the following statements to its post-GDPR terms & conditions:

> 'As with all technology companies, although we take steps to secure your information, we do not promise, and you should not expect, that your personal information will always remain secure.
>
> Keep in mind that even though our systems are designed to carry out data deletion processes according to the above guidelines, we cannot promise that all data will be deleted within a specific timeframe due to technical constraints. '

Statements like this suggest that some app developers are focused on the commercial value of users' data at the cost of complying with the true spirit of GDPR or with other privacy legislation, except where they are forced to do so.

These problems are compounded by user attitudes. An increasing number of mobile device users demonstrate a willingness to exchange their personal data and privacy for a free app. As stated in section 2.1, it is users who are now the weakest link in the chain and we must therefore focus on the 'human firewall'.

3. Fundamental Issues

3.1 Fundamentals of Cyber-Security

Learning Objective

1.3.1   Understand the fundamentals of cyber-security: policies and standards; identity and access management; threat and vulnerability management; outside service providers; IT risk management

3.1.1 Policies and Standards

Cyber-space has many excellent standards and guidelines. However, every organisation must make its own decisions on how to apply these various guidelines, based on its circumstances and the risks it faces, as well as on the requirements of regulators. Some of the most popular sets of guidance are described below.

The EU General Data Protection Regulation (GDPR)

The GDPR 2016/679 focuses on the issue of privacy for all individuals within the EU and the European Economic Area (EEA). It also addresses the export of personal data outside the EU and EEA areas. The GDPR gives EU citizens and residents theoretical control over their personal data and simplifies the regulatory environment for international business by unifying the regulation within the EU. Exercising practical control over one's data, in the context of a globalised search engine indexing model and the Big Data model, is less simple.

Ten Steps to Cyber-Security

In 2012, the UK's Department for Business, Innovation & Skills (BIS) published its *Ten Steps to Cyber-Security*. This guide provides an overview of cyber-security for senior executives. The guidance acknowledges that information is at the centre of business today and that cyber-space exists as a digital architecture upon which society and the economy depend. This relates to both the internet in general and the information systems that support and maintain infrastructure, business and services. The Ten Steps guide provides a sound framework for a high-level understanding of cyber-security.

Publicly Available Specification (PAS) 555

PAS 555 was released by the British Standards Institution (BSI) in 2013. While most guidelines and standards identify problems and offer solutions, PAS 555 describes the appearance of effective cyber-security. Rather than specifying the approach to a cyber-security problem, it describes what the solution might look like. While this is difficult to reconcile against a checklist of threats and vulnerabilities, it can be used to confirm that the solutions introduced are comprehensive and conform to expectations.

PAS 555 specifically targets the organisation's top management and is deliberately broad in its scope. It is primarily intended as a framework for the cyber-security governance which allows executives and senior management to compare the organisation's cyber-security measures against the established descriptions.

International Standards Organisation (ISO)/International Electrotechnical Commission (IEC) ISO/IEC 27001

ISO/IEC 27001 is an international standard for best practice information security management systems (ISMS). It is a detailed specification for protecting and preserving information assets using the core principles of confidentiality, integrity and availability (CIA).

The ISO/IEC 27001 Standard offers a set of best practice controls that can be applied by an organisation, using a risk-based approach. When implemented in a structured manner, limitations can be externally assessed and certified for compliance purposes.

ISO/IEC 27032

ISO/IEC 27032 is an international standard dealing explicitly with cyber-security. While the recommended controls are not as detailed and prescriptive as those provided by ISO/IEC 27001, this standard does identify the vectors that cyber-attackers use, including important non-technical vectors, such as social engineering. It also provides guidance for protecting information assets beyond the borders of the organisation, for example in partnerships, collaborations or other information-sharing arrangements with clients and suppliers, or in the cloud.

Cloud Controls Matrix (CCM)

The CCM is a set of controls designed to maximise the security of information for organisations using cloud technologies, developed by the **Cloud Security Alliance (CSA)**. The CSA developed the matrix in response to widely held concerns about cloud security.

ISO/IEC 27035

ISO/IEC 27035 is an international standard for incident management, which forms the first line of cyber -defence. When cyber-attacks occur, it is essential that organisations are prepared to respond quickly and effectively. The standard also includes guidelines describing how to update policies and processes to strengthen existing controls following root cause analysis of any event, thus minimising the risk of recurrence.

ISO/IEC 27031

ISO/IEC 27031 is an international standard for information and communications technology readiness for business continuity. Business continuity follows on logically from incident management, because any uncontrolled cyber or information security incident can rapidly morph into a threat to business continuity. The standard bridges the gap between the incident itself and general business continuity, and forms a key link in the cyber-resilience chain.

ISO/IEC 22301

ISO/IEC 22301 is an international standard for business continuity management systems (BCMS) and constitutes the final element of the cyber-resilience portfolio. The standard describes the processes for recovering from disasters and also for maintaining security and access to information in the wake of an incident.

3.1.2   Identity Access Management

In large organisations, there is a continual flow of people joining, transferring between and leaving departments. One of the biggest challenges businesses face in the modern era is ensuring that those with access to information systems have appropriate access and that access levels are changed or removed when they leave or move within the organisation.

An identity access management (IAM) system provides the framework and technology to support the business processes that facilitate the management of electronic identities. IAM solutions automate the initiation, capture, recording and management of user identities and their related permissions. The IAM will typically include a centralised directory service that scales appropriately as the organisation grows or shrinks. This central directory prevents credentials from being recorded haphazardly or insecurely as employees try to manage the burden of having multiple passwords or other **authentication** mechanisms for different systems.

IAM systems also facilitate the process of user enrolment and setup. If implemented correctly, they can decrease the time required for these processes by delivering a smooth workflow that reduces errors and the potential for abuse on misconfiguration.

A modern IAM system should automatically match employees' job titles, locations and business unit IDs to access rights. Depending on the employee's profile, some privileges may be automatically provisioned, while others may require special authorisation. All deviations to the standard should be subject to management approval in order to prevent privilege creep.

3.1.3   Cyber-Threat and Vulnerability Management

The concept of threat and vulnerability management refers to a process in which security is designed as a response to given threats that affect prioritised assets and which incorporates an awareness of existing vulnerabilities.

Threat and vulnerability management has four major elements:

1. **Asset inventory** – a log of all information system and data assets, scored by criticality and sensitivity.
2. **Threat analysis** – an assessment of the nature of the threat in relation to each class of asset.
3. **Vulnerability analysis** – an assessment of known or suspected cyber-security vulnerabilities, often based on penetration testing and cyber-resilience exercises.
4. **Vulnerability management** – the process of addressing and mitigating known vulnerabilities in order to reduce risk.

When conducted in unison, these four steps represent the interlocking parts of an integrated, effective threat and vulnerability management programme. We will revisit these points several times throughout the workbook.

3.1.4 Threat and Vulnerability Management

Vulnerability management uses the input from the threat and vulnerability analysis to mitigate the risk that has been posed by the identified threats and vulnerabilities. A vulnerability management programme consists of four key elements:

1. Countermeasure plans detailing the countermeasures to be implemented by the organisation with respect to specific risks.
2. Control frameworks describing the general cyber-security control plan to be used by the organisation.
3. Metrics and measurements listing the key indicators of performance or the red flags that might indicate manifest risks.
4. Threat intelligence capturing up-to-date intelligence information, for example in the form of a risk of threat register, in order to inform decision-making.

3.1.5 Outside Service Providers

Allied to the concept of globalisation is the outsourcing model. Whereas large corporations previously tended to provide many of the ICT services they required internally, in today's world most organisations use outside providers. However, the use of outsiders, while often more cost-effective, introduces additional risks. If data is to be transported for processing by third parties, then there may be attendant data protection issues, particularly if that data processing service is being conducted in another jurisdiction.

Risks also arise when third-party contractors work at the client's main site or make regular visits. The standards of security screening for contracted staff may not always conform to those of the client organisation and even former employees, who have been dismissed, sometimes find their way back in via the third-party provider route.

Hackers and other criminals regularly impersonate legitimate third-party providers in order to gain access to sites or to obtain sensitive information from employees. Financial services firms are not immune to this form of attack and there have been some high-profile examples in which large sums of money have been stolen as a result of such intrusions.

- One of the ways an external services organisation can communicate information about its controls is through a Service Auditor's Report. There are two types:
  - A **Type I** report describes the service organisation's controls at a specific point in time.
  - A **Type II** report not only includes the service organisation's description of controls, but also includes detailed testing of the service organisation's controls over a minimum of six months.
- Information provided by the independent service auditor. It includes a description of the service auditor's tests of operating effectiveness and the results of those tests.
- In a Type I report, the service auditor will express an opinion on whether the service organisation's description of its controls presents fairly, in all material respects, the relevant aspects of the service organisation's controls that were placed in operation as of a specific date, and whether the controls were suitably designed to achieve specified control objectives.
- In a Type II report, the service auditor will express an opinion on the same items noted above in a Type I report and also whether the controls that were tested were operating with sufficient effectiveness to provide reasonable assurance that the control objectives were achieved during the period specified.

3.1.6 Information and Communications Technology (ICT) Risk Management

Information and communication technology (ICT) risk management involves the application of traditional risk management thinking to ICT infrastructure and services to support a risk-based approach to information and **cyber-security**.

Risk management focuses on the business risks associated with the use, ownership, operation, involvement, influence and adoption of ICT by any enterprise. It is a component of the wider enterprise risk management domain.

A risk-based approach is a process that allows organisations to:

- identify, measure and prioritise potential risks using a scoring system
- develop strategies to mitigate each risk
- focus finite resources on risks in priority order, rather than attempting to address everything at once.

In simple terms, criminal hackers and rogue insiders exploit vulnerabilities to target assets. Organisations respond by implementing controls. A risk-based approach ensures that the controls which are implemented first are those that deal with the most dangerous criminal hackers and rogue insiders and the most sensitive assets, after taking the levels of control that already exist into account.

This can be expressed as:

$$\text{Risk} = (\text{Vulnerability x Threat}) / \text{Counter Measure}) \times \text{Asset Value}$$

Sometimes asset value is replaced by the term impact.

CRAMM Risk Management

CCTA Risk Analysis and Management Method (CRAMM) was created in 1987 by the then UK Central Computer and Telecommunications Agency (CCTA), a government body. It is consistent with most other risk management models and is valuable for its simple and logical approach.

Now in its fifth iteration, CRAMM comprises three stages, each supported by checklists and guidelines. The first two stages identify and analyse risks. The third stage recommends how identified risks should be managed.

- **CRAMM Stage 1**: Establishment of the security objectives:
  - defining the boundary for the study
  - inventory and valuation of physical assets
  - inventory and valuation of data assets
  - inventory and valuation of software application assets
  - analysis of the potential business impacts that could arise from non-availability, destruction, disclosure or modification of any asset.

- **CRAMM Stage 2**: Assessment of the risks to the system and the requirements for security:
  - identification and assessment of the type and level of threats
  - assessment of any vulnerabilities that might be exploited by the identified threats
  - concatenation of the threat and vulnerability assessments with asset values to calculate levels of risk.
- **CRAMM Stage 3**: Identification, selection and deployment of cost-effective countermeasures.

CRAMM provides a very large countermeasures library, consisting of over 3,000 detailed countermeasures organised into approximately 70 logical groupings.

CRAMM is widely used by NATO, the Dutch armed forces and some private corporations.

Access Versus Exploit

It is important to make a distinction between cybercrime access techniques and cybercrime exploits. Criminal hackers and rogue insiders employ access techniques to target assets. The assets they choose to target depend on their motives. For example, a single-issue extremist might wish to cause reputational harm to an organisation, while an organised criminal is more likely to be focused on financial gain.

Consider this in the context of home security. An intruder targeting your home has to consider several things. First, there is the geographic location of the property, its proximity to other residences and to major roads and police stations, as well as the extent to which it is overlooked by neighbours. There is also the question of how the intruder might gain physical access to your property, whether through socially engineering you and your family, stealing your keys or breaking in through a door, window or roof.

All the preceding considerations relate to gaining access. How a criminal might exploit vulnerabilities once access has been gained is another matter altogether. One class of intruder might search your bedroom for jewellery, while another might opt instead to take your television. An intruder with different motives may well target your computer or search for your wallet and only take your credit cards. In each case, the access technique and the method used to exploit that access can differ widely and each class of exploit is linked very closely to motive.

Understanding these distinctions is important. Not only must you protect the perimeter of your dwelling against intruders, but you must hide your jewellery, backup your computer files, insure your television and keep your wallet with you. Only by dealing with both the access and exploitation scenarios can you claim to live in a secure house.

Cybercrime and security are no different. If a hacker gains remote access to a computer system or network, they may choose from any number of exploits. The hacker might steal data or install **spyware** to monitor what users are doing, including their web-surfing habits, the emails they send and the applications they run. Alternatively, they might harvest contact lists or search for bank details. Another attacker might take over the machine and run it as part of a network of infected machines (a **Botnet**), or turn it into a server for illegal pornography. Or they might do all of these things at once. Cyber-security, therefore, requires those responsible for such systems to control access and also deal with the implications of every conceivable type of exploit in order to prevent, detect, mitigate and respond to attacks.

Failing to make a distinction between cyber-attack access techniques and cyber-attack exploits can lead firms to plan poorly in terms of security because they have not taken into account what their real vulnerabilities are. In many cases this has allowed attackers to remain active within the subverted system, long after the access event has been discovered, because investigators failed to follow the trail and to consider all the possible motives and exploit techniques. Taking up residence in a subverted system is known as persistence and it is becoming increasingly common.

4.   Technical Cybercrime Attacks

The model of network, device, application, data and user is a useful one to bear in mind when considering the many ways in which attackers steal data or attack systems. Unless they are physically present on your premises, attackers will typically need to gain access via some form of network. This first phase challenges the hacker and also offers the target its first opportunity to prevent unauthorised access.

Once network access has been obtained, the attacker may now need to gain entry to specific devices or install malicious applications on them. Once a device has been compromised, the applications running on the device are the next target. Therefore, the victim has two additional opportunities to prevent unauthorised activity: securing the devices and ensuring the security of the applications.

In the next phase, an attacker will often seek to copy, edit, delete or even encrypt the data held within the applications that sit on the devices across the network. They might even do more than one of these things, perhaps copying and extracting the data before deleting it. As we saw in the section 3.1.6, the attacker's motives will determine both how access is achieved and how the data is used. Similarly, the sensitivity of the data itself will affect the impact on the victim.

The fifth link in the chain, the user, can feature at each of the above points. Users working remotely, for example, might provide an attacker with a route across the network and into corporate systems, if both the user's habits and corporate security are lax. In a similar fashion, users who are able to select their own passwords and who choose poorly can provide opportunities for network and device access, as well as application access. Users who fail to update their applications, or who turn automatic updates off, further contribute to the problem by providing even more opportunities for attackers to exploit.

Finally, users who are cavalier in the way they treat data, for example placing sensitive information on external drives which they then leave behind on public transport or sending unencrypted file attachments containing share-sensitive data via email, all contribute to raised levels of risk.

So, we see that threats, vulnerabilities and controls all map onto the same basic framework, as do assets. Even the least technical of us can use this simple framework to guide discussions and to trigger common sense questions when the topic of cyber-security is being discussed.

4.1   Common Attack Objectives

Following on from descriptions of the various types of attacker given above, it is apparent that, while the objectives of cyber-attackers are quite varied, the great majority fall into one or more of five categories:

1. **Intrusions** into systems for the purpose of demonstrating or testing vulnerabilities, proving the attacker's own skills or setting the stage for a further exploit.
2. **Espionage** and data theft for personal, corporate or political gain, or to cause loss or harm. Recently, doxing (also spelled 'doxxing') has become a popular activity. This involves posting stolen data online about an individual, in order to cause reputational harm.
3. **Malicious alteration** of systems or networks in order to interfere with services, delete data or reconfigure systems for personal or corporate gain/harm.
4. **Denial of services** executed in order to prevent the targeted systems, and the organisations that rely on them, from operating effectively.
5. **Financial frauds** and other commercial abuses perpetrated primarily for financial gain, whether directly via fraud or as part of a market abuse scheme. On occasion, such attacks might also be intended to conceal a loss.

It is, of course, quite possible for an attacker to have more than one goal. For example, a hacker might be paid by a hostile state to conduct espionage on that state's behalf, but he may well use the opportunity to carry out a financial fraud for his own private benefit. Drawing firm conclusions about the hacker's identity based solely upon an assessment of motives can therefore be hazardous and a number of other identifiers tend to be employed, such as syntax within malicious code, indicators of the attacker's mother tongue and details of any devices used, when such data is available.

4.2   Evolution of Attack Models

As with any topic that attempts to describe and categorise the behaviour of large numbers of people across a wide span of time and a huge geographic area, simplistic segmentation and classifications only have an illustrative purpose. Each attacker is an individual and, while common themes have emerged, there are no hard and fast rules that dictate how cybercrime should or will be carried out. In fact, given the pace of change in internet technologies and services, it is hardly surprising that cybercrime attack methodologies are also evolving at lightning speed.

However, the following simple breakdown might serve to give you a sense of the general direction of travel. What it emphasises is the continuing move away from a small core of brilliant technical minds towards an environment in which cybercrime has been democratised and the internet has been weaponised, so that any interested party can download and use advanced attack tools that require relatively little technical skill.

There have been four main phases in the evolutionary process:

4.2.1   One-to-One Attacks

Most closely fitting the traditional image of the genius, pony-tailed hacker operating from a darkened room, one-to-one attacks also encompass insider data thefts and many forms of fraud, blackmail or e-crime attack. This remains an important type of threat.

In a typical one-to-one attack, a clever hacker targets a single system or organisation, driven solely by personal motives and without any requirement for outside assistance.

4.2.2   One-to-Many Attacks

Evolved over several decades, typical examples of the one-to-many attack model include malware or viral attacks, spread, for instance, via email. Spam and adware are also forms of a one-to-many attack in which a single source spews out unwanted marketing messages to millions of recipients.

Modern one-to-many attacks tend to have a financial motive.

4.2.3   Many-to-One Attacks

Typified by attacks against the US banking sector in 2013, as well as by the botnet scenarios described later, many-to-one attacks involve willing accomplices or hijacked devices launching mass attacks on a single target. These attacks are usually designed to deny services to the customers of the target or the users of the targeted machines and are often ideologically inspired.

4.2.4   Many-to-Many Attacks

A cyber-security nightmare, the conceptual many-to-many attack features millions of infected devices or willing participants simultaneously launching many millions of attacks on millions of targets across the internet, thus causing congestion and cascading internet failures.

One speculative scenario involves the citizens of a large, hostile state being co-opted by their government and persuaded to launch a co-ordinated attack on a long list of governmental and key private sector organisations in another state.

4.3   The Network is a Target

As we have seen in section 1.1.1, the internet is a complex web of billions of interconnected devices performing different functions. It is a network of networks and many of the devices are multifunctional. As a result, the model for easily defining risks and controls based on the delineation between network, device, application, data and user does tend to break down when confronted by real-life events.

Consequently, you will detect a degree of overlap and duplication, at least in terms of headings, while going through the text. **Access control** and authentication, for example, is relevant at almost every level and the principles of **multifactor authentication (MFA)** are equally relevant.

As explained at the start of chapter 1, the main components of the internet have been designed to support the switching, or direction, of data packets from senders to receivers, ensuring that packets go to the correct address by the best possible route without duplication or data loss. As the internet grew, the larger routers and domain name servers were joined by numerous cousins, such as retail routers, the likes of which you probably have in your home, and a plethora of data storage devices, including cloud storage.

Remote storage and data processing have served to increase the already critical dependence of all users on the network itself. When data is stored and processed locally, loss of network connectivity can be frustrating, but many operations can continue until the connection is restored. No doubt you are annoyed by a loss of internet access at home as this will prevent you from playing some of the games on your device or writing your great novel.

When both data and the applications used to process that data are hosted in the cloud, a loss of connectivity can bring all computing processes to a halt, unless there is a locally accessible backup in place. This utter dependence on connectivity is what makes the network as attractive a target for cybercrime as your servers, because:

- attacking your network connectivity can prevent your organisation from operating
- **sniffing** or otherwise intruding on your traffic as it transits the network can expose sensitive data
- inserting packets within the sessions initiated by yourself or your clients can result in fraud.

Think of the internet as a road network and the servers that it joins together as factories and warehouses. During a conflict between nations, or even during periods of civil strife, it is not necessary for your opponent to bomb or burn down all of your factories. It is sufficient for them to knock down the bridges or block the roads. This has long been the essence of military strategy and attacks against our network infrastructure are today the essence of a great deal of cyber-warfare and cybercrime strategy.

Even your home Wi-Fi router is now the target of cybercriminals. In fact, some of them have gone so far as to insert malware on gaming consoles and television sets in the living room. Numerous attacks of this nature have been reported, including attacks on Synology network-attached storage devices that were infected by ransomware in 2014.

In the previous year, Symantec researchers discovered a new Linux worm called Darlloz25 that targeted small internet-enabled devices such as home routers, set-top boxes, and security cameras; by March 2014, Symantec had identified 31,716 devices that were infected with this malware.

Attackers use the network to attack the network. Open source tools, such as the Shodan HQ search engine, allow them to search for internet-enabled devices, including security cameras and webcams. If these devices are not secured, attackers can view everything that the security camera or webcam picks up. This is even true of the webcam on your PC or laptop.

Experts believe that this is only the tip of the iceberg and that the internet of things will be a key target for cybercriminals in the coming years. Malware that targets Bitcoin has already been identified, as have denial of service attacks using hacked home routers. This will doubtless be compounded by the already busy mobile malware space.

4.4   Network-Level Threats (1)

Learning Objective

1.4.1   Identify the following types of network-level technical cybercrime attack: denial of service (DoS) and distributed denial of service (DDoS); distributed reflected denial of service attacks (DRDoS); man-in-the-middle attacks (MITM); sniffing attacks; session hijacks; botnets; malnets; spam

4.4.1   Denial of Service (DoS) and Distributed Denial of Service (DDoS)

One of the most popular techniques for attacking the network, or the servers that directly connect to it, is the infamous denial of service attack, which is more commonly seen in its distributed form (DDoS). All **denial of service** attacks aim to overload critical systems, such as web services or email, with internet traffic. If the target server cannot handle the volume of malicious traffic, then it is also unable to process legitimate traffic.

DoS attacks can wreak financial, reputational and operational havoc by disrupting normal business processes and communications and by preventing customers from using online services. While these forms of attack are not new, they are growing in frequency and intensity. During 2014, Symantec saw a 183% increase in attacks between January and August.

DDoS motives include extortion, the diversion of attention away from other forms of attack, **hacktivism** (ideologically motivated hacking) and revenge, often by former employees. Using the cloud and the crime-as-a-service model, would-be attackers can very easily purchase the skills and technology required without being technical experts themselves.

The **Low Orbit Ion Cannon (LOIC)** software used to launch the 2012 attacks on at least 14 major US banks was made available as a free internet download, amply supported by how-to videos on YouTube. One of the most popular of these videos, uploaded in November 2010 and still accessible years later, received over 264,000 views. Versions of this training tutorial are also available in other languages.

The LOIC application was downloaded 34,000 times in the UK alone over a period of just three days, according to the Metropolitan Police's head of e-crime investigations. This characterises the advanced nature of the threat and an apparent eagerness on the part of many individuals to acquire these cyber-warfare capabilities that no major body can afford to ignore.

Distributed Reflected Denial of Service (DRDoS) Attacks

In the standard distributed denial of service attack model, the attacker uses a master machine to control a large number of slave devices, also known as bots. This network of infected machines is therefore known as a botnet – a network of bots.

A **distributed reflected denial of service (DRDoS)** attack is a more sophisticated form of DDoS, although the fundamental principles are unchanged. In a DRDoS attack, the attacker configures his network of bots in such a way that they appear to be the victim's device. The attacker then uses his botnet to send packets to other machines (for example to DNS servers, requesting IP address translations) and when those machines respond, they send their responses not to the attacker but to the machine the attacker is pretending to be, ie, the victim's machine.

The servers that have been tricked into sending their packets of data to the victim are known as reflectors, so this form of denial of service attack is referred to as a reflected attack.

Main features of DRDoS attacks:

- The attacker is unable to make the reflectors forge IP addresses, so the source addresses in the response packets are the reflectors' actual addresses. Victims can therefore locate the reflectors directly.
- The source addresses in request packets sent by slaves are the victims' addresses, therefore the victim cannot get any information about the botnet slaves from the reflected data packets.
- The request packets generated by one slave are distributed to several reflectors, so that each reflector produces a relatively small number of response packets, making proactive prevention difficult.

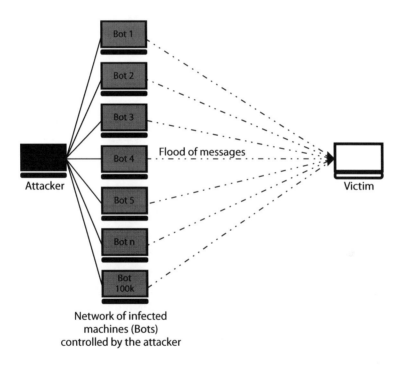

Figure 8: Distributed Denial of Service (DDoS) Attack

4.4.2 Man-in-the-Middle Attacks (MITM)

In **Man-in-the-Middle Attacks (MITM)**, an attacker intercepts all communications between two hosts. With communications between a client and server now flowing through the attacker, he or she is free to modify their content. Protocols that rely on the exchange of public keys to protect communications are often the target of these types of attacks.

Therefore, in ICT terms, an MITM attack occurs when an attacker secretly intercepts, relays, and possibly alters the communication between two parties who believe they are directly communicating with each other.

MITM attacks may have a variety of motives, for example active eavesdropping, where the attacker intercepts and relays messages in order to read their contents. Another motive is financial gain whereby the attacker edits the contents of financial transactions to his benefit, often by diverting part or all of the payment to his own account.

In order to conduct such an attack, the attacker must be able to intercept all relevant messages passing between the two victims and inject new ones. This is straightforward in some circumstances, for example, an attacker within range of an unencrypted Wi-Fi wireless access point can insert himself as a MITM. Other attackers use the ability to sniff IP sessions in order to conduct these attacks.

MITM attacks, by definition, must somehow circumvent the mutual authentication that often exists between parties communicating online. The attack can only succeed if the attacker can successfully impersonate both endpoints of the communication. Most communication sessions now employ encryption, including some kind of endpoint authentication, to prevent MITM attacks from occurring.

4.4.3   Sniffing Attacks

Sniffing IP sessions involves capturing, decoding and inspecting the information inside data packets on a TCP/IP network. If you cast your mind back to the postal analogy referred to in section 1.5.3, the sniffing of IP sessions is the equivalent of your landlord steaming open your letters, reading the contents and then sealing them again, leaving you unaware of the fact that your private correspondence has been read.

Sniffing is in fact a legitimate network management capability. It was originally intended to support traffic management and quality control. The most common objectives of unauthorised sniffing are to map networks in order to allow further hacking or to steal information from within packets, such as user IDs (identification documents), passwords, network details, credit card numbers and other sensitive data. Because sniffing is a passive attack in which the attacker remains silent on the network, effectively lying in ambush, it can be very difficult to detect, which is why it is a favourite tool of hackers.

Sniffing attacks are feasible primarily because the design of the TCP/IP protocol focuses on traffic management, ensuring that data packets are properly constructed and contain fields such as source and destination IP addresses, port numbers and sequence numbers, in order that they can be delivered correctly. Security lies at higher layers within the protocol stack and it is therefore possible for TCP/IP sessions to take place without the appropriate security controls being in effect.

4.4.4   Session Hijacks

Session hijacking can be described as the next level of attack after sniffing. During a session hijack, a hacker actually takes control of a user's web session. Having sniffed the session ID and the user's details (such as IP address), the hacker masquerades as the authorised user. The session ID is normally displayed within a cookie file or uniform resource locator (URL).

The attacker examines the format of the packets being sent and predicts the sequence number of the next packet in line. He then inserts his own packet, containing the correct sequence number, and once that is accepted by the receiving device, the hacker has control of the session and any packets sent by the legitimate user will now be ignored.

If an attacker assumes control of a session in this manner after the user has authenticated themselves with the destination server, the attacker can now masquerade as the legitimate user, for example transferring funds, ordering goods or sending correspondence.

Common symptoms experienced by users when their sessions are hijacked include a sudden change in the way a known website starts responding or a complete lack of response from a site that was previously working. Following a session hijack, victims may notice unexpected charges against their credit cards or online accounts and possibly unauthorised transfers from their bank accounts.

4.4.5 Botnets

More sophisticated than simple **scareware** (see section 4.8.7 of this chapter), a botnet is a network of infected computers or mobile devices, normally numbering in the tens of thousands and remotely controlled by an attacker (the botnet herder). The botnet herder is able to use his network of machines (bots) to launch a variety of exploits, the most common ones being DDoS attacks or the sending of spam. Some botnet owners offer their services online – one site claiming to offer such services provided an extensive price list, for example a spam broadcast of 100,000 messages was on offer for $150.

Symantec reports that the number of botnets declined by 18% in 2014 compared to the previous year, mainly because of the combined efforts of the FBI, the European Cybercrime Centre (EC3) at Europol, and other international law enforcement agencies, as well as the community of internet security firms.

Most notably, the Gameover Zeus botnet was shut down in 2014. This huge botnet was responsible for millions of infections worldwide since its debut in 2011 and is only one in a series of botnets taken down over recent years.

4.4.6 Malnets

Malnets are networks of infected web pages, rather than machines, that redirect visitors through a series of legitimate but infected pages towards a central malware server. By so doing, the main piece of malware does not need to be spread to a large number of pages, merely hosted on one, thus reducing the chances of it being detected. The only infections required are the redirect links which ensures that people visit the infected page.

Malnet attacks are often facilitated by a technique known as clickjacking. This involves the use of hidden functions placed over seemingly innocuous buttons or links that then redirect the user of a webpage away from that trusted page. Because these redirect functions are invisible, even the owner of the hijacked website might not easily detect their presence. Less secure websites, with passwords that can be easily guessed or cracked, are more likely to fall victim to this form of exploit.

4.4.7 Spam

Spam, or the distribution of unsolicited bulk email and other electronic messages, has been a long-standing headache for both users and service providers. Even in cases where users are protected from spam by efficient filtering, the spam messages themselves still need to be carried by the network and they can represent a very large percentage of all traffic. This means that even if you receive zero spam, your service provider, and you as a user, are still paying a financial penalty to support the additional infrastructure that exists only to carry spam.

Some spam is malicious in nature, containing links to infected web pages or directly to file downloads, but much of it is a genuine attempt at marketing. However, as the war on spam has progressed many spammers have also moved into the cloud or towards the use of botnet infrastructure in order to send out large volumes of messages that cannot be tracked back to them.

This distributed approach to the generation of spam is very similar to the approach taken to conduct DDoS attacks. In fact, those leasing botnet services will normally offer both DDoS and spam services as options.

Spam continues to evolve and grow in line with every new service offering and technical advancement. Spam is becoming a real problem in services such as WhatsApp, Twitter, Instagram and almost every other online service, to the extent that some users think that a significant proportion of their online followers have a purely commercial motive.

The links in spam messages often lead to hijacked domains and have a URL path that leads to a personal home page (PHP) landing page. If the user clicks on an infected link, they are led to a malicious file. These files are normally Trojan **malware** that is used to download additional infections (attack tools) onto users' compromised devices.

4.5   E-crime as a Service

Learning Objective

1.4.7   Identify the following types of technical cybercrime: crypto-extortion attacks or ransomware; web attack toolkits and scripts; data leakage and breaches; online frauds and other financially motivated e-crimes

According to one leading study, the thriving underground economy brazenly advertises easy-to-use DDoS tools and Botnets for hire. This means that anyone with a personal grudge, political grievance or criminal agenda can easily sponsor or launch an attack, and any organisation, large or small, can be targeted. Cyber-mercenaries represent a new class of financially motivated threat actor; they are guns for hire in the new Wild West of the internet, either attacking organisations or committing online frauds and other e-crimes.

Motivated either by revenge, competitive pressure, greed or ideology, instances of crime in the form of service-based attacks are steadily increasing. Volumetric attacks that use botnets as a source of network flooding have increased in size and frequency over the past few years, so that one quarter of attacks are now categorised as high-volume attacks.

To make matters worse, flooding or volumetric attacks on this scale often result in the failure of the very devices (firewalls and intrusion detection systems [IDSSs]) installed as key parts of the security layer. In fact, these platforms are often targeted in their own right. If the volume of traffic is sufficiently high, the security platform that handles or monitors inbound traffic falls over and the attacker might achieve his aims without actually penetrating beyond the perimeter.

The distribution and installation of malicious and unauthorised software has evolved consistently throughout the twenty-first century. The evolutionary path from annoying **viruses** to destructive malware and on to financially-oriented crimeware is well documented. The use of crypto-extortion tools to lock up a victim's data in order to extort payment for its release, is merely the latest in a series of money-making cyber-attacks.

While the individual technologies embedded within crimeware have evolved incrementally, the diversity with which these technologies are applied to fraudulent and criminal ventures has accelerated. Or, to put it another way, professional cybercriminals have been increasingly inventive in ways in which they use a standard toolset of malware features to conduct their criminal ventures.

4.5.1 Yesterday's Malware Lifecycle

In the past, the lifecycle of computer malware was relatively simple; a computer would become infected via an infection vector (such as an infected universal serial bus [USB] stick) and a solitary virus would be placed within the computer. Eventually, a copy of the virus would be obtained by the anti-virus vendors, detection signatures would be developed and clean-up scripts would be written. The anti-virus products would then be updated, assuming the users had not turned off automatic updating. As one commentator puts it, the net result was an endless but reassuring game of whack-a-mole.

For many years, the graceless dance of virus developers and anti-virus developers ran on in this fashion. Organisations and individuals began to understand the threat and the related controls and confidence grew in our collective ability to manage the problem. Malware was a nuisance but not a strategic risk. Then malware developers upped the ante, developing new ways in which to generate revenue from their activities. This revenue driver had the twin effect of drawing more people to the domain and providing a source of funding for more sophisticated software development and infrastructure. The malware Cold War went hot.

4.5.2 Web Attack Toolkits

A phase transition in the malware lifecycle occurred when the so-called '**dropper, reporter and wiper**' malware model was introduced, sometimes in the form of web attack toolkits that could be purchased and downloaded from the internet by would-be attackers:

- Malware contained in a toolkit is dropped onto a target machine through a vector (attack route) of some kind, such as an infected USB stick, an email attachment or a malicious web page.
- The malware reports back to its developer's command and control platform, informing the developer of the type of system it has infected, the applications that system is running and their patch or version numbers, as well as the security in place.

- More pieces of malicious code are then downloaded, based on the profile of the infected machine. These additional pieces of code execute the actual attacks on applications, data or devices and the network itself.
- Finally, once the attacks have been carried out, the malware removes itself from the infected platforms, deleting all evidence of its presence.

This sophisticated military grade attack model signalled the start of a new malware era. The modern malware threat is complex and sophisticated. It features a network of federated developers with a support infrastructure and monetisation model; the infamous crime-as-a-service (CaaS) model. A staggering range of technologies, applications and services are now on offer to anyone with a credit card, PayPal, or Bitcoin account, regardless of their nationality or their intentions. The world we live in has changed without us realising it, and it has changed beyond all imagination.

The CaaS ecosystem comprises a complex web of relationships and interdependencies. This includes cybercrime tool producers, content distribution service providers, hosting providers and highly resilient command and control topology. Some attacks involve as many as 80 separate compromised servers, used by the attack and concealment source, as attackers transit from one server to another. Modern crimeware is old-fashioned malware's Big Brother, as one commentator described it.

The crimeware marketplace is devoid of altruistic or ideological drivers and is motivated solely by profit. It is a large, underground, distributed corporate concern, the sole focus of which is the illegal extraction of funds from victims. It is organised crime online.

4.5.3   The Challenge for Cyber-Security

Anyone who fails to appreciate the complexity and sophistication of the CaaS model will find themselves hamstrung when they attempt to investigate or merely comprehend the nature and inner mechanics of a crimeware supported attack. Investigators may misinterpret forensic data and organisations are likely to draw the wrong conclusions about their adversaries' motives and the routes through which they have come.

Such failures of the imagination may lead organisations to implement inappropriate solutions, while failing to address their real vulnerabilities. They may also fail to appreciate the persistent nature of many such attacks, such as the fact that attackers may still be present within the network long after the victim imagines that they have cleaned up the mess. This issue of persistence was alluded to earlier in section 3.1.6, when we mentioned the advanced persistent threat and further examples will be provided in later sections.

Not only are the individual attacks much more advanced than previously, but attacks now also tend to happen in batches, with victims suffering multiple downloads of a wide range of malware simultaneously. This is facilitated by the aforementioned command and control infrastructure. Once the identity and configuration of an infected computer has been established, command and control can automatically download large numbers of different attack files to that machine without the threat actor needing to take any manual action. Modern cyber-attacks occur at the speed of light.

Leading security vendors report that today's installation lifecycle incorporates many checks, balances and security features as a means of maximising the success of the installation and protecting the attacker from detection and identification. The following list of typical attack stages provides a sense of how advanced the CaaS model is:

- A self-contained dropper binary is downloaded by the computer after falling victim to an exploit or succumbing to social engineering. In many cases, multiple droppers will be forced onto the victim's computer as part of a pay-per-install scheme.
- The dropper is executed and proceeds to unpack and install components – executing embedded commands. If multiple droppers were placed upon the victim's computer, then they too will be executed in parallel.
- Components of the dropper attempt to disable security settings, modify configuration settings and ensure that the main malware components will be executed automatically after the system restarts.
- A component of the dropper package then proceeds to confirm the installation success with an external crimeware update site. The update site ascertains whether the victim is real and whether it has been seen or compromised before.
- The update site will then return updated configuration and download location information to the installed dropper component – providing fresh instructions on how to acquire the core crimeware agent.
- A component of the dropper package now uses the fresh configuration information to locate the crimeware download site and then proceeds to download the main crimeware tool pack. In some cases this may be a separate downloader package or it may be multiple crimeware packages (representing a variety of cybercrime organisations and botnets).
- The downloader package is then executed and proceeds to unpack, install and replace key crimeware components. If multiple downloaders were retrieved, then they too will be executed in parallel.
- The original dropper package, along with non-essential components that were extracted from previous dropper and downloader phases, are deleted from the victim's computer and the core crimeware agent is ready to begin operation.
- The crimeware agent performs a number of built-in functions, such as collecting software licence keys, password files and other authentication credentials stored on the device or cached by the victim's web browser. It then automatically proceeds to upload an encrypted file containing the stolen data to a remote file server known as a drop server.
- These automatic functions are executed within seconds of the installation of the malware and are designed for quick exploitation and monetisation. Should the cybercriminal lose access (and control) of the victim, they will still have this valuable information which can be sold in its own right.
- The crimeware agent now begins to search for, locate and communicate with the frontline command and control servers. The crimeware will typically have a list of possible server locations or it may utilise an algorithm to locate candidate servers.
- The frontline command and control servers often operate as proxies for communication between the crimeware agent running on the victim's computer and a smaller network of core servers with which the cybercriminal regularly connects. These core servers are responsible for managing and organising the entire attack network.

- The cybercriminals regularly update the crimeware agent installed on the victim's computer, just as if it was a legitimate piece of software. In many cases the cybercriminal will also deploy pay-per-install crimeware packages belonging to other criminals, as a way of further monetising parts of their own attack network.
- The cybercriminals also regularly update the configuration files of the crimeware agents (for example by providing lists of new frontline command and control servers) and they may elect to send commands to the victim's computer interactively or through a batch queuing system.

4.5.4   Implications of the Crime as a Service (CaaS) Model

The crime-as-a-service model is a product of several factors that typify the modern internet-based economy. The first of these is the revolution of the cybercrime ecosystem described in section 4. This type of model is common to many software and technology markets and we see it exemplified by the App Store model in which many interrelated and even interdependent applications coexist, provided by unconnected developers, but dependent on a single set of technologies and customer drivers.

Federation provides efficiencies in distribution and management, thus driving down costs, but this may not be the primary reason for the emergence of this model. It is far more likely that malware and the services for monetising malware have evolved in this direction in response to security itself. Both the malware infections and the human developers behind them need to conceal their activities, hide their identities and maintain persistence for the longest possible period. The CaaS model allows attackers to remain one or more steps distant from the victims. It also allows those with the highest levels of expertise to focus on providing services to less skilled individuals, thus mitigating the risks arising from their own endeavours.

We can expect to see further expansion of this model with the internet of things driving the parallel development of an internet of attack tools and services.

4.5.5   The Blackhole Exploit Kit

In what could be construed as a demonstration of the combined effects of application vulnerabilities and federated malware, two Russian hackers, nicknamed HodLuM and Paunch, developed and then sold online an easy-to-use kit for launching cyber-attacks. The **Blackhole Exploit Kit** became one of the most popular and effective toolsets of its kind and, by 2012, internet security firm Sophos was reporting that 28% of all web threats it had detected during that year were facilitated by Blackhole.

How the Blackhole Model Works

An exploit kit is a software tool used by attackers to get further software installed on a victim's PC. This other software can perform a wide range of tasks, which are usually malicious. So, an exploit kit such as Blackhole contains a range of different **payloads** and the user selects the ones desired and the intended target or type of target. Blackhole then delivers the selected payload and the payload conducts its attack on the infected device, as described below.

Exploit kits are sold online to anyone who wishes to purchase one. The kits normally exploit known security holes in the versions of software installed on victim's devices, for example web browsers, to deliver the malicious payload selected by the user of the exploit kit. The older the browser version, the more likely it is to contain known holes and so updating browsers and other software regularly is a key defence against Blackhole-type attacks.

The people who wrote the Blackhole code are not the people who use it to attack targets. They are simply in the business of creating and selling their exploit kit as a service to other cybercriminals. Exploit kit developers deliver, package and sell their kits in a model that is very similar to the SaaS (software as a service) model, and this is therefore often referred to as CaaS (crime as a service). A would-be cybercriminal purchases a license to use Blackhole, or any other such exploit kit, for a period of time. The costs and licence options vary between different kits and some kits even include software updates, while others are available at a premium to include the most modern exploits that can bypass even up to date anti-malware applications.

Symantec comments that these SaaS toolkits are often located on bulletproof hosting services, with IP addresses that can change quickly and domain names that may be dynamically generated.

Blackhole and other exploit kits, therefore, represent the transfer of weapons-grade cyber-technology from the hands of a few to the hands of the many via a commercial channel. They empower relatively non-technical people to perform highly technical attacks against any chosen target or against targets of opportunity and, as such, they constitute a clear danger to all aspects of online activities and services.

The Five Stages of a Blackhole Attack

In simple terms, there are five main stages to a Blackhole attack:

- **Stage 1** – Initial contact with the victim.
- **Stage 2** – Drawing the victim to an exploit site.
- **Stage 3** – Investigation of the victim's device and software to identify possible exploits.
- **Stage 4** – Delivery of the appropriate malware to the victim's device.
- **Stage 5** – Execution of the malware payload. This in itself can be a multi-stage process.

As indicated in the list above, most exploit kit attacks start by getting a user's browser to point at an infected exploit site where the malicious payloads will be downloaded and installed without the user's knowledge or consent. Common ways of achieving this include:

- compromising legitimate, trusted web pages or servers and infecting them with code that redirects visitors to the malicious exploit site. Recently, large networks of compromised web pages have started to appear, all taking visitors to the same exploit site. These networks of infected pages are called malnets
- sending spam or targeted messages (email, short message service [SMS], instant messaging or social media messages) to people with links to the malicious site included in the message. Normally, these links are obfuscated so that they appear to go to non-threatening sites. A message asking, 'Is it you in this photo?' was circulated widely on Twitter and was linked to a Blackhole outbreak.

Attacks might also be conducted by hiding Trojan code in file downloads, such as popular music or games. In most of these scenarios, user ignorance or deliberate breaches of security guidelines are a major contributor to the problem.

At the Exploit Site

Once a victim arrives at the exploit site's landing page, the Blackhole software hosted there carries out several tasks automatically, such as:

- logging where the user was redirected from; in some cases, this will lead to a payment being made to a collaborating malicious site
- analysing the user's device remotely to determine its browser type and versions, operating system, other software types and versions (eg, Adobe, Java or Flash) in order to determine which types of attack have the best chance of success, based on the known vulnerabilities in each of these software types and versions. The Android OS, for example, is the target of over 90% of all malware attacks on mobile devices.

Execution of the Attack

Once its analysis is complete (and this requires only a split second), Blackhole determines the best available exploits and loads up the appropriate attack tools before directing them at the unwitting visitor. Payloads contained within these attack tools can include spyware that monitors users' actions, code that steals files or other data, worms that navigate from the infected device to other devices on the same network and many other attack techniques.

All of this is being controlled by the Blackhole users, of which there can be an unlimited number, not by the actual developers of Blackhole. In fact, the developers will have no specific knowledge of how or where their toolkit is being used.

4.5.6 Other Exploit Kits and CaaS Attacks

Blackhole is by no means the only kit of its type available for download, with others including the Phoenix and ZeroAccess exploit kits, the Low Orbit Ion Cannon and the High Orbit Ion Cannon. All are part of the new range of easy-to-use attack tools built by experts for deployment by less technical followers. Each of these tools has been widely distributed, downloaded and used in large numbers. Exploit kits such as these not only make the distribution of threats easier and more diffuse than ever before; some also represent a means for their creators to secretly take remote control of infected machines to create botnets – **robot** armies of malicious computers, sometimes numbering in the millions and capable of launching a variety of attacks or facilitating illicit money-making schemes.

Commenting in a report on the state of internet security, Verisign, a vendor of security solutions and services said:

You no longer need to be a sophisticated hacker to commit fraud on the internet. Anyone who is motivated can join in, thanks to the off-the-shelf phishing kits provided by a thriving cybercrime ecosystem. Cybercriminals are even migrating to a new business model where authors of exploit kits offer extra services to customers in addition to the exploit kit itself.

4.6   The Underground Cyber-Economy

It is all boom and bustle in the underground cyber-economy today. With much of the trade being conducted using the increasingly popular crypto-currency, Bitcoin, or other unregulated electronic currencies, people are buying and selling stolen data, attack toolkits and 'Stresser' DDoS services in volumes never seen before.

These activities occur far from the gaze of the public, most regulators and law enforcement officials, in an area of the web we read about in section 1.2.2 called the Darknet. Users of the Darknet further hide and anonymise their activities through the use of various online tools that allow them to conceal their IP addresses and to encrypt their sessions. Tools such as TOR have given anyone who has the time and inclination to download them the ability to cloak themselves in invisibility.

These hidden markets see an increasing division of labour. Some people specialise in writing malware or attack kits, while others focus on malware distribution, the management of botnets or the monetisation of stolen credit card and other personal financial details.

Symantec reports an increasing professionalisation of all of these elements. The prices charged are indicative of the perceived quality of service. A drive-by download web toolkit (including updates and 24/7 support) can be rented for between £60 and £500 per week or on a six-month lease at a rate of £800. An advanced DDoS attack can be ordered for as little as £20 per day, while stolen email addresses retail at £0.50.

Other examples[1] of offers and pricing reported from the Darknet include:

Item (from a Russian online price list)	Price
Email spam (per 1 million messages sent)	$10.00
SMS spam (per 100,000 messages)	$150.00
SOCKS bot (circumvents firewalls)	$100.00
Botnet (per 2,000 bots)	$200.00
DDoS botnet	$700.00
DDoS attack service (per day)	$70.00
Windows Rootkit (installs malicious drivers)	$300.00
Facebook account hack	$130.00
Twitter account hack	$170.00
Corporate mailbox hack	$500.00

---

1   www.trendmicro.com/cloud-content/us/pdfs/security-intelligence/white-papers/wp-russian-underground-101.pdf

4.6.1   Increasingly Varied Threats

Threats in the modern era are increasingly diverse and sometimes unforeseeable. Consequently, much of the emphasis within organisations will now need to be directed at responding to unavoidable incidents and managing their effects, in addition to preventing or attempting to avoid them.

Almost no company, whether large or small, is immune from this kind of attack. If the Antwerp example, seen earlier in section 2.1.3, strikes you as not being relevant to banking, pause for a moment. The Port management systems are transactional IT systems. A user is a user. What Antwerp demonstrates is the capacity of hackers to engineer human users (using spear-phishing techniques) into behaving foolishly, thus opening the gateway for malware. Whatever the type of transactional platform, if the data are sensitive and the hacker sufficiently determined, incredible harm can be done in any environment. Let us not forget that drug traffickers also launder funds and often fund terrorism. They may well be politically exposed persons (PEPs). The drug traffickers' skill sets are often identical to those of the financial criminals.

4.6.2   CaaS and SaaS Combined

Industry reports appear to support the notion that a significant percentage of websites have critical vulnerabilities that could allow hackers to take the sites over, without the knowledge of legitimate owners, in order to edit links so that visitors who trust the sites are in fact redirected to malicious pages.

The problem of compromised websites is growing. Even though there has been a decline in the number of compromised sites, the way in which they are being used by hackers is becoming far more sophisticated, as we saw in section 4.4.6 on malnets. Attackers are apparently moving away from crude volumetric methods towards much more surreptitious and intelligent techniques that elude security and which most internet users will struggle to comprehend.

There is also a move by attackers away from setting up their own malicious domains towards the use of cloud services. This could be described as CaaS using SaaS, or crime as a service using software as a service.

Criminals are also moving away from the use of email scams to send out malicious links and infected files, towards the use of social media and malicious advertising (malvertising) as channels for bringing victims to their domains or cloud-based systems. The prevalence of shortened URLs on most social media pages exacerbates the problem because users are unable to easily recognise malicious links.

Most social media users are now habituated to the practice of giving links to view funny videos, music videos or humorous content without a moment's hesitation. This provides attackers with a gold mine of gullible potential victims and it is now commonplace to see cases in which popular music videos are used as a mechanism for drawing victims to malicious pages. The other very popular technique for netting victims is the use of pornographic video and still images as a honey trap.

One key advantage to attackers of using the cloud is the relative anonymity it can provide combined with the fact that cloud servers can be based anywhere in the world and law enforcement investigations based on tracking IP addresses are therefore much more difficult to carry out. Some hosting services even offer rapid domain and IP address changes to the users. This represents a real boon to attackers.

4.7   Network-Level Threats (2)

Learning Objective

1.4.2   Identify the following types of network level technical cybercrime attack: remote code injection; structured query language (SQL) injection; cross-site scripting (XSS); format string vulnerabilities; user name enumeration

4.7.1   Remote Code Injection

Code injection does exactly what it says – it injects malicious code into a target system in order to produce an unwanted result.

A prime example of this type of attack occurred in 2011 when the log-on web page belonging to the online gaming company Sony Online Entertainment (SOE) was subjected to a code injection attack. Attackers apparently inserted code instructions into the username and password fields of an SOE page and these commands are believed to have given the attackers access to SOE customer data, including username and password lists and credit card details.

More than 77 million customer accounts were thought to have been compromised and, by its own account, SOE suffered a loss of over $178 million due to an extended period of downtime while the problem was investigated and resolved. The extent of the brand and reputational damage may never be known, but some analysts have estimated the total impact at over $1 billion.

4.7.2   Structured Query Language (SQL) Injection

Structured Query Language (SQL) injection was the code injection technique used to attack SOE, as described above. SQL injection targets database applications that use the SQL standard. Malicious SQL statements are inserted into an entry field for execution (eg, to dump the database contents to the attacker, delete the database, edit the database or insert new data within the database).

SQL injection exploits security vulnerabilities in software, eg, when user input is incorrectly filtered for disallowed commands.

4.7.3   Cross-Site Scripting (XSS)

Cross-site scripting (XSS) covers a range of technical issues. Essentially, it refers to a scenario in which an attacker exploits some vulnerability in a web page so that he can transmit malicious code from his own device via the web page to a victim's device when the victim is viewing the same page.

Alternatively, an XSS attack might allow an attacker to gather data from the other user's device without their knowledge or consent.

In both cases, XSS exploits security loopholes on the visited page and the victim may not necessarily be at fault in any way. The onus is on the administrators of web pages to maintain security and to scan regularly for vulnerabilities.

4.7.4 Format String Vulnerabilities

Within applications, for example a web form, format strings are pieces of code that trigger various application functions. Each application will include a library of format strings and the corresponding functions that they should execute.

Format string exploits occur when applications incorrectly allow format strings to be included in user data, for example when a field in a web form is filled in with text. If insecurely configured, a web form might accept that input as a command.

Common motives for attackers to enter format strings within text include:

- executing arbitrary or malicious code on the server
- reading values of the server
- triggering software crashes and denying service.

4.7.5 Username Enumeration

Username enumeration refers to a vulnerability in an application, normally a website, whereby the site delivers a response to a failed login attempt that indicates whether or not the username submitted is already on the system. This is a common feature on new account registration pages where entering an existing username will result in a statement to the effect that this name is already in use. In such scenarios, a hacker is already halfway to establishing the username and password combination for an account.

There are two classes of username enumeration exploit:

- **Bruteforceable** – confirmation that the username was valid although the password was incorrect allows an attacker to attempt a **brute force attack** using a dictionary of common passwords.
- **Dumpable** – the target application can be tricked into providing a dump (exportable list) of all valid user names on the system.

Blended Attacks

A blended threat combines elements of multiple types of malware, or other attack tools, and many employ multiple attack vectors in order to increase the severity of the attack and the speed of contagion.

Well-known examples of **blended attack** tools include:

- Nimda
- Code Red
- Bugbear
- Conficker.

A majority of modern attack scenarios involve blended threats. A blended threat typically involves:

- more than one means of propagation, for example by sending an email with a hybrid virus/worm that will self-replicate on the recipient's device and simultaneously infect the web server so that contagion will spread through all visitors to a particular site
- the exploitation of vulnerabilities which may be pre-existing or that might be caused by other malware distributed as part of the attack
- the intent to cause real harm, for example, by launching a DoS attack against a target, or by delivering Trojan malware to be activated at some later date.

Patch management, the use and maintenance of reliable firewall products, the employment of server software to detect malware threats and the education of users about proper email handling and online behaviour are essential countermeasures.

4.8 Malware Threats

Learning Objective

1.4.5   Identify the following types of technical cybercrime based on application exploits: application hacking; password cracks; code injection; malicious websites; drive-by downloads

1.4.6   Identify the main types of technical cybercrime arising from malware exploits, including: viruses; worms; Trojans; spyware; rootkits

4.8.1   Viruses

Viruses are the original form of malware. A virus is a piece of malicious code that requires some kind of user action before it executes itself on the infected system. Examples of user action include:

- opening a file attachment in an email
- clicking on a link to an infected web page
- downloading files (music, video or apps) from malicious web pages
- accepting an infected USB stick or other USB device, such as a camera
- purchasing ripped (pirated) software and films on DVDs.

The advent of the drive-by-download means that user action is no longer required to contract this kind of infection; merely visiting a malicious web page (a page hosting malware) is often sufficient to cause the infection to be installed.

4.8.2   Worms

A worm is a more sophisticated piece of malware that is programmed to navigate (or worm) its way around the network searching for a specific kind of device or software application.

The most famous worm to date is the Stuxnet worm, which navigated its way through the network used by the Iranian nuclear facility at Natanz and then, once it located the management system controlling the centrifuges, launched an attack that took the facility offline for 18 months.

4.8.3   Trojans

Trojan malware, as the name suggests, is malicious code that hides inside seemingly innocent code. Many modern apps contain Trojan malware.

4.8.4   Spyware

Spyware is malware that is designed to spy on user activities, capturing screenshots and keystrokes, and then sending this information back to the attacker across the internet.

4.8.5   Rootkits

A **rootkit** is a piece of malware that is able to assume system administrator privileges on the infected system. Once it has achieved this, the rootkit can install other pieces of malicious code, encrypt systems and even lock out legitimate users and administrators.

4.8.6   Ransomware

Ransomware, also known as crypto-extortion malware, allows attackers to communicate with victims after encrypting their data, or their entire hard drive, to demand the payment of a ransom in exchange for the decryption key.

WannaCry represents the most high-profile ransomware attack to date, but the issue is not new and has been growing steadily since 2012.

4.8.7   Maladvertising or Scareware

Another common online crime involves popping up a message when a visitor arrives at a malicious website that says: *your computer may be infected with the X virus. Download your free virus scan app here.*

If the user downloads and runs the free scan, the result is invariably positive and several infections are reported. In fact, no actual scan has taken place and the user is now being told to purchase a solution to a non-existent problem. They may also be downloading more malware with their new 'anti-virus' tool.

Numerous variations of this scenario exist and it is merely the online version of ancient conman techniques.

4.8.8   Malware Payloads

There are many other types of malware, but most malware has the capacity to deliver a common set of payloads. The term payload refers to the weapon carried by a vehicle of war. In this case, the malware is the vehicle and the payload is the particular technique it employs or the additional piece of malicious code that it downloads after it has infected a system.

The functions of typical malware payloads include:

- crashing the computer or taking control
- deleting or modifying files

- downloading unwanted files
- uploading files from the target machine
- encrypting files in a crypto-viral extortion attack
- installing a software 'back door'
- changing the way computer programs work
- using an attacked machine as part of a botnet
- logging keystrokes – phishing or espionage purposes
- monitoring the user's screen.

4.8.9 At War with the Anti-Malware Firms

Anti-malware firms tend to operate by collecting samples of malicious code, analysing the code in a sandbox in order to detect its signature, and then providing that signature as an update to every installation of their anti-virus products. A sandbox is a secure space in which the malware can execute and be studied without any risk to other systems.

If an anti-malware company cannot obtain samples of the malicious code easily, its work is greatly hindered. Malware developers, and others in the crimeware ecosystem, have become increasingly adept at spotting instances of anti-malware company machines (typically virtual machines) when they attempt to become infected. When such an instance is spotted, the malicious pages are configured in such a way that the malware infection will not be delivered to the investigator's device.

In this spy versus spy conflict, anti-malware practitioners need to take ever more inventive steps in order to conceal their links with the anti-malware organisation, doing their best to pose as naive victims with insecure laptops, rather than expert users with powerful machines loaded with sophisticated software.

4.9 Device Level Threats

Learning Objective

1.4.3   Identify the most common types of technical cybercrime attack at device level: device intrusions/hacking; password cracks; physical keyloggers; inbuilt infections at point of manufacture or sale; device sharing risks; device disposal and maintenance-related data breaches; device theft

1.4.4   Identify the most common technical cybercrime attack via peripheral devices: bring your own device (BYOD) risks; removable media risks; printer risks

---

4.9.1 Device Intrusions/Hacking

Hackers intrude into users' devices in numerous ways. Remote attacks via the internet are possible and occur frequently. One common scenario involves the attacker automatically scanning ranges of IP addresses on the internet, searching for open publication ports. When an open port is found, the attacker will attempt a brute force attack by trying various combinations of common usernames and passwords.

Devices are also susceptible to attack when they come into the physical possession of the attacker. This may happen because the device has been stolen, or because it is a shared device. Staff working at repair centres also have access to devices and have been known to insert malware or steal content.

Devices in the cloud, which are often located overseas, are also exposed to attack if operational security at the cloud service provider's site is lax. In one recent case, engineers visiting a leading service provider site to remove the computer assigned to one corporate firm were given access to the wrong area of the site by security. As a result, the engineers removed equipment belonging to another organisation, which resulted in the potential exposure of confidential data as well as a loss of service.

4.9.2   Password Cracks and Brute Force Attacks in Focus

Most systems that support password access store these passwords in tables, and not as plain text but in the form of 'hash' values. A hash is a mathematical description of a piece of data. You can generate a hash for any volume of data (eg, all the data on your hard drive) but the length of the resulting hash will always be the same. For example, the hash of the word 'Password' using the popular MD5 algorithm, is dc647eb65e6711e155375218212b3964. This will always be the same in any database using the same algorithm.

Hashes are used to validate users' passwords without ever storing the actual password itself. When you type a password in a form, it is converted to a hash value. The hash is then sent to the database and compared to the one stored there. If it matches, then you must have typed the correct term.

The vulnerability in this model occurs when someone selects a predicable password. Anyone who hacks, steals or buys a stolen database can precalculate the hash values for popular passwords (like (Password1234 or pA55W0rd1234*, for example). By searching the list of hashes in the exposed database, the hacker can find those users using guessable formats and then attempt to hack their accounts. The problem is made worse by the fact that many users employ the same username and password across several accounts, and attackers will test websites such as PayPal, Amazon, Netflix, Gmail and Facebook to see if they can also gain access there.

Brute Force Attacks

A brute force attack is designed to obtain a user's login details (username and password) by repeatedly trying common combinations of usernames and passwords. This is also known as a dictionary attack.

Brute force login tools exist for most services that allow remote access across a network. Attackers can use brute force applications, such as password guessing tools and scripts, to automate username and password login attempts. These applications often use default password databases, dictionaries, or rainbow tables that contain commonly used passwords, or they may try all combinations of a given character set to try to crack a password.

To find running Secure Shell (SSH) services on networks, attackers probe a large number of IP addresses on Port 22, the default SSH listening port. (SSH is a network protocol that allows data to be exchanged using a secure channel between two networked devices). If a response from the probe of Port 22 is received, the attacker will initiate a brute force attack.

Industrial Control Systems Cyber-Emergency Response Team (ICS-CERT) recommends that organisations monitor network logs for port scans as well as access attempts. Hundreds or thousands of login attempts over a relatively short time period is one common indicator of a brute force attack. High-volume scans tend to be quickly discovered, so attackers try to evade IDSs by making only a few careful attempts in any given time period.

Attacks of this nature have the greatest impact when they hit operational systems. They can be mitigated in the following manner:

- Configure SSH servers to use non-standard ports.
- Minimise network exposure for all key systems. Key systems should not directly face the internet.
- Locate key systems and devices behind firewalls and isolate them from the business network.
- Stay actively aware of what is on the network by performing periodic port scans and **penetration tests**.
- If remote access is essential, employ secure methods, such as virtual private networking (VPN).
- Remove, disable or rename any default system accounts (eg, root or sysadmin) wherever possible.
- Implement account lockout policies to reduce the risk of brute forcing attempts.
- Implement policies requiring the use of strong passwords. Make password lengths long and combine letters, numbers and special characters. Better still, introduce multi-factor authentication wherever possible.
- Monitor the creation of administrator level accounts by third-party vendors.
- Use intrusion detection/intrusion prevention. An IDS monitors networks for malicious activity or policy violations. IDS systems can aid in investigations of system breaches.

Dictionary Attacks

In a dictionary attack, the attackers test a large number of common names as possible account names on the target machine. Should they succeed in stumbling across a name for which there is actually an account on the target machine, they then proceed to test a large number of commonly used passwords. As described in section 4.7.5, username enumeration is a vulnerability that aids the attackers during this process.

Common user account names that an attacker might search for include:

- root
- webmaster
- webadmin
- linux
- admin
- ftp (File Transfer Protocol)
- mysql
- oracle
- guest
- postgres
- test
- sales
- staff
- user.

When an attacker finds an installed account on the target machine, the next challenge is to gain entry into the account by making guesses at the possible password for the account.

In the context of guessing the passwords, it is interesting to examine a subset of the 240 password guesses that were embedded in the binary code for the Conficker worm:

123, 1234, 12345, 123456, 1234567, 12345678, 123456789, 1234567890, 123123, 12321, 123321, 123abc, 123qwe, 123asd, 1234abcd, 1234qwer, 1q2w3e, a1b2c3, admin, Admin, administrator, Nimda, qwewq, qweewq, qwerty, qweasd, asdsa, asddsa, asdzxc, asdfgh, qweasdzxc, q1w2e3, qazwsx, qazwsxedc, zxcxz, zxccxz, zxcvb, zxcvbn, passwd, password, Password, login, Login, pass, mypass, mypassword, adminadmin, root, rootroot, test, testtest, temp, temptemp, foofoo, foobar, default.

Conficker successfully infected an estimated 12 million computers. This tells us something about the general state of username and password security.

4.9.3 Physical Keyloggers

Not all attacks are purely digital in nature. A number of physical devices can be purchased online that will aid attacks. A prime example of this is the physical keylogger.

Keyloggers often come in USB form, but they are sometimes seen in the form of serial devices that can be plugged into the serial ports on the back of a computer. A typical key logger will capture all keystrokes entered by a user, as well as other information, and store that in its physical memory.

The keylogger is programmed either to send the captured data to an internet address, or to allow the data to be transferred to another device when the attacker physically removes it. Devices like this are often left in place for long periods of time and the attacker will pay a member of staff, such as a security guard or office cleaner, to periodically remove the device and capture all the data stored on it, before putting the device back into the target machine.

4.9.4 Inbuilt Infections at Point of Manufacture or Sale

There have been innumerable instances of computer hardware apparently being infected at the point of manufacture. The US government alleged that it had found spyware pre-installed on servers that it had purchased from a Chinese manufacturer. Microsoft reported that test purchases of PCs and retail outlets in China resulted in the discovery of malware on 12% of those brand new, shrink-wrapped devices.

Companies that purchase lower cost grey market second-hand or reconditioned devices run even greater risks. Another long-standing practice is the installation of malware in repair facilities, or by engineers during site visits.

It is clear that the risk is not restricted to poor user habits while web browsing, reading email and using social media. Many of the attacks seen over the years appear to originate from corporate firms, foreign governments and people in their employ.

4.9.5 Device Sharing and Bring Your Own Device (BYOD) Risks

The potential risks of sharing devices are fairly obvious, but one facet of device sharing often escapes the attention of corporate security and risk management; the sharing of bring your own device (BYOD) devices with our children. Any parent who has had to endure the persistent clamour for a turn on the iPad while driving their children over a long distance to the countryside will know that there are few pressures more likely to lead to a breach of company policy than the shrill cries of two 6-year-olds!

As seen in section 4.8.3 on Trojan software, we can immediately see why allowing child users access in order to play games might expose the device owner, as well as the corporate network they might visit, to a range of malware infections.

In fact, this vector for infection is so commonplace that IT support staff use the phrase 'malware Mondays' to describe the dramatic increase in malware infections that is often observed at the end of every weekend.

Other device-sharing risks include the potential for personal details and financial data to be viewed by other users of the device. This may lead to fraud or, in certain cases, to reputational harm and the potential for blackmail.

4.9.6 Device and Removable Media Disposal

Electronic devices and media can hold vast amounts of information, some of which can linger indefinitely. The normal deletion of files does not remove data from a storage device; it simply tells the computer that the old data sectors are now available to be overwritten. The old data remains in place and is thus a major cause of data breaches and identity theft.

Even the trusty printer can represent a security risk, as files sent for printing may be stored in the printer's memory. If a repair technician works on the device, or if it is disposed of, that stored data could be exposed.

A formal data-removal process to securely delete sensitive data before disposal of old devices is essential. A sample list of relevant devices and media includes computers, laptops, hard drives, external hard drives, CDs, DVDs, USB drives, cameras, copiers and scanners, but other devices are also likely to hold data; even gaming consoles can hold email addresses and favoured passwords.

Secure disposal will ensure that sensitive data does not find its way into unauthorised hands. Most organisations will already have a secure disposal policy, which also extends to cover green issues by ensuring that heavy metals do not find their way into the environment.

Commonly, there are four basic types of sensitive data that need to be considered when disposing of devices or media:

- identity data
- financial data
- personal data (including photographs and anything else that might cause reputational harm)
- commercially sensitive data.

4.10   Advanced Persistent Threats

On 14 February 2012, the following text appeared as part of an article in the online publication CSO:

Former Nortel CEO Frank Dunn, now being tried for fraud, was among several senior company managers who were aware of a long-standing data breach into Nortel's computer systems, but chose to do nothing.

According to reports in the Wall Street Journal, former Nortel employee Brian Shields led an investigation and discovered the breach, but was prevented from taking any action by company executives.

Nortel, which has since declared bankruptcy, and which was cleared by the Department of Justice to sell $4.5 billion worth of patents to Apple, Microsoft and IBM on Monday, was deeply penetrated by hackers suspected of being from China. Sophos Senior Security Advisor, Chester Wisniewski, wondered if those companies would have paid so much for the patents if they'd known the data was likely already compromised. 'If the patents were known to have been potentially stolen or compromised, wouldn't they have to report that?' he asked.

Wisniewski criticized Nortel's response to the breach. 'I think the response is shameful. It doesn't look like they really cared,' he said. Wisniewski said that while many are blaming the Chinese government for the breach, there's really nothing to prove that China was really involved. While a Chinese internet site seems to have been the destination for data stolen from Nortel, 'Just because something appears to be from China doesn't mean it is,' Wisniewski said.

According to CSO, this cautionary tale highlights several important points:

- Threats can be very persistent – possibly over ten years in this case.
- Reporting is essential. In this case, a failure to report resulted in allegations of fraud.
- Due diligence by would-be buyers of intellectual property is equally important.
- Even major players in the high-tech industries can and do have their information assets ransacked by hackers.
- The apparent source of a sophisticated cyber-attack is unlikely to be the actual source.

4.10.1   Characteristics of Advanced Persistent Threats (APTs)

An advanced persistent threat (APT) is a form of cyber-attack normally directed at business and political targets. An APT employs stealth over a prolonged duration of operation in order to deliver whatever exploits the attacker has selected. The attackers' motives generally extend beyond simple financial gain to include religious, political, state or competitive advantage.

A key characteristic of most APTs is that the compromised systems continue to be of use even after they have been breached, hence the persistent facet of the attack. One could think of an APT in terms of a thief who enters your home in secret and then hides in the attic for weeks, waiting for the perfect moment to strike.

An APT can be summarised in the following fashion:

Advanced

Criminal operators behind the threat utilise the full spectrum of computer intrusion technologies and techniques. While individual components of the attack may not be classed as particularly advanced (eg, malware components generated from commonly available DIY construction kits, or the use of easily procured exploit materials), their operators can typically access and develop more advanced tools as required. They combine multiple-attack methodologies and tools in order to reach and compromise their target.

Persistent

Criminal operators give priority to a specific task, rather than opportunistically seeking immediate financial gain. This distinction implies that the attackers are guided by external entities. The attack is conducted through continuous monitoring and interaction in order to achieve the defined objectives. It does not mean a barrage of constant attacks and malware updates. In fact, a low and slow approach is usually more successful.

Threat

This means that there is a level of co-ordinated human involvement in the attack, rather than a mindless and automated piece of code. The criminal operators have a specific objective and are skilled, motivated, organised and well-funded.

Routes

Even in the presence of properly designed and maintained defence-in-depth strategies, an APT can breach enterprises through a wide variety of routes, for example:

- internet-based malware infection
- physical malware infection.

External Exploitation

Well-funded APT adversaries do not necessarily need to breach perimeter security controls from an external perspective. They can, and often do, use insiders and trusted connections to access and compromise targeted systems.

Abuse and compromise of trusted connections is a key ingredient for many an APT. While the targeted organisation may employ sophisticated technologies in order to prevent infection and compromise of their digital systems, criminal operators often tunnel into an organisation using the hijacked credentials of employees, business partners or remote offices. Almost any organisation or remote site may fall victim to an APT and be utilised as a soft entry or information harvesting point.

Low and Slow Attacks

A key requirement for an APT (as opposed to an every day botnet) is to remain invisible for as long as possible. The criminal operators of APT technologies tend to focus on low and slow attacks – stealthily moving from one compromised host to the next, without generating regular or predictable network traffic – to hunt for their specific data or system objectives. Tremendous effort is invested to ensure that malicious actions cannot be observed by legitimate operators of the systems.

Malware

Malware is a key ingredient in successful APT operations. Modern off-the-shelf and commercial malware openly available on the internet includes all of the features and functionality necessary to infect digital systems, hide from host-based detection systems, navigate networks, capture and extricate key data and provide video surveillance, along with silent and covert channels for remote control. If needed, APT operators can and will use custom-developed malware tools to achieve specific objectives and harvest information from non-standard systems.

Criminal Remote Control

At the very heart of every APT lies remote control functionality. Criminal operators rely upon this capability in order to navigate to specific hosts within target organisations, exploit and manipulate local systems and gain continuous access to critical information.

If an APT cannot connect with its criminal operators, it cannot transmit any intelligence it may have captured. In effect, it has been neutered. This characteristic makes an APT appear as a sub-category of botnets. While APT malware can remain stealthy at the host level, the network activity associated with remote control is more easily identified. APTs are most effectively identified, contained and disrupted at network level.

4.10.2 Simple APT Access Techniques

Security firm, Mandiant, remarks that while the APT threat continues to adapt and become more sophisticated, attackers still rely on simple techniques to gain access to a victim network. The following trends have been identified throughout the majority of engagements and **incident responses** the firm has conducted, since the APT continues to use a repetitive and identifiable targeting and exploitation cycle.

Step 1: Reconnaissance

Besides attacks using spear-phishing techniques, attackers also attack targeted organisations from several other angles, in order to gain a foothold in their network. They can do this by attacking the perimeter of the network, looking for holes in the defences and then exploiting them.

Reconnaissance plays a big part in an attacker gaining access to a targeted network, as they seek to gain information about the systems in operation and look for weaknesses. Once armed with information about the target network's host names, IP addresses and various internal path names, an attacker can more easily develop a plan of attack.

Zero Day exploits (exploits that have not yet been detected and dealt with by security vendors) can give attackers a big window of opportunity for hostile reconnaissance of this kind, often as much as a year or more. The best explanation for such extended periods of exposure is often the perceived severity of the threat. If a given exploit does not allow an attacker to directly take control of a vulnerable computer, it might not be considered as important to address as other vulnerabilities. Experienced attackers know this and configure their malware accordingly.

Mandiant states that this is a portion of the threat landscape that may deserve more attention from the security industry. While a vulnerability that simply returns information about the network, computer or device may not be considered as severe as one that allows privilege escalation, it can be just as dangerous if it points attackers toward vulnerable systems they would not have otherwise discovered.

During the reconnaissance phase, targeted individuals can range from an organisation's senior leadership to administrative assistants. Victims' contact information is regularly extracted from public websites and from services such as LinkedIn and Facebook and then used to format the social engineering messages sent to these people.

Staff awareness training is the only truly effective defence during the reconnaissance phase, as much of the process is non-technical and might never be detected or prevented by technological solutions.

Step 2: Full-Scale Intrusion into the Network

Once the reconnaissance phase is complete, an advanced persistent threat may use a range of techniques to gain initial access to an organisation. As stated in section 2.1, but worthy of repetition, the most common and effective method is the use of social engineering, via social media, telephone and face-to-face contact or via email.

Knowledge of the target is an essential prerequisite for a successful social media attack. For example, if a number of employees of the target organisation recently attended a well-publicised business conference, the attackers will often send fake or spoof emails apparently addressed from a speaker at the conference. The spoof email, which will refer to the speaker's awareness of the targets' attendance at the event, will include an attachment or a link to a ZIP file.

The ZIP file attached to the email will bear a name such as 'updated slide pack' and will contain one of several different intrusion techniques, including:

- a file containing malware
- a Microsoft Office document exploit
- some other form of software exploit, such as an Adobe Reader exploit.

Clever APT ploys of this nature are very difficult to distinguish from legitimate communications and many employees in a wide range of organisations and roles fall for such cons on a daily basis.

Step 3: Obtain User Credentials and Establish a Backdoor

Once the attacker has successfully infected a device in the target network, the next step is to attempt to acquire administrative user rights on that infected device. This allows the attacker to download and install further pieces of malicious code. This capability is commonly referred to as the installation or establishment of a backdoor.

There are many different ways by which attackers obtain administrative rights. In one example, the initial infection pops up a dialogue box on the user's screen stating that if the user wishes to proceed with whichever task it was they were undertaking (for example, running Microsoft Word), they now need to enter a system administration username and password.

If the user knows these credentials, they may well enter them, or they may summon an administrator and ask for assistance. Even fairly competent system administrators are known to simply enter the username and password requested, because such dialogues are not uncommon and system administrators are often under pressure and multitasking throughout the day.

Once the username and password combination has been entered, the dialogue box disappears and the malware saves those login details and possibly transmits them back to the attacker. The malware can now act as a system administrator, adding a new system admin account and installing additional applications.

Some malware takes further steps and deactivates anti-virus tools or the automatic update features of such tools, so as to increase the chances of a subsequent attack succeeding without detection. In other cases, attackers have been seen to capture the encrypted files that contain user or system administrator credentials on infected systems and transfer them out of the network, back to the attacker's domain. The attacker then runs decryption algorithms against those files and, once they have been cracked, the attacker now has the same system administrator privileges as described above.

The malicious code is updated regularly and attackers use encryption and concealment of the network traffic between the infected device and their own command and control systems to conceal their activities from network security.

Step 4: Install Various Utilities

APT attackers install a range of utility programs to perform common system administration tasks. They install backdoors, copy passwords and gather email messages from servers, or produce lists of running processes, among other tasks. The same utility applications are often found on systems that do not contain backdoors, which means that these activities are difficult to detect.

Step 5: Privilege Escalation/Lateral Movement/Data Exfiltration

Attackers will exploit the system admin rights to escalate, or increase, their privilege levels, allowing them to undertake ever-more sophisticated tasks on the victim's devices.

Using these and other techniques, attackers will now move laterally through the network acquiring similar privileges on one device after another. They may not install any malicious code on the other newly compromised devices, but their presence means that they can remain a persistent threat over an extended period of time within the compromised network. If the victim fails to detect this fact, they may spend months firefighting new infections on one device after another, without ever realising that the attacker has been present the entire time.

On average, it is reported that APT intruders access approximately 40 systems on a victim network using compromised credentials, although instances of 150 compromised systems have been seen.

Once a secure foothold is established within the victim's network, the attackers may proceed to exfiltrate, or remove and transmit, any data they have been able to collect, such as emails and attachments, or files residing on users' workstations and on file servers. In most cases, the stolen information is compressed using an archival utility such as password-protected ZIP, RAR or Microsoft Cabinet file. The stolen data may also be encrypted to further conceal its nature.

The data is often exfiltrated from the compromised network to a series of staging servers within the APT's command and control infrastructure, where the stolen data is aggregated and stored temporarily, before being downloaded to the attacker's own machine. This ensures that the attacker is one or more steps removed from the victim, making investigation more difficult. The drop servers will normally be other compromised hosts on other networks.

Once the data exfiltration and staging process is complete, the attackers will wipe the stolen files from staging servers, removing all evidence of their activities and the route taken.

Step 6: Maintaining Persistence

APT attackers closely monitor the activities of the victim. If they detect evidence to suggest that their presence has been spotted, they will move rapidly to delete their installed applications and, after lying low for a period of time, they will resume their attack from another of the compromised platforms on the network. In this fashion, attackers are able to stay in place for weeks and even months.

4.10.3 Famous APT Examples

Stuxnet

Stuxnet was a computer worm specifically adapted to target the Supervisory Control and Data Acquisition (SCADA) management systems used on some classes of Siemens industrial technology. Iran's nuclear programme uses Siemens SCADA systems and Stuxnet was able to infect the management systems at Iran's uranium enrichment facility at Natanz between 2009 and 2010. According to reports, Stuxnet changed the operating software at the plant, inflicting physical damage to the system by altering the frequency at which motors, connected to gas centrifuges that separate uranium isotopes, turned.

This was a rare example of a malware attack leading to a physical manifestation, although as an attack concept this is nothing new, with air traffic control, nuclear weapons command and control systems, power grids and water management all being the subject of previous analysis and speculation. While the sponsors of the Stuxnet attack are yet to be formally identified, the fact that over 60% of all reported Stuxnet infections have occurred in Iran leads most commentators to conclude that either Israel or the United States, possibly both, were behind the creation and use of Stuxnet.

Flame

Flame was another computer worm, apparently closely related to Stuxnet. While Stuxnet targets systems and alters their operations, Flame is primarily an espionage tool, stealing and exfiltrating data before wiping itself from the infected system. Flame bears several markers that suggest that it may have been developed by the same team as Stuxnet and it is believed to be the older of the two applications. These factors all point to the possibility that Flame was designed for cyber-espionage and reconnaissance, while Stuxnet followed up with an actual cyber-attack intended to cause physical or logical damage.

Shamoon

Possibly a Stuxnet copycat worm, Shamoon is best known for its infection of the Saudi Aramco computer network on 15 August 2012. Shamoon replaced files with images, thus deleting the original data irretrievably. Some 30,000 Aramco workstations were infected by Shamoon, representing 75% of the total, and these had to be removed and replaced. Signalling the growing power of attackers, who in Shamoon's case may not have been state-sponsored, this attack triggered fears that a major oil price increase might have been one result. Fortunately, Aramco was able to recover quickly and stability was restored to the market.

Hydraq

The Hydraq Trojan was in fact a family of threats, variously described as Operation Aurora, Google Hack Attack and Microsoft Internet Explorer Zero-day, that are reported to specialise in the use of features associated with a technology called virtual network computing (VNC). One exploit that this VNC technology enabled was for Hydraq to stream a video of the user's desktop to the attacker via the internet. This meant that the attacker was watching everything the user did on their machine in real time.

While this monitoring capability has been seen in other malware instances, Hydraq added some refinements. For example, the attacker controlling Hydraq could use the malware to download additional attack tools to the infected machine. They could also shut down and restart the machine remotely and collect a range of system data or search for and extract files from the target. Hydraq changed its identity each time the infected machine was restarted, thus making forensic detection more difficult to achieve and conforming to true APT type.

4.10.4 Watering Hole Attacks

Conceptually, a **watering hole attack** occurs when an attacker identifies, or guesses, the address of the website likely to be regularly visited and trusted by their targets. Malnet attacks often exploit this technique. For example, an attacker targeting the employees of the bank might guess that they visit a certain site in order to conduct background checks on potential clients.

In a watering hole attack, the attacker exploits a vulnerability on a popular, trusted web page and installs malware that will infect his target group. This has the same effect as a spear-phishing attack, but without running the risk of raising the target's suspicions by sending emails and other messages to them.

Once the victim has suffered the infections they are exposed to at the watering hole, attackers may carry out any of the relevant cybercrime exploits described in this workbook.

5. The Human Firewall

We have seen the extent to which the modern cybercriminal depends on social engineering to exploit human weaknesses (the 'human firewall') to gather intelligence on targets or to persuade people to exhibit risky behaviours.

Human users are the weak link in today's globalised network of information and communications technology platforms. While the capabilities of the technology are growing at an exponential rate, humans evolve very slowly and in a linear fashion, at best. We are entering an era in which the capacity of technology to transmit, store and process data in huge volumes has already far outstripped the capacity of most human users to adequately understand the technology and comprehend the volume and speed of the data it handles.

This comparative ignorance on the part of users in the face of highly complex technological solutions adds up to a significant area of risk.

5.1 User-Related Issues

Learning Objective

1.5.1 Identify the most common types of technical cybercrime stemming from user level issues: errors and accidental disclosures; rogue insiders; insider frauds; identity theft; phishing; vishing; pharming; physical intrusions; password sharing and weak passwords; self-provisioning

5.1.1 Errors and Accidental Data Disclosures

People working within organisations are a major cause of data breaches. A data breach is an incident in which sensitive, protected or confidential data is copied, transmitted, viewed, stolen or otherwise exploited by a person who does not have authority to access or process such data in that fashion. Sensitive, protected or confidential data includes financial information, such as credit card or bank details, personal health information (PHI), personally identifiable information (PII), trade secrets belonging to corporations, intellectual property and state secrets.

Various reports suggest that accidental data breaches by employees account for between 10%–20% of all incidents. Therefore, effective employee awareness training has the potential to cut exposure by up to one fifth.

Data breaches may be either intentional or accidental in nature. Accidental data breaches are also referred to as instances of unintentional information disclosure, data leaks or data spills. Most accidental data breaches do not involve a deliberate attack on the organisation, but attackers have proven themselves adept at quickly taking advantage of such errors, in order to exploit the data that has been exposed.

Regulated firms in the UK and across the EU are required to report data breaches involving sensitive data (see chapter 2, section 2.2.5 for details) to the office of the relevant Information Commissioner.

5.1.2   Rogue Insiders

When a data breach is deliberately caused by an employee, this is often referred to as a rogue insider case. A prominent recent example involved an employee at HSBC's subsidiary in Switzerland who removed and shared confidential bank records containing the details of offshore accounts held by a large number of European citizens. The allegation was that these account holders were either evading taxation or aggressively avoiding it in their home countries.

Whatever the motives of the insider, and whatever your personal views might be on a case-by-case basis, in information communications technology terms, a data breach is a data breach, and the individual responsible is either negligent or acting as a rogue insider.

5.1.3   Insider Frauds

Within the financial services sector, frauds committed by persons inside the organisation have been a long-standing issue. This is hardly surprising, given the fact that financial firms handle vast quantities of client funds and process the majority of their financial transactions. The temptations facing employees are therefore tremendous.

Cifas is the UK's counter-fraud body, responsible for collecting and disseminating data on fraud statistics. The Cifas internal fraud database looks at trends of various types, including those related to insider frauds (staff frauds). The database indicates an ongoing increase in both the number of insider frauds being committed and the number of cases being successfully detected and investigated.

In addition to frauds perpetrated against customers' accounts, fraudulent applications for employment (eg, containing false qualifications or omitting the details of previous convictions) have also increased sharply in recent years.

There is likely to be some correlation between the honesty and suitability of employees and other issues such as accidental data disclosure, insider fraud and the activities of rogue insiders. These statistics suggest, therefore, that more work needs to be done to address these issues and that insider frauds will continue to be a challenge for the foreseeable future.

5.1.4   Identity Theft and Fraud

Action Fraud, the national fraud and cybercrime reporting centre of the UK police force, defines data theft and fraud as follows:

- identity theft occurs when personal details are stolen
- identity fraud occurs when those details are used to commit fraud.

Action Fraud goes on to say that identity theft happens when fraudsters access enough information about someone's identity (such as their name, date of birth and current or previous addresses) to commit identity fraud. Identity theft can take place whether the fraud victim is alive or deceased.

A great deal of identity theft and identity fraud results from the actions of insiders. In the United States, it has been alleged that US Passport Agency contractors harvested Americans' personal data for identity theft purposes while working on government systems.

External fraudsters also go to great lengths to capture personal information. They may do this by hacking into databases, sending phishing messages, visiting social media pages to examine users' posts and profiles, socially engineering social media users through the use of fake profiles and even by using the ancient technique of dumpster diving – sifting through rubbish bins in search of discarded correspondence from banks, utility companies, for example.

The internet has facilitated a tremendous increase in levels of identity theft although cases of identity fraud, while on the rise, have not increased to quite the same degree. In other words, there is far more identity information out there and exposed online than ever before, but it is perhaps too much information for fraudsters to efficiently exploit.

5.1.5   Phishing, Pharming and Vishing

As seen in section 2.1.3, the practice of phishing, which involves sending carefully constructed messages in order to trick the recipient into giving up confidential information. Another variation of this ploy is known as pharming. The objectives of pharming are essentially the same, but pharming occurs when the victim visits a webpage and is tricked into entering confidential information on that page.

A common pharming technique is to somehow direct the victim to a page that promises some kind of prize or other financial reward. Before the victim can qualify for the reward they are told that they need to register their name, address and contact information. Once they have registered they are told that the reward can only be paid out if they provide their bank account details. They may then be told that, to qualify for the reward they also have to be a pre-existing customer and they are then asked to make a small credit card payment to purchase an innocuous-looking item.

Once this process has been completed, the fraudsters behind the website are in possession of all the information they need to commit identity fraud against their gullible 'customers'. Needless to say, no prize monies are ever paid.

Voice phishing is the practice of social engineering over any voice system, such as the telephone, Skype or WhatsApp, to gain access to private personal and financial information from victims. It is sometimes referred to as 'vishing' (ie, a combination of 'voice' and 'phishing'.

5.1.6   Physical Intrusions

Simply gaining physical entry to the premises of a target organisation remains a popular technique that even cybercriminals employ. This is essentially part of a blended attack; the physical access will normally be followed by the insertion of a device of some kind (eg, the insertion of an infected USB stick) as an attempt to hack the victim's Wi-Fi or physical network.

In 2013, the UK press reported a sophisticated cyber-attack against Santander bank in which an attacker posed as a maintenance engineer, gained access to a bank branch and fitted a keyboard video mouse device (KVM) to a computer in the branch, allowing transmission of the complete desktop contents of the bank computer over the network.

Criminals continue to demonstrate a willingness to take physical risks and to engage in a kinetic fashion with their targets. Such incidents are excellent examples of cyber-enabled crimes, in which technology serves as an enhancement to traditional methods, rather than completely replacing them.

5.1.7 Password Sharing and Weak Passwords

When we looked at brute force attacks in section 4.9.2 and the use of dictionary software to guess possible usernames and passwords, we saw that the strength of passwords is a key factor in security. Most corporate firms have moved away from basic username and password controls to secure sensitive information systems, moving instead towards **multifactor authentication**. However, username and password models continue to be used in many environments, for example when registering on a wide range of web services.

Because of the sensitive nature of the personal data that many users place in these online repositories, the vulnerability of the username and password control system remains very relevant. Weak passwords are an obvious problem and most modern systems will encourage, or even force, users to develop more complex passwords, normally containing a mix of lower and upper case letters and numbers at a minimum.

However, the human factor once again comes into play. Few people can remember more than one or two passwords and it is therefore quite natural that most users will use the same password across many different platforms. This means that a username and password need only be exposed once, for example via a Facebook hack, in order that it can be fraudulently used on a number of other services. If a user's Facebook username and password are the same ones they have opted to use on a PayPal-type account, or on their Bitcoin account, the exposure of their social media account can lead to serious financial harm for them.

The other common form of password sharing occurs when users on a network share their password with colleagues or visitors. This might take the form of explicit sharing or it can occur indirectly when a user gives up their seat to another person and allows them to operate the keyboard. On occasion, this happens accidentally when the user leaves the room for some reason and in many environments it occurs because users simply leave their login running at the end of a shift when they hand over to the new arrivals taking over their position.

Password sharing creates all manner of problems in terms of login user activities and maintaining audit trails. Controls that limit the scope for sharing are therefore essential for all organisations, along with raised employee awareness regarding the resultant risks.

5.1.8 Self-Provisioning

File transfer service provider Ipswitch claimed, in a June 2013 report, that 84% of employees in companies surveyed admitted to using personal email accounts to send sensitive files, often because the file size exceeded corporate email limits. Meanwhile, more than 50% of workers admitted they had uploaded company data to cloud services like Dropbox, without corporate approval.

Cloud self-provisioning is one of the most common challenges in this regard. If inappropriate cloud usage has the potential to expose the organisation to regulatory penalties, then employees responsible for such breaches must understand their personal exposure to punitive actions in the wake of such a failure.

There is also a need to tie cloud security policies in with BYOD policies, as the two issues are inextricably linked in the real world, and the self-provisioning of mobile devices and the apps that sit on them can also contribute to risk levels.

5.2 Social Media Threats

Learning Objective

1.5.2   Understand social media risk in relation to cybercrime: social engineering ploys; identity theft; contact network analysis; blackmail; harassment; stalking; grooming; data breaches; reputational harm and brand damage; target acquisition and reconnaissance.

5.2.1 Social Engineering Ploys

In 2015, Symantec reported that 70% of social media threats the previous year required end users to propagate them, compared with only 2% in 2013. The most popular scams are described below:

- **Manual sharing** – these rely on victims to actually do the work of sharing the scam by presenting them with intriguing videos, fake offers or messages that they share with their friends.
- **Fake offering** – these scams invite social network users to join a fake event or group with incentives such as free gift cards. Joining often requires the user to share credentials with the attacker or send a text to a premium rate number.
- **Likejacking** – using fake 'like' buttons, attackers trick users into clicking website buttons that install malware and may post updates on a user's newsfeed, spreading the attack.
- **Fake apps** – users are invited to subscribe to an application that appears to be integrated for use with a social network, but is not as described and may instead be used to steal credentials or harvest other personal data.
- **Comment jacking** – this attack is similar to likejacking where the attacker tricks the user into submitting a comment about a link or site, which will then be posted to their wall. This results in the infected link being shared more widely.

5.2.2 Identity Theft and Fake Online Profiles

Identity thieves and other fraudsters will go wherever there are people to be scammed and fake profiles, therefore, abound on sites like Facebook. Although not all of these are malicious fakes, some estimates put the total proportion of fake profiles at 5%. Facebook itself has admitted to malicious fake profiles on its site. When fake profiles from other social media sites are added to the mix, it is clear that there could be many millions, even tens of millions, of malicious fake online profiles.

This is important because of the trust many social media users place in these services. A number of businesses have already made the move away from email towards social media as their primary communications tool, but social media comes with none of the security controls now inherent in most modern corporate email services.

The ease with which attackers can assume fake identities online, or hack into valid accounts, compounded by the unwarranted trust of internet users, has far-reaching implications. The likelihood of data disclosure, and of brand or reputational harm, has increased by several orders of magnitude since the advent of social media services, but the full cost of this shift is yet to be understood.

Social media scammers are using their new-found skills to identify vulnerable targets and gather data about them, intrude into firms via naïve employees, investigate their contact networks and stalk people online, to harass victims and to groom others, sometimes for fraud and in other cases in preparation for predatory sexual activity. Inadvertent data breaches, committed by people who believe they are engaging in a genuine online relationship, are also a growing risk that can lead to extensive reputational harm and brand damage.

Hijacking Social Proof

Symantec remarks that criminals have hijacked the power of social proof; the idea that we attribute more value to something if it's shared or approved by others. The classic example the firm cites is of two restaurants: one with a big queue, the other empty. People would rather wait in the queue because popularity suggests quality.

Criminals exploit this observation by hacking genuine accounts on platforms like Snapchat so that when users see an endorsement for a scam product or link, they take it seriously because it seems to come from someone they actually know and trust.

Affiliate Scheme Scams

Affiliate schemes are a popular, and generally legitimate, means by which firms can expand their marketing reach. Affiliates are essentially sales channels for bigger brands. An affiliate will host a link to a product or service on their website. If a visitor to the affiliate site clicks on that link in order to purchase the good or service from the supplier's main site, the supplier is informed about the identity of the affiliate through which the click has come and the affiliate earns a commission on any resulting sale.

Fraud follows the money and there are large sums of money being generated by this affiliate click-through model. Unscrupulous affiliates attempt to trick users into signing up for premium services or product purchases that they do not want or need. If successful, the affiliate earns its commission and the customer may find it difficult to cancel the sale.

Another technique involves the offer of a discounted sign-up for an initial three-month period. A text message is then sent to confirm registration, but the text messages are charged at an exorbitant rate. Some online dating sites use this technique, providing an initial free trial period, but sending through confirmation text messages, each charged at a rate of £10. There is often little the consumer can do to challenge such charges and, in any event, most victims are too embarrassed to admit that they were using the site in the first place.

Social Media Authentication

Social media authentication mechanisms are generally weak and even the recent introduction of SMS-based two-factor authentication by Twitter, Facebook and others may have important shortcomings for the following reasons:

- Social media authentication is provided as a user option – nobody owning a malicious fake profile is likely to opt in, so optional two-factor authentication only addresses account takeover and does not deal with malicious fakes.
- Even in cases where providing a mobile phone number is mandatory for new accounts, research conducted by The Risk Management Group confirms that the use of an anonymous prepaid SIM (Subscriber Identification Module) is accepted by most sites, making an SMS-based authentication process meaningless as a mechanism for validating identity.
- Because of the opt-in nature of two-factor authentication in this model, anyone who has not opted in is now exposed to the risk of being locked out of their account completely by a hacker who uncovers their password and then opts in on their behalf for the SMS service by providing their (the hacker's) own phone number. This is a form of authenticated takeover that the legitimate customer will find even more difficult to counter.

In reality, in many cases weak username and password authentication are the primary culprit, often made worse by a lack of user awareness, with many being the victims of a variety of phishing attack methods. This is exactly what transpired when the so-called Syrian Electronic Army hacked the Twitter account of The Onion, a US spoof media outlet. The hacker first fooled Onion staff into clicking on a link to a news story in an email. This took them to what appeared to be a Google Apps login page and when two of the employees entered their usernames and passwords into this fake page, their credentials were captured. As one of these employees was apparently an administrator of some kind, The Onion's full set of Twitter account logins was then exposed, the list being stored within Google Apps itself.

5.2.3   Personal and Social Effects

The example of social media highlights the potential of cybercrime incidents to have both corporate, personal and even social costs. Once again, fraud is an obvious risk, but others exist. Online harassment, grooming, stalking and bullying have frequently been an outcome of account takeovers, as have burglary and robbery. These issues are added to the potential for data breaches and disclosures, blackmail and reputational harm and social engineering that these sites give rise to.

In its 2010 *Digital Criminal Report*, Legal & General described how burglars and other criminals are using various cyber-techniques, including fake social media identities, to acquire targets. Very often, the children of homeowners are approached online by what appear to be other children and discussions about holiday plans, parents' jobs and personal wealth then follow. Once trust has been developed, name and address information is requested. Armed with this data, criminals can make informed choices about where and when to act.

At the level of society, the murder of soldier Lee Rigby on a street in Woolwich in May 2013 once again demonstrated the negative potential of social media, when numerous examples of incitement to racial hatred via Twitter and Facebook were reported in the aftermath of the event. In Latvia in 2012, a run on the automated teller machine (ATM) system was sparked by false rumours on Twitter about the impending collapse of Swedbank – over €30 million in cash was then withdrawn from Swedbank accounts via the ATM system during the course of a single weekend.

5.2.4   Tracking and Privacy

Internet users and their personal data are not solely the focus of criminals. Many service providers have identified identity capital as a key business asset. Identity capital takes a variety of forms and can be sourced directly via sign-up forms or users' profiles, or via analysis of patterns of activity, contacts, message content and behaviours.

A large gap exists between the principles of European data protection and privacy law (current and proposed) and the online practices of social media providers. In many instances, this is simply a product of the global nature of the internet; it is difficult to enforce EU rules beyond the borders of the EU. Nevertheless, many large online providers of goods and services find it necessary to establish operations regionally, Google and Facebook being only two examples, and it would seem that more can and should be done to protect European consumers from privacy and data breaches.

Collusion Reports

A key feature of online tracking and behavioural analysis is the collusion that occurs between online sites. In addition to first-party tracking, in which a user's profile is captured and stored by a visited site, most sites also exchange data with other interested parties. Facebook is a good example, not because its intentions are any better or worse than any other business, but because it has created one of the most advanced models and because this is a model that others are likely to emulate.

When a Facebook user visits a Facebook page and clicks a 'like' button, that click is stored by Facebook and it becomes a source of behavioural data that can be used to refine Facebook's profile of that user. It might be argued that the user should anticipate this possibility and that in clicking the 'like' button, they are obviously communicating their opinion to Facebook. Conversely, it could also be argued that the user is doing no such thing – their intention is solely to communicate with the person or business on whose Facebook page the 'like' button appears. This point is open to debate.

What is less well understood by most users is the possibility that when they visit another web page outside Facebook that contains a Facebook 'like' button, Facebook is informed about the visit even if the visitor does not click the button. There are many other examples of this form of surreptitious third-party tracking and, to the legal layman at least, the practice does seem to conflict with the spirit, if not the text, of European legislation and values.

Social network usage analysis is also widely deployed and private firms are able to scoop up vast amounts of Twitter and Facebook content without the users of those sites being explicitly alerted to the fact that their profiles, connections and posts are being archived by third parties. Twitter, for example, provides a commercial Firehose API (software interface and data feed) that allows organisations to enter into an agreement with the site and then suck up all tweets posted by users for analysis in any manner of their choosing.

The privacy issues related to this already widespread practice of collecting and storing tweets without explicit user consent, and without an enforceable right to be forgotten, are yet to be fully explored.

5.3 Open Source (Desktop Attack) Threats

Learning Objective

1.5.3 Know key desktop attack and concealment techniques used in cybercrime: keylogging; screen-scraping; advanced online searching and reconnaissance; Google and Pastebin; LinkedIn, Facebook and Twitter searches; security and privacy vulnerabilities; image and reverse-image searching methods; mapping and geolocation vulnerabilities

5.3.1 Online Investigations

The internet is a vast repository of information and some of that information may include negative or sensitive facts about an organisation's brand, owners and employees. Rather than waiting for those hostile to the brand to uncover such data, organisations need to be proactive in searching for potentially damaging online content in order that such content can either be removed or responded to in other ways.

Enhanced due diligence (EDD) or politically exposed person (PEP) checks can also be conducted through the effective use of online tools and the following table provides a summary of some of the main considerations.

Table 1: Online Investigation Checklist

Activity	Purpose or Guidance
Keyword searches	Use the relevant search operators for each search engine to find references to the brand, products and similar items.
File types	Consider searching by file type, based on the type of data sought, for example .xls tables of usernames and passwords.
Advanced	Use advanced search techniques, including links searching, Boolean or enforced term operators and forced-phrase searching.
Name searches	Search for every possible name configuration and variation for senior personnel and other key employees, suppliers and contractors.
Nicknames	Make guesses as to possible nicknames.
Website visits	Conduct *Who is* lookups on any domain names located that hold negative references to the brand or to key staff.
IP address lookups	Ascertain physical IP address locations, but always bear in mind the fact that IP address geolocation may be inaccurate or that it may be spoofed.
Traces	Ascertain physical server locations.

Activity	Purpose or Guidance
Emails	Trace hostile emails to their point of origin.
News media searches	Search within news media sites using the site search functions normally provided.
Social media searches	Search social networking sites and online communities such as Facebook, Periscope, LinkedIn, Twitter, Myspace, Convicts Reunited, Bebo, for mentions.
Maps	Search using geolocation mapping of social media posts.
Chats, forums and ads	Search message forums, groups and Usenet newsgroups for mentions.
Community	Examine online classified and community sites using names, phone numbers and email addresses.
Blog searches	Search blogs and free domain hosting sites.
Themes	Search blogs by theme as well as by username.
Deep Web searches	Search the Deep Web and locate relevant databases including electoral register, telephone directories, business databases, maps and genealogy sites.
Geography	Use the Deep Web engines most appropriate for the organisation's geographic location(s).
Associations	Also search in the geographic areas your subjects come from, visit or otherwise engage with.
Image searches	Search media sites such as Flickr, YouTube and Pinterest.
Search terms	Use a wide range of search terms, as images may not be stored with the name of the search subject in the file name.
Search options	Explore the available search options such as colour, file size, type of image.
Reverse-image search	Use reverse image searches to search by image rather than keywords, metadata or watermarks.

5.3.2   Keylogging and Screen-Scraping

Some forms of malware are designed to stay resident without causing obvious harm to systems. Collectively referred to as 'spyware', these key loggers and screen scrapers do exactly what their names suggest; they spy on users, capturing every keystroke and monitoring everything displayed on their screens.

5.3.3   Advanced Online Searching

Most search engines (eg, Google, Yahoo, Bing) provide a default basic search function and the majority of users are unaware that a far more powerful set of advanced search features is available one mouse click away.

Search engine results are far more restricted than we realise. Even if you get 1 million hits on a search term, your search engine will never allow you to view more than the first 25 or 30 pages of results – that's about 300 hits.

In order to discover more, three key techniques are needed:

- the use of advanced search features
- the use of multiple search indexes
- the use of multilingual searches.

Google provides a good example. Its advanced website search facilities (located at http://www.google.com/advanced_search) allow users to define several additional search parameters not available on the basic search screen:

- **Language** – defines the source language of the web content to be searched for.
- **Region** – specifies a geographic region for the search.
- **Last updated date** – allows the user to focus on specific dates.
- **Site or domain** – allows the user to specify a website or domain name for the result.
- **Where the search terms appear on the page** – allows the user to specify the location on the page to search.
- **Safe search** – provides filtering options to eliminate indecent images.
- **File type** – lets users specify the format of any files they are seeking.
- **Usage rights** – finds pages that users have permission to use.

Another popular site, providing everything from password lists to stolen credit card details, is Pastebin.com.

For financial services compliance teams performing online searches for the purpose of due diligence, know your customer (KYC) or PEP checks, anything less than an advanced Google search is grossly inadequate. In fact, even the advanced surface web search has severe limitations and compliance teams are advised to make extensive use of Deep Web search engines, such as 192.com.

5.3.4   LinkedIn, Facebook and Twitter Searches

Social media sites also provide advanced search capabilities:

- Advanced searching on LinkedIn is also available and it allows users to apply numerous filters, with additional capabilities being offered to premium users.
- Facebook has a graph search service.
- In similar fashion, Twitter offers an advanced search capability: https://twitter.com/search-advanced?lang=en

Even in the wake of the Cambridge Analytica scandal of 2018, the majority of sites of this nature still have such advanced search features that compliance teams should be making maximum use of. Some sites have a wide range of hidden search capabilities that expert investigators and criminals use on a regular basis. Be careful what you post and what you like; it can often be seen by someone outside your circle.

5.3.5   Security and Privacy Vulnerabilities

Another frequently overlooked feature of social media sites is their security settings, an oversight that contributes to privacy risks. Users generally have a reasonable degree of control over how much personal data they enter into the site and also who can view their data. In LinkedIn, users can even set themselves to anonymous so that when they visit the profile of a person of interest, their own identity is withheld.

Anyone working in a sensitive role, particularly if they are responsible for investigations, should ensure that they have examined all of the security settings available on every site that they use. These settings change frequently and users should be aware of the fact that the service providers occasionally reset new settings to their default values. It is therefore very important that you revisit your settings page on a regular basis to ensure nothing has changed.

When searching through tools like Google, clicking on a link to a webpage will take you to the live page. Your visit will be detected and logged by that page and so, once again, if you wish to keep a low profile, or minimise your footprint, the secret is to select the small green arrow below the link in the Google results and view the cached version of the page.

Cached pages are recent copies of the live page that are stored on Google's own servers. When you visit a cached version of the page, you create no footprint on the actual web page, although the material you are viewing will be slightly out of date. The actual date on which the cache was created will be displayed, so you will know how much time has elapsed. Most search engines provide identical features for viewing cached content.

5.3.6   Image Searching Methods

As with webpage searches, there are also advanced search options for image searching, eg, www.google.com/advanced_image_search

The additional search features provided include:

- size
- aspect ratio
- colour
- type (eg, face or animated)
- site or domain
- file type
- safe search
- usage rights (find images that you have permission to use).

Another extremely powerful search feature is the reverse image search. Inexplicably, this is not provided from Google's advanced search page but rather from the basic image search page, where the user needs to click on the small black camera icon on the extreme right of the search bar. This will allow the user to either specify the URL, or to upload a photograph from their hard drive, in order to search the internet for other instances of the same picture.

Image and reverse image searching, when conducted as a two-step process, are very powerful techniques for due diligence and background checking. The author runs reverse image searching on all new friend requests and contact requests in social media and LinkedIn in order to find possible evidence of fake profiles.

5.3.7 Mapping and Geolocation Vulnerabilities

There are now numerous apps and websites that will display users' locations on maps. Snapchat is a good example, if the user responsible for the post has location services activated on their device. These sites come and go and you are advised to conduct a Google search to find the latest ones.

The geolocation of users is a very effective way of tracking threats to an organisation or the movements of persons of interest and it illustrates the growing sophistication of online searching and intelligence operations, many of which can be directed at a firm and its employees, just as they can be used by firms to aid compliance and fraud enquiries.

End of Chapter Questions

Think of an answer for each question and refer to the appropriate section for confirmation:

1. What is the World Wide Web?
   Answer reference: Section 1.1.2

2. What was Silk Road?
   Answer reference: Section 1.2.3

3. What are the three main classes of cloud service model?
   Answer reference: Section 1.4

4. What are the four main categories of cloud deployment model?
   Answer reference: Section 1.4.1

5. What is the meaning of the term DBMS?
   Answer reference: Section 1.5.1

6. Name two examples of a cryptocurrency.
   Answer reference: Section 1.6.1

7. What three key concepts form the Information Security Triangle?
   Answer reference: Section 1.7.1

8. Name any two cybercrime attack objectives.
   Answer reference: Section 4.1

9. What is a DDoS attack?
   Answer reference: Section 4.4.1

10. What is an exploit kit?
    Answer reference: Section 4.5.5

11. Name any three device level threats.
    Answer reference: Section 4.9

12. What is the common first phase of an APT attack?
    Answer reference: Section 4.10.1

Chapter Two
The Legislative Environment

1. Legal Concepts   83

2. UK Legislation   87

3. Relevant Foreign Legislation   103

This syllabus area will provide approximately 8 of the 50 examination questions

He can compress the most words into the smallest ideas better than any man I ever met. Abraham Lincoln, referring to a lawyer

1. Legal Concepts

In its 2013 *Comprehensive Study on Cybercrime*, the United Nations Office on Drugs and Crime (UNODC) cited *Fragmentation at the international level, and diversity of national cybercrime laws* as important hindrances to the effective management of cybercrime. According to the UN, while the evolution to this fragmented state is understandable in that it reflects varying socio-cultural and regional or geographic variations, fragmentation also results in *country cooperation 'clusters' that are not always well suited to the global nature of cybercrime.*

This is the other side of the globalisation coin – the one on which the capacity of governments to act effectively and collaboratively to address a globalised threat is hindered by the very nature of commercial globalisation itself.

1.1 Internet Law

Learning Objective

2.1.1   Understand the key concepts influencing internet law: net neutrality; free speech on the internet; internet censorship; privacy expectations; intelligence services surveillance; responsibilities of internet service providers (ISPs)

1.1.1 Net Neutrality

Net neutrality refers to the idea that internet service providers and governments should treat all data on the internet equally, meaning that there should be no pricing differentiation by user, type of content, site identity, class of platform, type of application, type of attached equipment or means of communication.

One example of a violation of net neutrality principles occurs when a service provider intentionally slows uploads from peer-to-peer file sharing applications, gaming or **voice over IP** (VoIP) calls. There is an ongoing battle between those who believe that the market should determine pricing on the internet and those who regard it as a shared public resource that everyone should be able to access at a fixed cost.

The relevance of this topic to cybercrime lies in the fact that a non-neutral internet, with higher prices for premium services, is likely to attract even more fraudsters and other criminals than are already present today.

1.1.2   Free Speech and Censorship on the Internet

The debate over the delicate balance between free speech and responsible behaviour is becoming increasingly complex. The use of the internet by extremist propagandists, the contentious foreign policies of some leading nation states, the rise of trolling and the increased use of channels like Wikileaks to expose corporate and governmental activities all add to the mix.

Historically, the majority of technical minds driving the evolution of the internet appear to have regarded it as a common tool, to be used freely by everyone. The assumption was that everyone would use it responsibly. These original thinkers on the topic of internet culture may have been hamstrung by a lack of understanding regarding how most of humanity thinks and functions; or they may simply have failed to anticipate the global take-up of internet services that has occurred. The internet was, after all, originally designed for defence and academic uses.

Ironically, one of the greatest inhibitors of free speech on the internet is free speech itself. The malicious and very damaging activities of internet trolls regularly inhibit or silence the voices of other commentators, particularly women, who are sometimes threatened with rape or even murder.

The Protection from Harassment Act 1997 has sometimes been employed to protect victims of both online and real-life stalking, while the Malicious Communications Act 1988 has been used against trolls who send *indecent or grossly offensive* messages, despite this Act predating widespread access to the internet. Section 127 of the Communications Act 2003 makes it an offence to send grossly offensive, obscene, indecent or menacing electronic communications. This law has been invoked in a number of trolling cases, including in the cases of two harassers who were sentenced, in January 2014, to eight and twelve weeks in prison respectively.

In 2012, Matthew Woods posted several grossly offensive comments on Facebook about the missing child April Jones, who was later found to have been murdered. Woods was sentenced to 12 weeks in prison, although the decision was criticised and not long afterwards the then-director of public prosecutions, Keir Starmer, published guidelines for the Crown Prosecution Service designed to limit the number of cases brought under the Act.

UK law relating to trolling is controversial. As suggested, it is difficult to simultaneously protect victims from online abuse and uphold free speech; it is also difficult to determine exactly how offensive a message needs to be to merit criminal prosecution. In other words, how do we define what is grossly offensive and what is not, given the many value systems held by different sectors of society?

Most people would agree that a rape threat is not protected by free speech, but many may feel that making jokes about a missing child, while despicable, is not actually criminal. Either way, the trolling phenomenon shows no sign of abating and the courts' power to deal with it continues to grow. On 13 April 2015, the Criminal Justice and Courts Act 2015 took effect, increasing the maximum penalty for abusive online messages to two years in prison.

1.1.3   Internet Censorship by Search Engines

When you search the internet, you are actually searching the indexes previously built up by the search engine provider you have chosen to use, eg, Google, Yahoo, Bing. This gives search engine providers the power to remove or otherwise conceal any topic, phrase or word of their choosing.

There is a tension between the national nature of laws governing free speech and censorship and the global nature of the internet and internet search engine providers. Providers run many different indexes located all around the planet. Any censorship of those indexes is a function of at least three central factors:

· local laws and formal or informal government pressure
· the internal policies of the search engine provider
· public pressure and pressure from lobbying groups or corporate entities.

Although most search engine providers maintain the position that they work to defend free speech and censorship is in the main objectionable, the rise of organisations like Islamic State (IS) and the impact of various WikiLeaks releases, may well serve as ammunition for governments and corporate interests that see unrestrained free speech as a threat to democracy or to their own position.

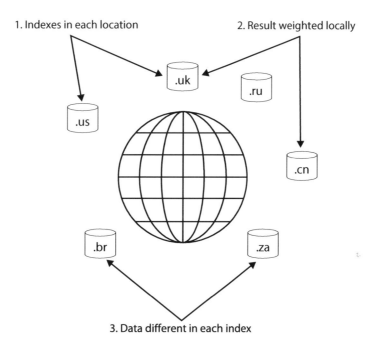

Figure 9: Search Engine Indexes

1.1.4　Privacy Expectations

The large increase in the number of data breaches reported over recent years has also had an impact on internet users' attitudes with regard to their own privacy. Recent surveys indicate that almost 60% of internet users fear that their personal data is unsafe online. An even larger percentage indicated that data security is an important factor in determining which companies they choose to do business with. This, in the financial services sector, is particularly true.

Only a small fraction of those surveyed said that they were happy for their data to be shared with third parties. This statistic disregards the fact that the big data market has already taken virtually everyone's information, packaged it up and resold it thousands of times worldwide. Simply put, internet users are largely unaware of the extent to which their privacy has already been undermined by a combination of global corporate pressures to create increasingly sophisticated marketing databases and the failure of national regulators to comprehend this change and to intervene on behalf of their citizens.

The simple truth is that the privacy horse has already bolted and we are still struggling to close the door to the empty stable. That is not to say that we should abandon all efforts to protect privacy. New personal data is created every minute and new users go online at an ever-increasing rate. Both need to be protected far more effectively than preceding generations have been if the internet is to remain a safe place to operate and do business.

One factor serves to compound this issue: the traditional security perimeter for any organisation is no longer as clearly defined as it used to be. Mobile devices and the cloud have blurred the boundaries, but even though most large firms have reached a level of maturity in which encryption and secure authentication are the norm within the perimeter, very few mobile devices are encrypted and the username and password model still persists in the cloud.

1.1.5   Intelligence Services Surveillance

Ever since the advent of modern communications systems, government agencies in almost every nation have engaged in surveillance of telecommunications and data transmissions. Depending on the nature of the government in question, and the views of its electorate, such surveillance is either regarded as necessary to maintain public safety or an intrusion by the state.

In recent times, the best known example of such surveillance within the Western democracies has been the PRISM programme. Launched in 2007, PRISM is a clandestine surveillance programme under which the United States National Security Agency (NSA) collects the internet communications of foreign nationals from at least nine major US internet companies. The programme collects stored internet communications based on information requests made to internet companies, such as Google, to hand over any data that match court-approved search terms. The NSA can use these requests to access communications that were encrypted when they were transmitted across the internet and to retrieve stored data from telecommunications systems.

Details regarding the operations of the programme were leaked in 2013 by an NSA contractor named Edward Snowden. He cautioned that the extent of mass data collection was far greater than reported and outlined what he characterised as 'criminal' activities by the NSA.

In May 2015, a panel of three US Court of Appeals federal judges ruled that the bulk collection of telephone metadata by the NSA was unlawful. This decision appeared to clear the way for a full legal challenge against the NSA.

However, the judges opted not to end the US domestic bulk collection of data while Congress decides the fate of the programme, calling judicial inaction a lesser intrusion on privacy.

The judges ruled:

> *In light of the asserted national security interests at stake, we deem it prudent to pause to allow an opportunity for debate in Congress that may (or may not) profoundly alter the legal landscape ... We hold that the text of section 215 cannot bear the weight the government asks us to assign to it, and that it does not authorise the telephone metadata program.*

Whatever the outcome of this process, it is likely to have implications for the practices of intelligence agencies within many democratic states, which often take a lead from the policies promulgated by the United States.

1.1.6 Responsibilities of Internet Service Providers (ISPs)

The question of defining the responsibilities of ISPs has always been complex and challenging. At a minimum, an ISP has a clear responsibility to provide:

- a working communications channel for its users
- a quality of service that matches agreed contractual and marketing commitments
- customer service to support the management of complaints and claims regarding inaccurate charging.

Over the years, many other issues have emerged, including:

- ISPs' responsibilities with regard to child protection
- their role in supporting authorised intelligence services and police investigations
- spam filtering
- resilience to and detection of DoS flooding attacks
- responsibility for content published online
- data retention to support law enforcement and other agencies.

Once again, the national nature of legislation means that ISPs are subject to different rules in different jurisdictions. In the EU, data retention law has been successfully challenged in the courts, although the transposed laws remain in effect in most European states.

2. UK Legislation

The UK is home to an extensive list of acts that govern or influence the practice of cyber-security, data protection and the responsibilities of firms and service providers. Some of the most relevant codes of relevance to cybercrime cases, include:

- The Computer Misuse Act (CMA)1990
- The Data Protection Act (DPA) 2018
- The Police and Justice Act (PJA) 2006
- The Fraud Act (FA) 2006
- The Regulation of Investigatory Powers Act (RIPA) 2000.

In this chapter, we will explore the main provisions of these and other pieces of legislation from within the UK and internationally.

2.1   The Computer Misuse Act (CMA)1990

Learning Objective

2.2.1   Know the offences created under the Computer Misuse Act 1990: Offence 1: unauthorised access to computer material; Offence 2: unauthorised access with intent to commit or facilitate commission of further offences; Offence 3: unauthorised acts with intent to impair

2.2.2   Know the maximum penalties applicable to Offence 1

2.2.3   Know the maximum penalties applicable to Offence 2

2.2.4   Know the maximum penalties applicable to Offence 3

2.1.1   Terms of the CMA 1990

The Computer Misuse Act (CMA) 1990 is an Act of the UK Parliament that makes computer misuse a criminal offence. This Act has become a model from which several other countries, including Canada and the Republic of Ireland, have drawn inspiration when subsequently drafting their own information security laws.

The CMA does not provide a definition of a computer because it was feared that any definition would soon become outdated due to the rapidity with which technology evolves. Such definitions are, therefore, left to the courts, which are expected to adopt the contemporary meaning of the word.

In 1997, Lord Hoffman defined a computer as a *device for storing, processing and retrieving information*, but given the changes in technology that have already occurred, a better definition might be:

> *a device, whether mechanical, electronic, chemical or biological (including quantum materials) or any combination thereof, that either stores, displays, processes, retrieves, shares or allows the creation of data, or otherwise facilitates any use of, or interactions with data, whether in digital or other formats.*

Things have become far more complex since 1997.

Following its amendment by Section 35 of the Police and Justice Act 2006 and Schedule 15 of the Serious Crime Act 2007, the CMA now defines the following four offences:

*   **Section 1 CMA** – Unauthorised access to computer material.
*   **Section 2 CMA** – Unauthorised access with intent to commit or facilitate commission of further offences.
*   **Section 3 CMA** – Unauthorised acts with intent to impair, or with recklessness as to impairing, operation of computer, etc.
*   **Section 3A CMA** – Making, supplying or obtaining articles for use in offences under Sections 1 or 3.

These offences are summarised in figure 10.

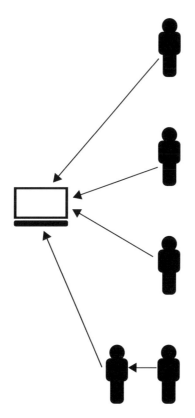

Section 1:
- **Intends** to access programme or data
- Is **unauthorised**
- **Knows** at the time that they are unauthorised.

Section 2:
- Commits a **Section 1 offence**, and:
  - intends to commit a **further offence**, or
  - intends to **facilitate** a further offence.

Section 3:
- **Knowingly** commits an **unauthorised** act
- Intending to **impair** or **hinder**:
  - **access** to programme or data
  - **operations** of programme or data, or
  - **reliability** of programme or data.

Section 3A:
- **Makes available** an article (eg, item of software):
  - **intending** it to be used in an offence
  - **believing** it is likely to be used, or
  - for it to be **supplied** to commit an offence.

Figure 10: Offences under the Computer Misuse Act

2.1.2 Additional Offences

In 2015, two further offences were added to the Computer Misuse Act by the Serious Crime Act 2015:

- unauthorised acts causing, or creating, risk of serious damage
- obtaining articles for purposes relating to computer misuse.

2.1.3 Jurisdiction of the CMA

Questions of jurisdiction are likely to become ever more challenging as the internet and the world wide web expand and fragment. The UK's CPS advises that there is jurisdiction to prosecute all CMA offences if there is *at least one significant link with the domestic jurisdiction* of England and Wales in the circumstances of the case.

Section 2(5) of the CMA defines 'significant link', and the CPS cites the case of *R v Waddon* (6 April 2000) when the Court of Appeal held that the content of American websites could come under British jurisdiction when data was downloaded in the UK.

2.1.4   Effectiveness of the CMA

Although the CMA was enacted more than 20 years ago, relatively few cases have actually been prosecuted under the Act. Even when cases do go to trial, those convicted have tended to receive lenient sentences. The primary challenge has been proving intent. Many of those charged simply claim that they were unaware that what they were doing was illegal or they did not realise that they were in possession of malware. Proving awareness is often difficult.

A further challenge has been that of attribution – conclusively establishing a connection between the devices used to carry out a crime and the person who used the device. Merely establishing ownership is generally insufficient because, by their very nature, computing devices can be accessed and shared by many different people.

Ultimately, in computer crime cases, the prosecution of offenders does little to address the fact that the damage has already been done. The solutions to cybercrime lie in areas of prevention and the minimisation of risk, rather than in policing and the prosecution of offenders. That is not to say that offenders should remain unpunished but merely to point out that pursuing offenders *after* the crime has been committed is not a sustainable or cost-effective response.

2.2   The EU General Data Protection Regulation (GDPR)

Learning Objective

2.2.8   Know how the European Union (EU) General Data Protection Regulation relates to cybercrime

Since it came fully into effect on 25 May 2018, the European Union's GDPR forms a key part of the data protection regime in the UK, together with the new Data Protection Act 2018 (DPA 2018).

The GDPR applies to processing carried out by organisations operating within the EU. It also applies to organisations outside the EU that offer goods or services to individuals in the EU.

2.2.1   Personal

The GDPR addresses the processing of personal data that is:

*   wholly or partly by automated means, or
*   the processing other than by automated means of personal data which forms, or is intended to form, part of a filing system.

According to the UK **Information Commissioner's Office (ICO)**, personal data only includes information relating to natural persons who:

*   can be identified or who are identifiable, directly from the information in question, or
*   who can be indirectly identified from that information in combination with other information.

The GDPR applies to data 'controllers' and data 'processors'.

A controller determines the purposes and means of processing personal data. A processor is responsible for processing personal data on behalf of a controller.

The GDPR places specific legal obligations on processors, who are required to maintain records of personal data and processing activities. They have legal liability if they are responsible for a breach. Controllers are not relieved of their obligations where a processor is involved – the GDPR places further obligations on them to ensure that contracts with processors comply with its regulations.

The GDPR does not apply to certain activities, including:

- processing covered by the Law Enforcement Directive
- processing for national security purposes, and
- processing carried out by individuals purely for personal or household activities.

The GDPR applies to personal data in any form. This is any information relating to a person who can be directly or indirectly identified from the data. Examples include a person's name, identification number, location data or online identifier, reflecting changes in technology and the way organisations collect information about people.

Even personal data that has been pseudonymised can fall within the scope of the GDPR depending on how difficult it is to attribute the pseudonym to an individual.

2.2.2   Sensitive Personal Data

Certain types of personal data are particularly sensitive, including genetic data and biometric data.

2.2.3   Rights

The GDPR provides the following rights for individuals:

- the right to be informed
- the right of access
- the right to rectification
- the right to erasure
- the right to restrict processing
- the right to data portability
- the right to object, and
- rights in relation to automated decision making and profiling.

2.2.4   Accountability

Accountability is one of the key data protection principles – it makes data custodians and processors responsible for complying with the GDPR and says that they must be able to demonstrate compliance by:

- adopting and implementing data protection policies
- taking a 'data protection by design and default' approach

- putting written contracts in place with organisations that process personal data on their behalf
- maintaining documentation of their processing activities
- implementing appropriate security measures
- recording and, where necessary, reporting personal data breaches
- carrying out data protection impact assessments for uses of personal data that are likely to result in high risk to individuals' interests
- appointing a data protection officer, and
- adhering to relevant codes of conduct and signing up to certification schemes.

2.2.5 Acting on Data Breaches

The GDPR introduces a duty for all organisations to report certain types of personal data breach to the relevant supervisory authority. They must do this within 72 hours of becoming aware of a breach, where feasible.

If a breach is likely to result in a high risk of adversely affecting individuals' rights and freedoms, they must also inform those individuals without undue delay.

Organisations should ensure they have robust breach detection, investigation and internal reporting procedures in place. This will facilitate decision making about whether or not they need to notify the relevant supervisory authority and the affected individuals. They must also keep a record of any personal data breaches, regardless of whether they are required to notify.

2.2.6 Penalties

The regulation also introduces increased penalties equating to 4% of annual global turnover or fines of up to €20 million, whichever is highest. The Information Commissioner's Office website provides more information on penalties - https://ico.org.uk/for-organisations/guide-to-law-enforcement-processing-part-3-of-the-dp-act-2018/penalties/.

2.3 The Police and Justice Act (PJA) 2006

Learning Objective

2.2.5 Know the amendment to 'unauthorised access' and the two additional offences defined in the Police and Justice Act 2006: Section 36: unauthorised acts with intent to impair operation of computer; Section 37: making, supplying or obtaining articles for use in computer misuse offences

2.3.1 About the Police and Justice Act

The Police and Justice Act (PJA) 2006 served, among other things, to strengthen the CMA by adding a new offence and stronger penalties. Specifically, Sections 35–38 of the PJA 2006 amended the CMA under Miscellaneous Part 5 Computer Misuse Amendments. Beyond these amendments the PJA has little direct relevance to the management of cyber-security.

The Police and Justice Bill 2006 was given royal assent and therefore the PJA came into force on 8 November 2006.

2.3.2　The Amendments in Detail

The following amendments to both offences and penalties were introduced by the PJA.

Section 35 – Unauthorised access to computer material:

1. In the CMA 1990 (c. 18) ('the 1990 Act'), Section 1 (offence of unauthorised access to computer material) was amended as follows.
2. In subsection (1):
   a. in paragraph (a), after 'any computer' there is inserted, or 'to enable any such access to be secured'
   b. in paragraph (b), after 'secure' there is inserted, or 'to enable to be secured'.
3. For subsection (3) there is substituted:

   '(3) A person guilty of an offence under this section shall be liable:

   a. *on summary conviction in England and Wales, to imprisonment for a term not exceeding 12 months or to a fine not exceeding the statutory maximum or to both*
   b. *on summary conviction in Scotland, to imprisonment for a term not exceeding six months or to a fine not exceeding the statutory maximum or to both*
   c. *on conviction on indictment, to imprisonment for a term not exceeding two years or to a fine or to both.'*

2.3.3　The Additional Offence – Section 36

An additional offence (already included in the earlier text on the CMA in this document) was also stipulated:

Section 36 – Unauthorised acts with intent to impair operation of computer, etc.

For Section 3 of the 1990 Act (unauthorised modification of computer material) there is substituted:

'Unauthorised acts with intent to impair, or with recklessness as to impairing, operation of computer, etc.

1. *A person is guilty of an offence if:*
   a. *he does any unauthorised act in relation to a computer*
   b. *at the time when he does the act he knows that it is unauthorised, and*
   c. *either subsection (2) or subsection (3) below applies.*
2. *This subsection applies if the person intends by doing the act:*
   a. *to impair the operation of any computer*
   b. *to prevent or hinder access to any program or data held in any computer*
   c. *to impair the operation of any such program or the reliability of any such data, or*
   d. *to enable any of the things mentioned in paragraphs (a) to (c) above to be done.*
3. *This subsection applies if the person is reckless as to whether the act will do any of the things mentioned in paragraphs (a) to (d) of subsection (2) above.*
4. *The intention referred to in subsection (2) above, or the recklessness referred to in subsection (3) above, need not relate to:*

a. *any particular computer*

b. *any particular program or data, or*

c. *a program or data of any particular kind.*

5. *In this section:*

a. *a reference to doing an act includes a reference to causing an act to be done*

b. *'act' includes a series of acts*

c. *a reference to impairing, preventing or hindering something includes a reference to doing so temporarily.'*

2.3.4 Penalties under Section 36

'A person guilty of an offence under this section shall be liable:

a. *on summary conviction in England and Wales, to imprisonment for a term not exceeding 12 months or to a fine not exceeding the statutory maximum or to both*

b. *on summary conviction in Scotland, to imprisonment for a term not exceeding six months or to a fine not exceeding the statutory maximum or to both*

c. *on conviction on indictment, to imprisonment for a term not exceeding ten years or to a fine or to both.'*

2.3.5 A Second Additional Offence – Section 37

A second additional offence was added with respect to 'making, supplying or obtaining articles for use' in computer misuse offences. After Section 3 of the 1990 Act the following was inserted:

'3A – Making, supplying or obtaining articles for use in offence under Sections 1 or 3

1. *A person is guilty of an offence if:*
   a. *he makes, adapts, supplies or offers to supply any article*
   b. *he intends it to be used to commit, or to assist in the commission of, an offence under Sections 1 or 3.*

2. *A person is guilty of an offence if he supplies or offers to supply any article believing that it is likely to be used to commit, or to assist in the commission of, an offence under Sections 1 or 3.*

3. *A person is guilty of an offence if he obtains any article with a view to its being supplied for use to commit, or to assist in the commission of, an offence under Sections 1 or 3.'*

The term 'article' includes any programme or data held in electronic form.

2.3.6 Penalties under Section 37

'A person guilty of an offence under this section shall be liable:

a. *on summary conviction in England and Wales, to imprisonment for a term not exceeding 12 months or to a fine not exceeding the statutory maximum or to both*

b. *on summary conviction in Scotland, to imprisonment for a term not exceeding six months or to a fine not exceeding the statutory maximum or to both*

c. *on conviction on indictment, to imprisonment for a term not exceeding two years or to a fine or to both.'*

2.4 The Fraud Act (FA) 2006

Learning Objective

2.2.6 Understand how the Fraud Act 2006 relates to cybercrime: fraud by false representation

2.2.7 Know the maximum penalty stipulated under the Fraud Act 2006

2.2.9 Understand the core principles of the Regulation of Investigatory Powers Act (RIPA) with respect to communications meta-data and message content

2.4.1 Terms of the FA 2006

Section 1 of the Fraud Act (FA) 2006 created a new general offence of fraud, the maximum penalty for which is ten years' imprisonment and a fine. There are three ways of committing the offence:

- false representation
- failing to disclose information
- abuse of position.

This general offence relies heavily on dishonesty and abolishes any requirement to prove deception. The FA targets fraudulent behaviour, not the consequences of that behaviour. It has moved from assessing whether the victim was deceived to what the defendant intended to happen as a result of their dishonest behaviour.

Section 2 makes it an offence to commit fraud by false representation.

Subsection (1) (a) makes it clear that the representation must be made dishonestly. The test also applies to Sections 3 and 4.

The definition of dishonesty was established in *R v Ghosh* [1982] 3 WLR 110. That judgment set a two-stage test. The first question is whether a defendant's behaviour would be regarded as dishonest by the ordinary standards of reasonable and honest people. If answered positively, the second question is whether the defendant was aware that his conduct was dishonest and would be regarded as dishonest by reasonable and honest people.

Subsection (1) (b) requires that the person must make the representation with the intention of making a gain or causing loss or risk of loss to another. The gain or loss does not actually have to take place. The same requirements apply to conduct covered by Sections 3 and 4.

Subsection (2) defines the meaning of 'false' in this context.

Subsection (3) defines the meaning of 'representation'.

A representation is defined as false if it is untrue or misleading and the person making it knows that it is, or might be, untrue or misleading. A representation means any representation as to fact or law, including a representation as to a person's state of mind.

Subsection (4) provides that a representation may be expressed, or implied by words or communicated by conduct. An example is where a person dishonestly misuses a credit card to pay for items. By tendering the card, he is falsely representing that he has the authority to use it for that transaction. The offence would also be committed by someone who engages in phishing, ie, where a person disseminates an email to large groups of people, falsely representing that the email has been sent by a legitimate financial institution and prompting the recipient to provide personal information.

Subsection (5) provides that a representation may be regarded as being made if it is submitted in any form to any system or device designed to receive, convey or respond to communications (with or without human intervention). The main purpose of this provision is to ensure that fraud can be committed where a person made a representation to a machine and a response can be produced without any need for human involvement (eg, when a person enters a number into a chip and PIN machine).

Section 3 makes it an offence to commit fraud by failing to disclose information to another person where there is a legal duty to disclose the information. This may include duties under oral or written contracts. It includes where a person in a fiduciary position has a duty to disclose material information when entering into a contract. An example would be the failure of a solicitor to share vital information with a client in order to perpetrate a fraud on the client. Another example would be where a person intentionally failed to disclose that he had a heart condition when making an application for life insurance.

Section 4 makes it an offence to commit a fraud by dishonestly abusing one's position. It applies in situations where the defendant has been put in a privileged position and, by virtue of this position is expected to safeguard another's financial interest or not to act against those interests. An example is where a person who is employed to care for an elderly or disabled person has access to that person's bank account and abuses their position by transferring funds for their own use.

Section 5 defines gain and loss in terms of money or other property. Property covers all forms of property including intellectual property, although, in practice, intellectual property is rarely gained or lost.

Section 6 makes it an offence for a person to possess or have under his control any article for use in the course of or in connection with any fraud. The intention was to apply the case law on Section 25 of the Theft Act 1968, which established that proof is required that the defendant had the article for the purpose of using it or with the intention that it be used in the course of or in connection with the offence, and that a general intention to commit fraud will suffice. Unlike Section 25, which made it an offence for a person to go equipped to commit a burglary, theft or cheat but does not apply when the person is at home, Section 6 of the FA applies everywhere, including the home address.

Subsection (2) provides that the maximum custodial sentence for this new offence is five years.

Section 7 makes it an offence to make, adapt, supply or offer to supply any article, knowing that it is designed or adapted for use in the course of or in connection with fraud or intending it to be used to commit or facilitate fraud. An example is where a person makes devices which, when attached to electricity meters, cause the meters to malfunction resulting in a loss to the provider.

Section 8 extends the meaning of 'article' for the purposes of sections 6 and 7 to include any programme or data held in electronic form. Examples are a computer program generating credit card numbers, computer templates for producing blank utility bills, computer files containing lists of people's credit card details or draft letters in connection with advance fee frauds.

Section 9 extends the offence of fraudulent trading to businesses carried on by sole traders. A person commits the offence of fraudulent trading under companies' legislation if they are knowingly party to the carrying on of a company's business whether with intent to defraud creditors or for any other fraudulent purposes.

Fraudulent trading is in effect a general fraud offence, comparable to conspiracy to defraud, but requiring use of a company instead of the element of conspiracy. Case law has established that:

- dishonesty is an essential ingredient of the offence
- the mischief aimed at is fraudulent trading generally, and not just insofar as it affects creditors
- the offence is aimed at business carried on over time but can be constituted by a single transaction
- it can be committed only by persons who exercise some kind of controlling or managerial function within the company.

Section 10 increases the maximum custodial sentence for fraudulent trading to ten years.

Section 11 makes it an offence for any person to obtain services dishonestly, ie, to obtain services for which payment is required but with the intent to avoid payment. The person must know that the services are chargeable, or that they might be. A person dishonestly using false credit card details or other false personal information to obtain the service would be committing an offence under this section.

Section 12 repeats the effect of Section 18 of the Theft Act 1968 by making company officers liable for offences committed by a company.

Section 13 provides the most recent example of the removal of privilege against self-incrimination. Subsection (4) provides that a 'related offence' means conspiracy to defraud and *'any other offence involving any form of fraudulent conduct or purpose'*. If section 13 applies, a person may be compelled to answer questions and provide documents notwithstanding the fact that he would (but for the section) be able to avail himself of the privilege. However, the information obtained cannot be used against that person in criminal proceedings. The only case to consider the phrase 'related offence' under the Act is *Kensington International Ltd v Republic of Congo* [2007] 65, in which the courts considered whether the Act suspended the privilege in debt proceedings and whether bribery was a related offence.

It is clear that many of the frauds that are now being perpetrated by the use of computers are not new but rather old-style frauds that have been reinvented and are being committed in a sophisticated and technological way. This is because much of commerce is now reliant on the use of computerised networks and office desktop software. Global business and, indeed, the entire global economy, are now based upon the electronic transfer of information.

2.4.2   The FA 2006 and Cybercrime

Many sections of the Fraud Act 2006 have direct relevance for cybercrime cases.

Section 1 – the general offence of fraud by:

- **false representation** – this could be construed to include the use of the internet and/or computer devices to mislead a distant party
- **failing to disclose information** – for example, digital information regarding identity or other information held by the remote perpetrator of an offence
- **abuse of position** – for example, when a computer is inappropriately made accessible to an offender based on them abusing their senior position within an organisation.

Subsection (5) provides that a representation may be regarded as being made if it is submitted in any form to any system or device, clearly covering the use of computers and the actions of cyber-attackers and e-crime fraudsters.

Section 5 defines gain and loss in terms of money or other property, including intellectual property. This addresses cybercrime data breaches, including but not limited to hacking, and the theft or disclosure of a range of data types.

Section 6 makes it an offence for a person to possess or have under his control any article for use in the course of, or in connection with any fraud, including possession within the home. This clearly encompasses the possession of computing devices and accessories, such as USB sticks and other peripheral tools.

Section 7 makes it an offence to make, adapt, supply or offer to supply any article, knowing that it is designed or adapted for use in the course of or in connection with fraud or intending it to be used to commit or facilitate fraud. The example previously given was where a person makes devices which, when attached to electricity meters, cause the meters to malfunction resulting in a loss to the provider. Installing malware on a device or peripheral piece of equipment, or hacking and changing software code, would be covered by this section when Section 8 (see below) is also considered.

Section 8 extends the meaning of 'article' for the purposes of Sections 6 and 7 to include **any programme or data held in electronic form**.

Section 11 encompasses fraudulent credit card transactions, the most common form of e-crime.

2.4.3   Fraud by False Representation

As we have seen in section 2.4.1, Section 2 of the Fraud Act 2006 makes it an offence to commit fraud by false representation, and this has obvious relevance in terms of cybercrime offences.

Dishonesty

The Act states that representation must be made dishonestly and cites the judgement in *R v Ghosh* [1982] 3 WLR 110. That judgment specified a two-stage test for dishonesty:

1. The first question is whether a defendant's behaviour would be regarded as dishonest by the ordinary standards of reasonable and honest people.
2. If the first question is answered positively, the second question is whether the defendant was aware that his conduct was dishonest and would be regarded as dishonest by reasonable and honest people.

Intent

The accused person must make the false representation with the **intention** of making a gain or causing loss, or risk of loss, to another. The gain or loss does not actually have to take place.

Falsehood

A representation is defined as false if it is **untrue or misleading** and the person making it **knows** that it is, or might be, untrue or misleading.

A false representation may be express or implied. It can be stated in words or communicated by conduct. There is no limitation on the way in which the representation must be expressed. So it could be written or spoken **or posted on a website**, meaning that the phrase covers various forms of cybercrime event, including social engineering activities where there is intent to cause a loss or the risk of a loss.

Implied by Conduct

A representation may also be implied by conduct. An example of a representation by conduct is where a person dishonestly uses a credit card to pay for items, knowing that he is not authorised to use the card. By tendering the card, he is falsely representing that he has the authority to use it for that transaction.

It is immaterial whether the merchant accepting the card for payment is deceived by the representation. Merely by attempting to use the card, an offence is committed.

In cybercrime terms, this definition could perhaps be extended to cover failed attempts to hack into a computer system using guessed passwords.

Submission

A representation may be regarded as being made if it (or anything implying it) is submitted in any form to any system or device designed to receive, convey or respond to communications (with or without human intervention). The main purpose of this provision is to ensure that fraud can be committed where a person makes a representation to a machine and a response can be produced without any need for human involvement.

Again, this clearly addresses a range of cybercrime activities, including remote attacks across the internet.

2.4.4   Crown Prosecution Service (CPS) Guidelines

The CPS provides a checklist of 'Aggravating and Mitigating Factors' (from *Sentencing Guidelines Council Definitive Guideline*) for use by the courts in relation to fraud by false representation.

Step One – Assess the Culpability of the Offender

Factors indicating higher culpability:

- planning of an offence
- an intention to commit more serious harm than actually resulted from the offence
- offenders operating in groups or gangs
- professional offending
- high level of profit from the offence
- an attempt to conceal or dispose of evidence
- deliberate targeting of vulnerable victim(s)
- abuse of a position of trust.

Investigators working on relevant cases should bear these points in mind.

Factors indicating significantly lower culpability:

- mental illness or disability
- youth or age, where it affects the responsibility of the individual defendant
- the fact that the offender played only a minor role in the offence.

Step Two – Assess the Harm Caused by the Offending

Factors indicating a more than usually serious degree of harm:

- multiple victims
- victim is particularly vulnerable
- high value (including sentimental value) of property to the victim, or substantial consequential loss.

Aggravating Factors

The Sentencing Guidelines Council also identifies four particular factors which may aggravate culpability and harm:

- The number of persons involved in the offence and the role of offender (eg, if the offender was an organiser, planner or prime mover in a fraudulent enterprise carried out by a number of individuals).
- The offending was carried out over a significant period of time.
- Use of another person's identity occurred:
  - using the identity of a living person is likely to cause emotional distress and practical difficulties of untangling the financial consequences of the fraud
  - using the identity of a deceased person is likely to indicate a higher degree of planning (as it can be an attempt to make the fraud more difficult to uncover) and is likely to cause considerable distress to the relatives of the deceased, especially if that person has only recently died.
- The offence has a lasting effect on the victim (eg, the loss of most or all of their savings, being unable to make mortgage and loan repayments, or having to work beyond retirement age).

Mitigating Factors

The Sentencing Guidelines Council has identified four personal mitigating factors that are relevant to this type of offending:

- **Voluntary cessation of offending**, especially where accompanied by a genuine expression of remorse.
  - This may depend upon the time that has elapsed since the commission of the last offence and the reasons why an offender stopped offending.
  - Where it was because of a heightened fear of discovery or the fact that the additional funds were no longer needed, a court may conclude that the degree of mitigation is negligible or that this factor should not be taken into account at all.
- **Complete and unprompted disclosure** of the extent of the fraud.
  - This amounts to ready co-operation with the authorities, which the Council has recognised as offender mitigation.
  - The point at which the disclosure is made and the degree of assistance given to the authorities should determine the amount of mitigation.
- **Voluntary restitution** – the point at which an offender voluntarily returns property or money obtained through fraud will be important. The earlier it is returned, the greater the degree of mitigation the offender could receive.
- **Financial pressure** – while many are motivated by greed or a desire to live beyond legitimate means, others may be motivated by financial pressure.
  - In principle, financial pressure is a factor that neither increases nor diminishes an offender's culpability in relation to any type of dishonesty offence, including fraud.
  - However, where financial pressure is exceptional and not of the offender's own making, it may, in very rare circumstances, constitute offender mitigation.

2.4.5 Penalties Stipulated Under the FA 2006

The maximum penalties for offences under Sections 1, 7 and 9 of the FA 2006 are:

- 12 months' imprisonment upon summary conviction
- ten years' imprisonment upon conviction on indictment.

Section 10 of the Act increases the maximum penalty for offences contrary to Section 458 of the Companies Act 1985 to ten years' imprisonment.

The maximum penalties for an offence under Sections 6 and 11 are:

- 12 months' imprisonment upon summary conviction
- five years' imprisonment upon conviction on indictment.

2.5 Core Principles of the Regulation of Investigatory Powers Act (RIPA) 2000

In a 1998 ruling, the European Court of Human Rights stated that surveillance laws in the United Kingdom were unclear. The Court found that there was a lack of legislation in force to prevent abuses of power by law enforcement agencies, and others, in relation to the interception of electronic communications.

It was decided that UK surveillance laws, and their attendant practices, needed to be significantly strengthened and tightened in order to protect the rights to privacy of UK citizens. This was achieved through the creation of the Regulation of Investigatory Powers Act (RIPA) which was passed in 2000.

RIPA is an extremely important and powerful piece of legislation that has had a huge impact on the day-to-day operations of most, if not all, public sector organisations. The Act includes five sections to address the main principles of lawful interception:

1. unlawful interception
2. meaning and location of interception
3. lawful interception without an interception warrant
4. power to provide the lawful interception
5. interception with a warrant.

2.5.1 The Terms of RIPA

RIPA was designed to provide a legal framework within which organisations such as the security services and the police can lawfully carry out surveillance and gain access to electronic, postal and digital communications.

RIPA also makes it a crime for anyone who is **not** authorised under the Act to carry out surveillance and monitoring of communications. This does not exclude firms from monitoring what happens on their own proprietary internal data and communications networks, but refers more broadly to the private communications of others outside of a business context.

The primary authorised purposes for which the monitoring or interception of communications by authorised firms is permitted to occur, are to:

- prevent or detect crimes
- prevent public disorder from occurring
- ensure national security and the safety of the general public
- investigate or detect any abnormal or illegal use of telecommunication systems.

The final point might be interpreted as encompassing cybercrime investigations, but caution should be exercised as most ICT professionals and regulators make a clear distinction between the rules governing the communications voice services and data services, which may not pass through a telecom operators' hands at all.

2.5.2 Mission Creep?

When RIPA was originally passed in 2000, it only covered the operations of nine organisations, including MI5 and the police. Today, the number of organisations operating under the terms of the Act has risen above 1,000. Whether this is indicative of a massive increase in the scope of surveillance and data collection or merely indicates increased levels of control over organisations that were already carrying out such activities is not absolutely clear. However, many in society are firm in their belief that the frequency and intrusiveness of surveillance by public sector organisations of numerous types has increased dramatically, is excessive and poses a threat to privacy and civil liberties in the UK.

2.5.3   Adherence to the Terms of RIPA

On the other side of the coin, operational experience strongly supports the claim made by the police and others that they adhere very strictly to the terms of RIPA. In fact, RIPA represents a bureaucratic stumbling block that frustrates and annoys many of those who are honestly and strenuously going about the business of fighting crime. It is, unfortunately, a necessary stumbling block.

3.   Relevant Foreign Legislation

Learning Objective

2.3.1   Know key US regulation and guidance that relates to Cybercrime: Homeland Security Act (2002); The Department of Homeland Security (DHS) Critical Infrastructure Cyber-Community (C-cubed) Voluntary Program; Electronic Communication Privacy Act (1986); Privacy Act (1974); Federal Information Security Management Act (2002); Executive Order 13636, Improving Critical Infrastructure Cyber-Security

3.1   The US Homeland Security Act (HSA) 2002

The primary purposes of the Homeland Security Act (HSA) are to:

*   aid the prevention of terrorist attacks within the United States
*   reduce the vulnerability of the United States to terrorism
*   minimise damage and assist in recovery for terrorist attacks that occur in the United States.

The Homeland Security Act of 2002 provides the Secretary of Homeland Security with the authority to direct and control investigations that require **access to any information** needed to investigate and prevent terrorism. The Act therefore has real implications for persons and organisations operating within the United States, or directly with US-based companies, and which are subject to other data protection laws, such as UK or EU data protection regulations.

The authority provided by the Act has been interpreted to include requests for personal data of any type, without the express consent of the data subject. The Act does state that data is protected from unauthorised disclosure and is to be handled and used only for the performance of official duties.

The HSA also established the US Department of Homeland Security (DHS). The DHS includes many other organisations, such as the Federal Emergency Management Agency, US Coast Guard, US Secret Service and Transportation Security Administration.

3.1.1   Privacy and the Homeland Security Act

The DHS boasted the first statutorily required privacy office within a federal agency. A chief privacy officer and chief Freedom of Information Act (FOIA) officer were appointed in March 2009. The privacy office is primarily responsible for evaluating privacy's effect on the department's programs, systems, and initiatives. It is further required to mitigate any anticipated risks to privacy.

The privacy officer's objectives include:

- evaluating the department's legislative and regulatory proposals that involve the collection, use and disclosure of personally identifiable information
- centralising and providing program oversight and implementing all FOIA and Privacy Act operations
- operating a privacy incident response program that addresses incidents involving personally identifiable information
- responding to, investigating and addressing complaints of privacy violations
- providing training, education and outreach that build the foundation for privacy practices across the DHS and create transparency.

3.2 US Executive Order (EO) 13636, *Improving Critical Infrastructure Cybersecurity*

Issued by US President Barack Obama on 12 February 2013, Executive Order (EO) 13636, *Improving Critical Infrastructure Cybersecurity*, called for government to collaborate more closely with critical infrastructure owners and operators to strengthen cyber-security, particularly by sharing information about cyber-threats and by jointly developing a framework of cyber-security standards and best practices. The expectation was that elements of the framework would later be incorporated into government regulations or voluntarily adopted by industry.

3.2.1 The Implications of EO 13636

The EO highlighted the fact that the threat of cybercrime was now recognised at the highest levels of government. The White House stated that it had issued the EO to counter growing threats to the nation's 16 critical infrastructure sectors from state and non-state actors, hacktivists, organised crime, extremists and others.

The EO stated that:

> *Repeated cyber-intrusions into critical infrastructure demonstrate the need for improved cyber-security... The cyber-threat to critical infrastructure continues to grow and represents one of the most serious national security challenges we must confront. The national and economic security of the United States depends on the reliable functioning of the Nation's critical infrastructure in the face of such threats.*

3.2.2 The 16 Critical Infrastructure Sectors

The US Department of Homeland Security defines the 16 critical infrastructure sectors, as follows:

1. chemicals
2. commercial facilities
3. communications
4. critical manufacturing
5. dams
6. defence industrial bases
7. emergency services
8. energy

9. financial services
10. food and agriculture
11. government facilities
12. healthcare and public health
13. information technology
14. nuclear reactors, materials and waste
15. transportation systems
16. water and wastewater systems.

A successful cyber-attack against any of these sectors would constitute a real and present danger to the United States; indeed to any nation that suffered such an attack.

3.2.3 Directives

The EO directs the US DHS, the Department of Justice and the Office of the Director of National Intelligence to produce and share unclassified and classified cyber-threat reports which identify specific targeted and victim entities.

The DHS would expand the Enhanced Cyber-Security Initiative to all critical infrastructure sectors, thereby making classified cyber-threat data and technical information available to eligible critical infrastructure owners and operators.

The DHS would also expand programs that provide security clearances to private sector employees of critical infrastructure and bring private sector subject matter experts into the US federal government.

3.3 US Cyber-Security Framework

Another major goal is to develop a cyber-security framework of standards and best practices for reducing risk to critical infrastructure. Under the EO, the National Institute of Standards and Technology (NIST) will work with the sector-specific agencies (SSAs), sector coordinating councils (SCCs) and other stakeholders to develop the cyber-security framework.

NIST officials want owners and operators to actively participate in this process. The EO also calls for the DHS to establish a voluntary program for framework adoption by owners and operators.

3.3.1 The DHS Critical Infrastructure Cyber-Community (C³) Voluntary Program

The C³ Voluntary Program (pronounced 'C-Cubed') is a public–private partnership that aligns US business enterprises with State, Local, Tribal, Territorial (SLTT) and Federal governments. It is designed to assist the efforts of all these parties to use the NIST cyber-security framework to manage their cyber-security risks more effectively.

The C³ Voluntary Program provides a central place to access the information and resources available to critical infrastructure sectors and organisations that need to improve their cyber-risk resilience. The resources are provided by many DHS and government-wide agencies and offices. The C³ Voluntary Program is the co-ordination point within the Federal government for efforts designed to promote use of the cyber-security framework.

3.3.2 The National Institute of Standards and Technology Cyber-Security Framework

The NIST cyber-security framework incorporates proven best practices from a number of standards bodies. While the framework targets organisations that own or operate critical infrastructure, some commentators have opined that adoption may prove advantageous for businesses across virtually all industries.

The NIST cyber-security framework yielded no surprises for critical infrastructure executives who had monitored its development. The framework did not introduce new standards or concepts; rather, it leveraged and integrated industry-leading cyber-security practices that had been independently developed.

The framework was inspired by a February 2013 Executive Order entitled *Improving Critical Infrastructure Cyber-Security* and ten months of collaborative discussions with more than 3,000 security professionals. It comprises a risk-based compilation of guidelines that are intended to help organisations identify, implement and improve their cyber-security practices.

3.4 The US Electronic Communication Privacy Act (ECPA) 1986

The Electronic Communication Privacy Act 1986 (ECPA), was enacted by the United States Congress to extend government restrictions on the surveillance of telephone calls. The scope of ECPA extends to the interception of transmissions of electronic data by computers.

The primary purpose of the Act, therefore, is to reinforce privacy and it is primarily intended to prevent unauthorised government access to private electronic communications.

ECPA was later amended by the Communications Assistance for Law Enforcement Act (CALEA) of 1994, the Uniting and Strengthening America by Providing Appropriate Tools Required to Intercept and Obstruct Terrorism (USA PATRIOT) Act 2001, the USA PATRIOT reauthorisation Act 2006 and the FISA Amendments Act 2008, the last three of which were enacted after the events of September 11, 2001. Those attacks on America had a significant effect upon attitudes towards privacy at that time.

Criticisms of the ECPA include the comment that it is now outdated and that it does not adequately cater for the manner in which modern communications and internet services operate and the ways in which consumers use devices and applications.

3.5 The US Privacy Act 1974

The Privacy Act 1974 provides safeguards against invasion of personal privacy through the misuse of records by federal agencies. It is a United States federal law that establishes a Code of Fair Information Practice governing the collection, maintenance, use and dissemination of personally identifiable information (PII) about individuals maintained in systems of records by US federal agencies.

This Act established controls over what personal information can lawfully be collected, maintained, used and disseminated by these agencies.

The Privacy Act only applies to records that are located in a system of records. As defined in the Privacy Act, a system of records is:

a group of any records under the control of any agency from which information is retrieved by the name of the individual or by some identifying number, symbol, or other identifying particular assigned to the individual.

The Privacy Act guarantees every US citizen three primary rights:

- The right to see records about themselves, subject to Privacy Act exemptions.
- The right to request the amendment of records that are not accurate, relevant, timely or complete.
- The right to be protected against unwarranted invasions of privacy resulting from the collection, maintenance, use and disclosure of personal information.

In this sense, the Privacy Act shares some key characteristics of EU (and UK) data protection law.

Any US citizen, or any alien lawfully admitted for permanent residence of the United States, may make a request for personal information about themselves under the Privacy Act.

3.6 The US Federal Information Security Management Act (FISMA) 2002

The Federal Information Security Management Act (FISMA) 2002 is a piece of US legislation that defines a comprehensive framework to protect government information, operations and assets against natural or man-made threats. FISMA was signed into US law as part of the E-Government Act of 2002.

FISMA assigns responsibilities to various agencies to ensure the security of data stored anywhere within departments of the federal government. It requires program officials, and the head of each agency, to conduct annual reviews of information security programs designed to keep risks at or below specified levels in a cost-effective, timely and efficient manner.

NIST outlines nine steps toward compliance with FISMA:

1. Categorise the information to be protected.
2. Select minimum baseline controls.
3. Refine controls using a **risk assessment** procedure.
4. Document the controls in the system security plan.
5. Implement security controls in appropriate information systems.
6. Assess the effectiveness of the security controls once they have been implemented.
7. Determine agency-level risk to the mission or business case.
8. Authorise the information system for processing.
9. Monitor the security controls on a continuous basis.

Any firm engaging with any part of the US Federal Government should take into account the requirements of this Act.

End of Chapter Questions

Think of an answer for each question and refer to the appropriate section for confirmation

1.   Explain the concept of net neutrality.
      Answer reference: Section 1.1.1

2.   Name one of the offences created by The Computer Misuse Act 1990.
      Answer reference: Section 2.1.1

3.   Name one type of information protected by the Data Protection Act 1998.
      Answer reference: Section 2.2

4.   What was the focus of the amendment to Section 35 of the Police and Justice Act 2006?
      Answer reference: Section 2.3.2

5.   List the two main steps specified in the CPS checklist of aggravating and mitigating factors.
      Answer reference: Section 2.4.4

6.   What is the maximum penalty stipulated under the Fraud Act 2006 on summary conviction?
      Answer reference: Section 2.4.5

7.   What is the maximum penalty stipulated under the Fraud Act 2006 on indictment?
      Answer reference: Section 2.4.5

8.   What is the purpose of RIPA?
      Answer reference: Section 2.5

9.   Name one of the three primary goals of the US Homeland Security Act 2002.
      Answer reference: Section 3.1

Chapter Three
The Public-Private Interface in Combating Cybercrime

1. Law Enforcement Agencies   111

2. Standards and Best Practice   122

3. Cyber-Security and the Financial Services Industry   129

This syllabus area will provide approximately 5 of the 50 examination questions

Hey John, get out of the car and come over here to say 'thank you'. We just stopped the man who pays our salary! Unknown police officer

In section 3 of chapter 2 we briefly reviewed the relevant legislative landscape in the US, which emphasises the importance of a public–private partnership in combating cybercrime. Such an approach represents one of the most important facets of current thinking, not least because of the wave of privatisations that have occurred over the last few decades and which have delivered the responsibility for operating and securing many parts of our critical infrastructure into the hands of private firms. Firms operating in the financial services arena, while they may never have been public entities, are also included on the list of critical infrastructure that needs to be defended in the interests of national security.

Consequently, the interface between regulated firms and law enforcement arms of government is particularly important. Not only do firms face critical infrastructure attacks, but they have pre-existing responsibilities for reporting suspicious transactions and for conducting due diligence which is designed to identify accounts operated by organised criminals, terrorists and PEPs.

1.   Law Enforcement Agencies

Learning Objective

3.1.1   Understand the role and activities of the following UK and EU agencies: The National Crime Agency (NCA); the Metropolitan Police Service (Met) & SO15; the City of London Police; regional police forces; Europol.

1.1   The Home Office

In the UK, the **Home Office** is responsible for national security, the police services of England and Wales, administration of the justice system and immigration policy and controls. The Home Office is therefore the sponsoring department for the promulgation and efficient implementation of criminal legislation.

In particular, the Home Office is responsible for UK primary legislation and for international co-operation with overseas governments and agencies, with respect to the criminal law on numerous matters of international concern.

As the sponsoring agency for much legislation addressing international organised crime, money laundering and terrorism, the Home Office works closely with HM Treasury, the **National Crime Agency** (NCA) and the **Financial Conduct Authority (FCA)**.

1.2   The National Crime Agency (NCA)

The National Crime Agency (NCA) replaced the Serious Organised Crime Agency (SOCA) in late October 2013. The NCA is a national law enforcement agency and is a non-ministerial government department. It is the UK's lead agency in the fight against organised crime, which encompasses people trafficking, drug trafficking, weapons trafficking, cybercrime and economic crimes committed across regional and international borders. However, the NCA can be tasked to investigate any crime.

The NCA's role is strategic. The agency is charged with looking at the bigger picture across the UK and analysing how criminal networks are operating and how they can potentially be hindered or even stopped. In order to achieve this, the NCA must work closely with the regional organised crime units (ROCUs), the Serious Fraud Office (SFO) and with individual police forces.

The NCA is also the UK point of contact for foreign agencies such as Interpol, Europol and other international law enforcement agencies. The NCA is organised into several operational branches, overseen by directors, who are in turn overseen by a Director-General, assisted by a Deputy Director-General. The key commands are as follows:

- Border Policing Command
- CEOP (Child Exploitation and Online Protection Centre) Command
- Economic Crime Command
- Organised Crime Command
- National Cybercrime Unit (NCCU).

It is the NCCU which makes the NCA particularly relevant as a public interface for cyber-security managers.

1.2.1   The National Cybercrime Unit (NCCU)

The NCCU brings together specialists from the Police Central e-Crime Unit in the Metropolitan Police Service and the original SOCA Cyber-Unit to create a pool of expert technical, tactical intelligence and cybercrime investigation teams. It is described as being able to respond quickly to rapidly changing threats.

The NCCU defines its role as collaborating with a range of partners in order to reduce cyber and cyber-enabled crime by:

- providing a powerful and highly visible investigative response to the most serious incidents of cybercrime: pursuing cybercriminals at a national and international level
- working proactively to target criminal vulnerabilities and prevent criminal opportunities
- assisting the NCA and wider law enforcement to prevent cyber-enabled crime and pursue those who utilise the internet or ICT for criminal means
- driving a step change in the UK's overall capability to tackle cyber and cyber-enabled crime, supporting partners in industry and law enforcement to protect themselves better against the threat from cybercrime.

Using the NCA's consolidated national intelligence picture, the NCCU works with its partners to identify and understand the growing use of cyber as an enabler across almost all types of crime. The unit can then select the most effective ways of tackling each emerging threat. The NCCU also supports the delivery of enhanced cybercrime awareness across all police forces and provides expert investigative capabilities and dedicated operational support on cyber and cyber-enabled crime nationwide.

The NCA in Summary

The NCA is a powerful organisation. Its Director-General has the authority to direct regional police chiefs to concentrate their resources on specific issues and cases, effectively making him the most influential police officer in the country. The British media regularly refers to the NCA as the UK version of the American FBI.

Figure 11: The NCA's Definition of Organised Crime

1.3 The Metropolitan Police Service (MPS) and SO15

Founded in 1829, the Metropolitan Police Service (MPS), commonly known as **the Met**, is the police force responsible for Greater London, which is defined as all areas of London excluding the Square Mile. The Square Mile is the responsibility of the **City of London Police**.

Although the size of the Met varies, it is generally in the region of 55,000 officers and other staff. Approximately 75% of its membership comprises sworn police officers. The remainder are non-police staff, traffic wardens, volunteers and police community support officers.

The Met polices an area of 620 square miles, which is home to more than 7 million people, as well as the UK's largest commercial centre. In addition to manning police stations in every part of Greater London, the Met contains a number of specialist units, of which the most relevant to this workbook are the:

- Specialist, Organised and Economic Crime Command (SOECC).
- Online Crime and Fraud Unit (FALCON).

1.3.1 The Specialist, Organised and Economic Crime Command (SOECC)

The Command has lead responsibility for investigating all types of economic crime, including e-crime, corruption, human trafficking and prostitution. It also provides a national response to extradition cases, mutual legal assistance and art and antiques crime.

Additionally, the Command deals with asset recovery through the London Regional Asset Recovery Team and the Criminal Finance Team. It is also responsible for investigating all serious organised crime, such as kidnap, robbery and drug trafficking.

The main elements of the Command are:

- **Art and Antiques Unit** – gathers intelligence on art crime and conducts proactive operations using specialist knowledge for investigations ranging from art faking and forgery to theft and money laundering.
- **Branch Intelligence Unit** – provides fast-time 24/7 intelligence support to the SOECC, especially for kidnappings, and delivers tactical intelligence analysis.
- **Criminal Finance Team (CFT)** – exists to improve the MPS response to the Proceeds of Crime Act (POCA) 2002. It assists borough operational command units in improving their asset recovery activity, taking the cash out of crime.
- **Dedicated Cheque and Plastic Crime Unit** – a joint MPS and City of London Police unit, which works with, and is sponsored by, the banking industry to manage serious cheque and credit card fraud.
- **Extradition and International Assistance Units** – these have national responsibility for locating and arresting wanted fugitives worldwide. They also conduct enquiries on behalf of and at the request of other countries.
- **Financial Investigation Development Unit** – provides a corporate response to intelligence from hundreds of thousands of SARs received by the NCA from within the financial community.
- **Flying Squad** – reactively and proactively investigates every allegation of robbery, whether armed or not, affecting cash-in-transit companies, building societies, betting offices, post offices, jewellers, casinos and banks. They also investigate all robberies at commercial premises where a firearm is produced or intimated and all tiger kidnaps – a kidnapping that is followed not by a ransom demand but by a demand that a crime be committed on behalf of the kidnappers.
- **Fraud Squads** – responsible for combating serious and complex fraud and corruption within the public and private sectors. The teams work together with public sector partners including local councils, Transport for London and immigration services, to protect London from financial crime.
- **Project Genesius** – a partnership between the MPS and the printing industry, designed to reduce the access of criminals to the equipment and supplies they require to produce false identity documents.
- **Kidnap Unit** – provides fast-time responses to life-threatening crime in action, for example, kidnap for ransom where the hostage has not been recovered and extortion, blackmail and any other serious crime impacting on the metropolis.
- **London Regional Asset Recovery Team (London RART)** – a multi-agency unit, funded by seized assets, comprising staff from the MPS, the NCA, London City Police and Her Majesty's Revenue and Customs (HMRC). It was set up to deal with the seizure of criminal assets on a national basis under the Proceeds of Crime Act 2002 (POCA).

- **Operation Maxim** – a joint partnership between the MPS and the UK Border Agency (UKBA) which targets organised immigration crime networks across London that are involved in the facilitation of legal and illegal immigrants into the UK and the production and supply of forged identity documents.
- **Middle Market Drugs Partnership** – a joint partnership between SOECC and the NCA, which tackles Class A drug supply in London within minimum levels of ½ kg of heroin and 1 kg of cocaine.
- **Operation Nexus** – set up to tackle foreign national offenders of any nationality who are committing crime in the UK (including EU nationals).
- **Police Central e-Crime Unit (PCeU)** – a highly skilled team that deals with computer and cybercrime offences committed under the CMA (primarily the offences of hacking, denial of service and maliciously creating computer malware).
- **Proactive Money Laundering Investigation Team** – conducts intelligence-led investigations to proactively disrupt organised criminal networks and seize their financial assets under POCA 2002 and other money laundering legislation. The team includes specialist subunits, one of which is a team of officers working on fraud cases with an international element.
- **Projects Team** – conducts operations against organised crime which is pan-London or of a national or international level but impacting on the capital to a major degree. This includes the issuing of contracts to kill, activities of major drugs suppliers and multi-dimensional crime groups, including ethnically composed gangs, as well as serious large-scale firearms trafficking.
- **Operation Sterling** – the MPS strategy for combating economic crime in London. It has made significant inroads into preventing economic crime, which costs the UK economy billions of pounds every year. It has done this through establishing partnerships with other public bodies and with private industry. Operation Sterling is also at the forefront of the fight against the growing threat of identity theft.
- **Stolen Vehicle Unit (SVU)** – has responsibility for investigating and disrupting serious and organised vehicle crime. It includes the Vehicle Fraud Unit, which investigates financial frauds designed to purchase vehicles from car dealerships. It is entirely funded by the Finance & Leasing Association (FLA), which represents a number of major finance companies. Since October 2008, the Plant and Agricultural National Intelligence Unit (PANIU), with national responsibility for plant theft, has been based within the SVU.
- **Special Intelligence Section (SIS)** – tasked with dealing with serious organised crime, targeting those persons directly affecting the safety and well-being of Londoners through the use of highly specialised teams. The SIS seeks to use high-quality intelligence actively both to prevent harm and to enforce legislation against organised criminal networks.

1.3.2 SO15 Counter Terrorism Command (CTC)

Prior to 2006, counter-terrorist investigations and operations were carried out by the Special Branch (SO12) and the Anti-Terrorist Branch (SO13). As the threat of terrorism increased and became more sophisticated, collaboration between these separate organisations became increasingly complex. It was, therefore, decided that a unified command structure would offer greater efficiency.

In 2006 the unified Counter Terrorism Command, or SO15, was launched. Exclusively focused on fighting terrorism, SO15 brings together expertise in intelligence analysis and development, investigations and operational support activities.

SO15 is responsible for bringing to justice anyone engaged in terrorism or domestic extremism and related offences. By gathering and exploiting intelligence on terrorism and extremism in London, the unit is intended to provide a proactive and reactive response to these offences, including preventing and disrupting terrorist activity targeting London. SO15 necessarily includes the surveillance of terrorist communications and some aspects of cybercrime and online terrorist-related activity within its remit.

1.4   The City of London Police

The City of London Police has responsibility for the Square Mile, the original City of London. The Square Mile is home to much of the capital's financial services sector, including the Bank of England. As such, it is a major target for fraudsters, organised crime and terrorism.

The force is divided into five directorates:

- **Corporate Services** – comprised of a number of departments, all providing a support function to the operational activities of the force and its staff. The Directorate includes Human Resource Services, General Services, Financial Services, Shared Services and Information Technology.
- **Crime Investigation Directorate** – encompasses a number of departments that provide the force with the ability to respond to all tiers of criminality. This Directorate also deals with the threat of serious and organised crime and terrorism as well as day-to-day acquisitive criminality (theft, robbery and burglary) and violent crime.
- **Economic Crime Department** – dedicated to preventing and investigating fraud and is the lead UK force for economic crime investigation.
- **Intelligence and Information Directorate** – a single co-ordinating hub responsible for all intelligence and information management. It provides all contact management and is the first point of contact for the initial reporting, assessment, screening and allocation of crimes.
- **Uniformed Policing Directorate** – delivers all aspects of uniformed policing, including response, and provides specialist skills and support, on a regular basis, to other directorates within the force and to outside forces.

1.5   Regional Police Forces

Policing in the UK is largely organised on a regional basis. There are also several pan-UK departments or forces. Currently, the composition of the UK's regional forces is as follows:

England

- Avon and Somerset Constabulary
- Bedfordshire Police
- Cambridgeshire Constabulary
- Cheshire Constabulary
- City of London Police
- Cleveland Police
- Cumbria Constabulary
- Derbyshire Constabulary
- Devon & Cornwall Police

- Lincolnshire Police
- Merseyside Police
- Metropolitan Police Service
- Norfolk Constabulary
- North Yorkshire Police
- Northamptonshire Police
- Northumbria Police
- Nottinghamshire Police
- South Yorkshire Police

- Dorset Police
- Durham Constabulary
- Essex Police
- Gloucestershire Constabulary
- Greater Manchester Police
- Hampshire Constabulary
- Hertfordshire Constabulary
- Humberside Police
- Kent Police
- Lancashire Constabulary
- Leicestershire Police

- Staffordshire Police
- Suffolk Constabulary
- Surrey Police
- Sussex Police
- Thames Valley Police
- Warwickshire Police
- West Mercia Police
- West Midlands Police
- West Yorkshire Police
- Wiltshire Police.

Northern Ireland

- Police Service of Northern Ireland (PSNI).

Scotland

- Police Scotland.

Wales

- Dyfed-Powys Police
- Gwent Police
- North Wales Police
- South Wales Police.

Non-geographic

- British Transport Police
- Central Motorway Policing Group
- Civil Nuclear Constabulary (CNC) – formerly United Kingdom Atomic Energy Authority (UKAEA) Constabulary
- Ministry of Defence Police
- Port of Dover Police
- National Crime Agency (NCA).

The various British Overseas Territories (BOT) and Crown Dependencies also have their own police forces, faintly delineating the extent of Britain's former empire and, as some of these territories are now home to major centres of offshore banking, it is useful to be aware of the existence of these forces:

- Bermuda Airport Security Police
- Bermuda Police Service
- British Indian Ocean Territory Police
- Royal Cayman Islands Police Service
- Royal Falkland Islands Police
- Gibraltar Defence Police
- Royal Gibraltar Police
- Pitcairn Islands Police (a single officer)

- Royal Montserrat Police Service
- Saint Helena Police Service
- Sovereign Base Areas Police Service (SBA Police)
- Royal Virgin Islands Police Force.

In the main, these overseas administrations follow a combination of local law and adopted English statute law, while their police forces comply with Home Office and Association of Chief Police Officers (ACPO) guidelines.

1.6   Europol

The European Police Office (Europol) is the EU's federal law enforcement agency. Post-Brexit, Europol's interactions with UK law enforcement are unlikely to change dramatically for the simple reason that collaboration between agencies is well-established and that it mirrors the collaboration UK agencies already have in place with many non-EU agencies and forces. Europol will probably remain an important partner in the fight against cross-border organised crime and terrorism. Europol's stated primary goal is the achievement of a safer Europe for the benefit of all EU citizens. The organisation does this by assisting the EU's member states in their fight against serious international/ organised crime and terrorism.

The establishment of Europol was one of the activities defined in the Maastricht Treaty which came into effect in November 1993. The agency began limited operations in 1994, as the Europol Drugs Unit (EDU). The Europol Convention was later signed in July 1995 and came into force in October 1998, after being ratified by all of the member states. Europol finally commenced its full operational activities on 1 July 1999.

Europol serves as Europe's centre of expertise in key fields of law enforcement activity and Europol is the European centre for strategic intelligence on organised crime. The agency reports that large-scale criminal and terrorist networks pose an important threat to the internal security of the EU and to the safety and livelihood of its people. According to Europol, the biggest security threats today come from:

- terrorism
- international drug trafficking
- money laundering
- organised fraud
- counterfeiting of the euro currency
- people smuggling.

But other dangers are also on the agency's radar, particularly cybercrime, people trafficking and other modern-day threats such as weapons of mass destruction (WMD), trafficking and child sexual exploitation.

1.6.1   Tackling Organised Crime in Europe

Organised crime in Europe is a multi-billion euro business. Criminals are quick to adapt to new opportunities and are resilient in the face of traditional law enforcement measures. Approximately 800 Europol staff work closely with law enforcement agencies in each of the EU member states from Europol headquarters in The Hague, the Netherlands. The agency also collaborates closely with other non-EU partner states such as Australia, New Zealand and Canada, parts of the former Soviet Union (most notably the Ukraine), as well as the USA, Israel and Norway.

Europol states that it uses its information capabilities to identify and track the most dangerous criminal and terrorist networks in Europe, implying that its primary focus is on intelligence operations. Law enforcement authorities in the EU exploit the agency's intelligence product and the services of Europol's operational co-ordination centre and secure information network, to carry out over 13,500 cross–border investigations annually.

Europol reports that these national follow-up operations have led to the disruption of many criminal and terrorist networks and the arrest of thousands of dangerous criminals. National forces have also recovered millions of euros in criminal proceeds and have rescued hundreds of victims from harm, including children trafficked for sexual exploitation.

1.6.2 Powers

Europol has no executive powers. Officials of the agency are not entitled to conduct investigations in the member states or to arrest suspects but they can provide support and intelligence to the police forces of member states; this support capacity extends to joining operations on the ground.

The primary means for providing support to its EU law enforcement colleagues consists of gathering, analysing and disseminating information and coordinating international operations. Europol's partners use its intelligence inputs to prevent, detect and investigate offences, and to track down and prosecute those who are suspected of committing them. Europol experts and analysts also participate in the activities of joint investigation teams (JITs), helping to solve criminal cases in EU member states.

Europol personnel are drawn from a wide range of EU law enforcement agencies, including regular police forces, border police, customs and the security services. This multi-agency approach means that the agency has a rich network of connections all across the region and a decidedly multicultural and multilingual capability set, which helps it to close information gaps and minimise the space in which criminals can operate.

1.6.3 Liaison

Approximately 150 Europol Liaison Officers (ELOs) are also based at Europol headquarters. These ELOs are seconded to Europol by the EU member states and by other non-EU partners of Europol. They guarantee fast and effective co-operation, based on personal contact networks and mutual trust.

In this fashion, Europol acts as a support centre for law enforcement operations, a hub for crime intelligence and a centre for law enforcement expertise.

1.6.4 Intelligence Analysis

Analysis is at the core of Europol's activities. The agency employs approximately 100 crime intelligence analysts, giving Europol one of the largest concentrations of crime intelligence analytical capability in the EU. These analysts support member states' investigations on a daily basis.

In order to provide its partners with the deepest possible insight into the criminal problems they face, Europol produces regular intelligence assessments of crime and terrorism in the EU:

- The European Organised Crime Threat Assessment (OCTA) identifies and assesses emerging threats. It describes the structure of organised crime groups and the way they operate, and the main types of crime affecting the EU.
- The EU Terrorism Situation and Trend Report (TE-SAT), published annually, provides an account of the state of terrorism in the EU.
- Europol serves as an EU centre of expertise, providing a central platform for law enforcement experts from the EU countries.

1.6.5 Europol and Financial Crime Investigations

Several Europol units deal directly or indirectly with the challenges of money laundering and the financing of terrorism. The main responsibility for these matters, however, belongs to the Terrorism Unit of the Serious Crime Department (SC5) and the Financial Crime Unit of the Serious Crime Department (SC4).

The anti-money laundering (AML) activities conducted by Europol encompass a wide range of competences and working areas of multidisciplinary law enforcement agencies within the EU, including various Customs and Financial Intelligence Units with either judicial or police structures. Europol acts as a focal point for the exchange of dedicated financial data in support of money laundering investigations, performing its tasks in co-operation with EU member states. It does so by facilitating the exchange of such information and ensuring analytical assistance for complex cases generated by suspicious transaction reports (STRs) and currency transaction reports (CTRs) as well as ongoing money laundering investigations, regardless of the predicate offence committed.

Europol also works proactively in the development of counter-terrorism goals that adhere to the Hague Programme response of 2004. This promoted four parallel strands:

- prevent
- protect
- pursue
- respond.

These goals, in turn, follow four axes, namely:

- strengthening national capabilities
- facilitating European co-operation
- developing collective capacity
- promoting international partnerships.

Combating the financing of terrorism forms part of the pursue strand of the Hague Programme. The key elements of this strategy are a targeted intelligence approach, improved designation and listing of terrorist organisations and individuals associated with terrorist groups, improved tracing of financial assets, ongoing monitoring of developing trends and support for EU counter-terrorism financial investigation units. The issue of money laundering – the process of turning the proceeds of crime into laundered funds – is a key area of focus for the agency.

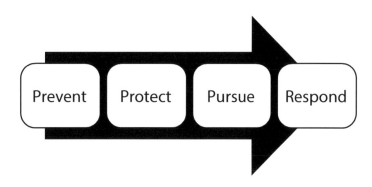

Figure 12: The Hague Programme Response

1.6.6   Europol and Cybercrime Investigations

Europol's European Cybercrime Centre (EC3) commenced operations in January 2013. It was designed to strengthen the EU law enforcement response to cybercrime and to help protect European citizens, businesses and governments from cyber-attacks and online frauds. Its establishment was listed as a priority under the EU Internal Security Strategy.

The threat from cybercrime is increasing and the EU is seen as a key target, mainly due to its advanced internet infrastructure and its internet-based economies and payments systems.

By situating EC3 within Europol, it is able to draw on Europol's existing law enforcement capacity and is tasked to focus on the following cybercrime categories:

- Cybercrimes committed by organised groups, particularly those generating large criminal profits.
- Cybercrimes that cause serious harm to the victim, such as online child sexual exploitation.
- Cybercrimes (including cyber-attacks) affecting critical infrastructure and information systems within the EU.

- In relation to these three areas, Europol's EC3:
    - serves as the central hub for criminal information and intelligence
    - supports member states' operations and investigations by means of operational analysis, co-ordination and expertise
    - provides a variety of strategic analysis products enabling informed decision-making at tactical and strategic level concerning the combating and prevention of cybercrime
    - establishes a comprehensive outreach function connecting cybercrime-related law enforcement authorities within the private sector, academia and other non-law enforcement partners
    - supports training and capacity building, in particular for the competent authorities in the member states
    - provides highly specialised technical and digital forensic support capabilities to investigations and operations
    - represents the EU law enforcement community in areas of common interest, such as research and development requirements, internet governance and cyber-security policy development.

2. Standards and Best Practice

Learning Objective

3.2.1 Know the purpose and content of the main international standards for information security management

3.2.2 Know the purpose and content of the UK Government Communications Headquarters (GCHQ) information assurance 'Cyber-Essentials' scheme

3.2.3 Understand the purpose and content of the UK Government Communications Headquarters (GCHQ) guidance entitled '10 Steps to Cyber-Security'

3.2.4 Understand the role of the European Network and Information Security Agency (ENISA)

3.2.5 Understand the role of the UK National Cyber Security Centre (NCSC)

Details of cyber-security best practice are provided in chapter 5 of this workbook. This section provides an overview of the organisations responsible for developing and promulgating many of the practices described in chapter 5.

2.1 The Main International Standards for Information Security Management

As with most multi-jurisdictional challenges, cybercrime and information security are the subject of a plethora of regulations and guidelines emanating from several different, and often unconnected, centres of excellence and regulatory bodies. Some of these are described below:

2.1.1 International Organisation for Standardization (ISO)

The International Organisation for Standardization (ISO) is a consortium of national standards institutes from over 155 nations. The ISO is coordinated via its secretariat, located in Geneva, Switzerland.

The ISO is, without question, the world's most prolific developer of international standards. The following ISO standards cover the issues of information security and cybercrime.

ISO/IEC TR 15443 is a multi-part technical guide designed for IT security professionals to aid them in the selection of appropriate assurance and security methods and the production of effective specifications. The aim of the guide is to understand the assurance type and amount required to achieve confidence that the deliverable satisfies the stated IT security assurance requirements and consequently its security policy.

ISO/IEC TR 15443-1:2005 describes the fundamentals of security assurance and its relation to other security concepts. This guide clarifies why security assurance is required and dispels common misconceptions, for example, that increased assurance is gained by increasing the strength of a security mechanism.

The framework includes a categorisation of assurance types and a lifecycle model intended to identify the appropriate assurance types required. The model also demonstrates how security assurance must be managed throughout its lifecycle.

The framework has been developed to be general enough to accommodate different assurance types and map into any lifecycle approach so as not to dictate any particular design.

ISO/IEC TR 15443 targets IT security managers and other security professionals responsible for developing a security assurance program, engineering security into a deliverable, determining the security assurance of their deliverable, entering an assurance assessment audit (eg, ISO 9000, SSE-CMM (ISO/IEC 21827), ISO/IEC 15408-3) or other assurance activities.

ISO/IEC 20000-1:2011 is a service management system (SMS) standard. It specifies requirements for the service provider to plan, establish, implement, operate, monitor, review, maintain and improve an SMS. The requirements include the design, transition, delivery and improvement of services to fulfil agreed service requirements.

ISO/IEC 20000-1:2011 can be used by the following:

- an organisation seeking services from service providers and requiring assurance that their service requirements will be fulfilled
- an organisation that requires a consistent approach by all its service providers, including those in a supply chain
- a service provider that intends to demonstrate its capability for the design, transition, delivery and improvement of services that fulfil service requirements
- a service provider to monitor, measure and review its service management processes and services
- a service provider to improve the design, transition, delivery and improvement of services through the effective implementation and operation of the SMS
- an assessor or auditor as the criteria for a conformity assessment of a service provider's SMS to the requirements in ISO/IEC 20000-1:2011.

ISO/IEC 27000 is part of a growing family of ISO/IEC information security management systems (ISMS) standards, commonly known as the ISO/IEC 27000 series.

The standard was developed by sub-committee (SC) 27 of the first Joint Technical Committee (JTC1) of the ISO and the IEC.

ISO/IEC 27000 provides:

- an overview of and introduction to the entire ISO/IEC 27000 family of ISMS standards
- a glossary of fundamental terms and definitions used throughout the ISO/IEC 27000 family.

ISO 27001:2013 provides the actual specification for an ISMS, as defined by ISO/IEC 27000. On successful completion of a formal audit process, organisations meeting the requirements of the 27001 standard are awarded ISO certification issued by an independent, accredited body.

The official title of this standard is *Information technology – Security techniques – Information security management systems – Requirements*.

The standard comprises ten short clauses and a detailed annex, covering:

- scope of the standard
- how the document is referenced
- reuse of the terms and definitions in ISO/IEC 27000
- organisational context and stakeholders
- information security leadership and high-level support for policy
- planning an ISMS, risk assessment and risk treatment
- supporting an ISMS
- making an ISMS operational
- reviewing the system's performance
- corrective action
- Annex A: list of information security controls and their objectives.

ISO/IEC 27002 is a code of practice for information security management that provides guidelines for organisational information security standards and information security management practices. It includes the selection, implementation and management of controls, taking into consideration an organisation's information security risk environment.

The standard is designed to be used by organisations that intend to:

- select controls during the process of implementing an ISMS based on ISO/IEC 27001
- independently implement commonly accepted information security controls
- devise their own information security management guidelines and controls.

2.2 The US National Institute of Standards and Technology (NIST)

The US **National Institute of Standards and Technology (NIST)** is a non-regulatory federal agency that forms part of the US Department of Commerce. The Computer Security Division within the NIST develops a wide range of information and computer security standards, metrics, tests and validation programs. It also publishes standards and guidelines to improve secure IT planning, implementation, management and operation.

2.3 The Internet Society (ISOC)

The **Internet Society (ISOC)** is a professional membership society with more than 100 organisation memberships and over 20,000 individual members in approximately 180 countries.

Whereas most standards bodies address current technologies and security challenges, ISOC aims to provide leadership in addressing issues that confront the future of the internet. It is the home for various groups responsible for the internet's infrastructure standards, including:

- the Internet Engineering Task Force (IETF)
- the Internet Architecture Board (IAB).

ISOC also hosts the Requests for Comments (RFCs). These include the official Internet Protocol Standards and the RFC 2196 Site Security Handbook.

2.4   The Information Security Forum (ISF)

The Information Security Forum (ISF) is a not-for-profit organisation with a membership of several hundred leading organisations in financial services, manufacturing, telecommunications, consumer goods, government and other areas.

The ISF conducts research into information security practices and offers advice, as well as more detailed regular circulars for its members.

2.5   The Institute of Information Security Professionals (IISP)

The Institute of Information Security Professionals (IISP) is another independent, not-for-profit body governed by its members. Its principal objective is the advancement of the professionalism of information security practitioners and thereby the professionalism of the industry as a whole.

The Institute has developed the IISP Skills Framework©, which describes the range of competencies expected of information security and information assurance professionals in the effective performance of their roles. This framework was developed based on collaboration between private and public sector organisations and world-renowned academics and security leaders.

2.6   The UK Government's GCHQ Information Assurance *Cyber Essentials* Scheme

Cyber Essentials is a government-backed, industry supported scheme to help organisations protect themselves against common cyber-attacks.

The scheme provides the following core content that organisations may freely use:

- *Cyber Essentials* Scheme: Summary
- *Cyber Essentials* Scheme: Requirements for basic technical protection from cyber-attacks
- *Cyber Essentials* Scheme: Assurance Framework.

While the *Cyber Essentials* Requirements document sets out the necessary technical controls, the Assurance Framework describes how the independent assurance process works and the different levels of assessment that organisations can apply for to achieve certification. It also contains guidance for security professionals carrying out those assessments.

In setting up the scheme, the government worked with the Information Assurance for Small and Medium Enterprises (IASME) consortium and the ISF to develop *Cyber Essentials*, a set of basic technical controls for organisations to use.

The full scheme, which was launched in June 2014, enables organisations to gain either of two new levels of *Cyber Essentials* certification:

- *Cyber Essentials*
- *Cyber Essentials* Plus.

The scheme is backed by leading associations representing UK industry, including the Federation of Small Businesses (FSB) and the Confederation of British industry (CBI), as well as a number of insurance organisations which offer insurance products for businesses who demonstrate compliance.

Since 1 October 2014, the UK government has required all suppliers bidding for certain sensitive and personal information handling contracts to be certified against the *Cyber Essentials* scheme.

2.7 The UK Government Communications Headquarters (GCHQ) Guidance Entitled *10 Steps to Cyber Security*

First launched in 2012, GCHQ's popular guide, *10 Steps to Cyber Security*, was updated and reissued in 2014 and linked to the UK *Cyber Essentials* scheme as a supporting document. The ten-step guide is advertised as a critical resource for UK businesses aiming to protect themselves in cyber-space.

The guidelines actually comprise several related documents, all of which are free to download:

- 10 Steps: Summary
- 10 Steps: A Board Level Responsibility
- 10 Steps: Executive Companion
- 10 Steps: Ten Critical Areas
- 10 Steps: Advice Sheets
- 10 Steps: Infographic
- Common *Cyber Essentials*: Summary
- Common *Cyber Essentials*
- Common *Cyber Essentials*: Infographic.

The ten cyber essentials steps are as follows:

1. **Information Risk Management Regime** – this primarily addresses the issues of governance, **policy** and practices.
2. **Secure configuration** – explaining why ICT systems need to be configured correctly in order that security is maintained.
3. **Network security** – addresses the security of the networks that tie systems together, including the internet.
4. **Managing user privileges** – describes why the establishment and management of appropriate levels of access and other user privileges are essential to information security.
5. **User education and awareness** – explains the critical need for a properly trained user base.
6. **Incident management** – describes the basic processes required once an incident occurs, in order to assure business continuity.
7. **Malware prevention** – explains why up-to-date anti-malware controls are a key part of the cyber-defence portfolio.
8. **Monitoring** – summarises the need for continuous monitoring of alerts, statistics and other symptoms indicative of a data breach or cyber-attack.
9. **Removable media controls** – addresses the numerous risks that arise from the widespread use of USB enabled devices, CD and DVD drives and a multitude of other removable media.
10. **Home and mobile working** – addresses the related issue of employees working from home, while on the move and using portable devices or personal equipment for business purposes.

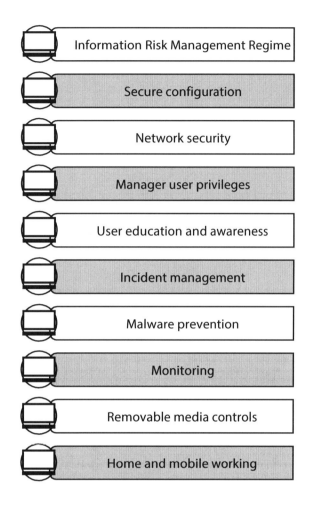

Figure 13: GCHQ's Ten Steps to Cyber-Security

2.8 The UK National Cyber Security Centre (NCSC)

Launched in October 2016, the NCSC has headquarters in London and brings together expertise from Communications-Electronic Security Group (the information assurance arm of GCHQ), the Centre for Cyber Assessment, CERT-UK and the Centre for Protection of National Infrastructure (CPNI).

The NCSC is tasked with helping to protect the UK's critical services from cyber-attacks, helping to manage major incidents, and improving the underlying security of the UK's internet through technological improvement and advice to citizens and organisations.

The NCSC supports the most critical organisations in the UK, the wider public sector, industry and SMEs. When incidents do occur, it aims to provide effective incident response to minimise harm to the UK, to help with recovery, and to learn and communicate lessons for the future.

The NCSC also represents a single point of contact for SMEs, larger organisations, government agencies and departments. It works collaboratively with other law enforcement, defence, the UK's intelligence and security agencies and international partners.

Specifically, the NCSC states that it:

- understands cyber-security
- distils this knowledge into practical guidance that it makes available to all
- responds to cyber-security incidents to reduce the harm they cause to organisations and the wider UK
- uses industry and academic expertise to nurture the UK's cyber-security capability
- reduces risks to the UK by securing public and private sector networks.

2.9 The European Union Agency for Network and Information Security (ENISA)

The **European Union Agency for Network and Information Security (ENISA)** – formerly the European Network and Information Security Agency – works across all EU institutions and member states. Despite the name change, the organisation still refers to itself as ENISA.

ENISA is the EU's response to the ever-increasing cyber-security challenges confronting the EU. As such, it claims to be a pacesetter for information security and a pan-European centre of expertise, as well as a hub for the exchange of information, best practices and knowledge.

Together with the institutions and member states of the EU, ENISA strives to develop and foster a strong cyber-security culture for the benefit of citizens, consumers and businesses, as well as public sector organisations.

The agency also assists the EC in the conduct of technical preparatory work to support the development or updating of European Community legislation in the field of network and information security. This particular role may well disappear after the UK leaves the EU.

The agency provides numerous valuable free guidelines and other resources on its website. These cover a number of key issues, including:

- Computer Emergency Response Team (CERT) practices
- privacy and confidentiality
- identity and trust
- resilience
- critical information infrastructure protection
- cyber-security
- cooperation
- good practice
- electronic identification and authentication (eID).

3. Cyber-Security and the Financial Services Industry

Learning Objective

3.3.1   Know the role of UK and EU Information Commissioners in relation to cybercrime

3.3.2   Understand the obligations of financial services firms to the Information Commissioner

3.3.3   Know the role of the Financial Conduct Authority (FCA) and Prudential Regulation Authority (PRA) in relation to cybercrime

3.3.4   Understand the obligations of financial services firms to the FCA and PRA with regard to a cybercrime event

3.1   Background

With information security now penetrating into mass consciousness, the brand and reputational effects of increased cyber-security governance are even more pronounced. A 2012 UK Information Commissioner's Office study into public attitudes in relation to data protection found that:

- 97% of those surveyed were concerned that organisations would pass or sell on their personal details
- 53% considered details of the products they had bought to be personal information.

Public sector bodies are strongly influenced by such measurements of public sentiment and the commercial sector must heed the warning contained in these figures. Speaking in 2013, the UK's Information Commissioner, Christopher Graham, said:

Education and empowerment have been two of the key areas we've focused on in the past 12 months. That work is having real benefits: consumers' awareness of their rights remains strong, and that is empowering people to demand more in return for their data.

One result is that consumers increasingly expect organisations to handle their personal data in a responsible and ethical way.

I think 2013 is the year that organisations will realise the commercial imperative of properly handling customer data. The stats we've seen about public concern around personal data show that, as does a company the size of Microsoft choosing privacy as a theme of a national advertising campaign.

The message to business is simple: consumers understand the value of their personal data, and they expect you to too.

Some important influences affecting the evolutionary path taken by information security and cyber-security-related regulation in the UK are summarised in Table 3.1.

Table 3.1 Influences affecting the evolutionary path taken by information security and cyber-security-related regulation in the UK

Time period	Situation and/or new developments
2005 and earlier	Public sector and critical infrastructure risks dominate the agenda.
2006	The phone hacking scandal triggers calls for a legal review, based in large part on the content of the report issued by the Information Commissioner's Office, entitled *What Price Privacy?*
2007	The HMRC loss of computer disks holding personal data takes data handling to the top of the political agenda.
2008	Private sector cyber-security risks start to emerge as being of at least equal importance and the law begins to address the matter of controls. Corporate cyber-security policies start to mature as a result.
2009	The Wikileaks Pentagon scandal breaks, underscoring the nature of the insider threat in a digital age. Meanwhile, the UK Information Commissioner was granted the power to levy fines of up to £500,000 for serious breaches of the DPA occurring on or after 6 April 2010, or serious breaches of the Privacy and Electronic Communications Regulations occurring on or after 26 May 2011.
2010	Hacktivism, characterised by the LulzSec and Anonymous movements, becomes risk number one as the democratisation of cybercrime moves the world into the era of the many-to-one attack.
2011	Awareness of the role of state actors and their proxies, characterised by the advanced persistent threat model (Hydraq, Shamoon, Flame and Stuxnet) illustrates a new threat vector in which a foreign public sector is the attacker and the local or globalised private sector is the target.
2012	The UK Information Commissioner imposes a record number of fines (25) for regulatory breaches.
2015	The EU prepares to issue strengthened data protection laws, with greatly increased penalties and a consumer's right to be forgotten. Facebook is taken to court in the UK in a class action case about privacy issues.
2018	The enforcement of the EU General Data Protection Regulation comes into effect.

3.2 The UK Information Commissioner's Office (ICO)

The Information Commissioner's Office (ICO), reports directly to Parliament and is sponsored by the Ministry of Justice. ICO is an independent regulatory body responsible for DPA, and other legislative acts and regulations, as outlined below.

The Information Commissioner's decisions are subject to the supervision of the Courts and an information tribunal. ICO's official mission is to *uphold information rights in the public interest, promoting openness by public bodies and data privacy for individuals.*

3.2.1 Relevant Legislation

ICO deals primarily with the following acts and regulations:

- Data Protection Act (DPA)
- Freedom of Information Act (FOIA)
- Privacy and Electronic Communications Regulations (PECR)
- Environmental Information Regulations (EIR) 2004
- Infrastructure for Spatial Information in Europe (INSPIRE) Regulations.

3.2.2 The Register of Data Controllers

One of the primary operational activities undertaken by ICO is the maintenance of a national register of data controllers. The DPA requires that every organisation which processes personal information must register with the ICO unless it can successfully claim to be exempt. Failure to register is a criminal offence.

There are currently more than 370,000 registered data controllers on the ICO database. The ICO publishes the name and address of each data controller as well as a description of the kind of data processing they do.

3.2.3 Handling of Concerns

Part of the ICO's role is to improve the information rights practices of organisations by gathering and dealing with concerns raised by members of the public. Each year the office addresses tens of thousands of enquiries from the public, written concerns and complaints about information rights issues.

Once a concern is raised the ICO will record and consider it. In some cases, the office collates further information on similar issues, looking at the concern alongside others raised about the organisation in question. All concerns raised contribute to the ICO's understanding of an organisation's performance against its obligations and facilitates decision-making on any improvements to be made.

3.2.4 Penalties and Other Measures

A number of additional tools are available to the ICO that enable it to take action to change the behaviour of organisations and individuals that collect, use and retain personal information. They include criminal prosecution, non-criminal enforcement and audit. The Information Commissioner also has the power to serve a monetary penalty notice on a data controller.

In cases where a clear and serious breach of the legislation has taken place, the ICO will generally take direct action on the specific concern raised. If it is decided that there has been a serious failure to comply with the law, the ICO provides advice and instruction to help ensure that the organisation complies with the relevant law going forward. If an organisation is not taking its responsibilities seriously, the ICO may also take enforcement action.

The tools already available to the ICO are not mutually exclusive and they may use them in combination, where justified by the circumstances.

The main options are:

- serving information notices that require organisations to provide the ICO with specified information within a certain time period
- issuing undertakings that commit an organisation to a particular course of action in order to improve its compliance
- serving enforcement notices and stop now orders where there has been a breach, which requires organisations to take (or refrain from taking) specified steps in order to ensure they comply with the law
- conducting consensual data security assessments (audits) to check that organisations are complying with the regulations
- serving assessment notices to conduct compulsory audits to assess whether organisations' processing of personal data is in keeping with best practice
- issuing monetary penalty notices that require organisations to pay up to £500,000 for serious breaches of the DPA occurring on or after 6 April 2010
- prosecution of those who commit criminal offences under the Act
- reporting to Parliament on issues of concern.

3.2.5   The Privacy and Electronic Communications Regulations (PECR)

Additionally, there are a number of tools available to the ICO for taking action to change the behaviour of anyone who breaches the Privacy and Electronic Communications Regulations (PECR). They include criminal prosecution, non-criminal enforcement and audit. The Information Commissioner again has the power to serve a monetary penalty notice and once more these powers are not mutually exclusive.

With respect to the PECR, the ICO can:

- issue an undertaking committing an organisation to a particular course of action in order to improve its compliance
- conduct an audit to check a service provider is complying with its security obligations, and make recommendations
- serve an enforcement notice or stop now order where there has been a breach, requiring an organisation to take specified steps to comply with the law. Failure to comply is a criminal offence
- issue a monetary penalty notice, requiring an organisation to pay up to £500,000 for serious breaches
- impose a fixed penalty of £1,000 on a service provider who fails to notify the ICO of a security breach
- apply to the court for an order under section 213 of the Enterprise Act 2002 requiring a person to cease conduct harmful to consumers

- prosecute if the breach also involves a criminal offence under the DPA, or if an organisation fails to comply with an enforcement notice (except in Scotland, where the procurator fiscal brings prosecutions)
- report to Parliament on issues of concern.

On 6 April 2015, the threshold for issuing monetary penalties under PECR changed. An amendment to the Regulations removed the requirement for the ICO to consider whether the contravention is likely to have caused substantial damage or substantial distress. The ICO can issue a penalty for any serious contraventions of regulations 19 to 24 of PECR (these provisions cover automated calling and direct marketing).

3.2.6   Other Acts and Regulations

There are a number of tools available to the ICO to take action to ensure that organisations adhere to the terms of the FOIA, Environmental Information Regulations, INSPIRE Regulations and other associated codes of practice. These include non-criminal enforcement and assessments of good practice.

Specifically, where authorities repeatedly or seriously fail to meet the requirements of the legislation or conform to the associated codes of practice, the ICO can:

- conduct assessments to check organisations are complying with the Act
- serve information notices requiring organisations to provide the ICO with specified information within a certain time period
- issue undertakings committing an authority to a particular course of action to improve its compliance
- serve enforcement notices where there has been a breach of the Act, requiring organisations to take (or refrain from taking) specified steps in order to ensure they comply with the law
- issue practice recommendations specifying steps the public authority should take to ensure conformity to the codes
- issue decision notices detailing the outcome of the ICO's investigation to publicly highlight particular issues arising out of an authority's handling of a specific request
- prosecute those who commit criminal offences under the Act
- report to Parliament on freedom of information issues of concern.

3.2.7   International Duties

As a statutory body, the ICO has a duty to cooperate with European and other international partners, including the EC and other data protection authorities. This cooperation includes:

- sharing information and good practice
- helping with complaints, investigation and enforcement
- working together to improve understanding of data protection law and the production of common positions and guidance, where appropriate and necessary.

In the European Union (EU), for the time being, the ICO still cooperates with other bodies across all areas, including activities related to the internal market, justice, freedom and security, and to police and judicial cooperation.

3.3   European Law Enforcement

As there are several law enforcement agencies operating across the EU, which are not governed by the UK DPA or the data protection laws of other EU countries, the ICO helps to supervise data protection arrangements for these law enforcement agencies to safeguard data protection and uphold the privacy rights of UK residents.

With respect to the Europol Convention, cooperation between the agency and national police forces involves sharing sensitive information about individuals. As a result, a number of data protection safeguards were built into the Convention to ensure that people's privacy rights are properly taken into account during investigations and intelligence work.

Apart from the data and services available to member states, **Europol** also provides support to co-operation partners. Cooperation partners currently include Iceland, Norway and the USA. The operations of Europol are supervised by the Europol Joint Supervisory Body (JSB), which ensures it complies with data protection rules.

3.3.1   Schengen Information System (SIS)

The Schengen Convention, 1990, was intended to facilitate the goal of creating a Europe without internal borders, specifically relating to the free movement of persons within the EU. At present 25 member states, as well as Norway and Iceland, are part of this free travel area. The UK is not a full member, and though it had asked for limited participation as allowed under the Treaty of Amsterdam 1999, their 2016 EU referendum has almost certainly put paid to that endeavour.

The Schengen Convention applies, among other things, to the areas of visa policy, asylum policy, police co-operation, drugs policy and the free movement of persons. An information system, the Schengen Information System (SIS), was established to facilitate the exchange of data in these areas. As the data is of a personal nature, data protection safeguards have been put in place. These safeguards include supervision by the data protection authorities, including the ICO.

3.3.2   Schengen Information System II (SIS II)

In order to cope with the enlargement of the EU, a new Schengen Information System (SIS II) was developed. This was intended to have the capacity to deal with the increased membership and has required the implementation of an EU regulation and an upgrade to the SIS IT infrastructure.

On 13 April 2015 the UK connected into SIS II, but this country only participates in the law enforcement aspects of the system. SIS II allows participating countries to share and receive law enforcement alerts in real time for:

- persons wanted for arrest for extradition purposes, for which a warrant has been issued (Article 26)
- missing persons who need to be placed under police protection or in a place of safety, including minors and adults not at risk (Article 32)
- witnesses, absconders and subjects of criminal judgments to appear before the judicial authorities (Article 34)
- people and vehicles requiring specific checks or discreet surveillance (Article 36)
- objects that are misappropriated, lost, stolen and which may be sought for the purposes of seizure or for use as evidence (eg, firearms and passports) (Article 38).

Supplementary Information Request at the National Entry (SIRENE) Bureaux are set up in all SIS II participating countries, to provide supplementary information on alerts and co-ordinate activities in relation to alerts in SIS II. In the UK's case this is still managed by the NCA. How the Brexit vote will impact these arrangements is still unclear.

A coordinated supervisory group, which includes the European Data Protection Supervisor and all member states, has been established under the new SISII Regulation and the ICO is currently represented on this body.

3.3.3   Customs Information System (CIS)

The abolition of border controls following the formation of the Single Market in 1993 triggered a requirement to find new and more effective means of combating various forms of smuggling across the borders of EU states.

The response was the Customs Information System (CIS), which was established under a special CIS Convention. Its aim is to assist in combating customs-related crime by facilitating co-operation between European customs authorities.

The centralised CIS, located in Brussels, can be accessed by member states and, as this involves the processing of personal data, a number of data protection safeguards have again been built into the system. The CIS only records data relating to the Customs and Excise area and the types of personal data held are limited to that specified in the Convention.

The CIS operates with two separate databases. One relates to matters which are subject to European law, while the second relates to matters which are solely subject to national law. Data held on the CIS may be accessed by the relevant authorities in the member states. However, only the party which has input the original data is authorised to correct, amend or delete such data. It seems likely that the UK will eventually lose access to this system after the country exits the EU, but this will certainly be one of many points for negotiation during the exit process.

3.3.4   Eurodac

Eurodac is a centralised EU database for analysing and comparing the fingerprints of asylum seekers. This is consistent with the Dublin Declaration of 1990 which seeks to standardise the manner in which applications for asylum are dealt with in member states. One of its main uses is to identify people who have previously made an application in another member state, or whose application has been rejected by another member state, in order to facilitate the identification of the state properly responsible for dealing with the application.

The Council Regulation which established Eurodac required that a national supervisory authority exists in each member state in order to monitor the operation of the system. The ICO is the national Eurodac supervisory authority for the UK.

Once again, departure from the EU will inevitably have some effect on these arrangements, subject to what terms the UK is able to negotiate over the coming months or years.

3.3.5 United States Department of the Treasury – Terrorist Finance Tracking Program (TFTP)

The TFTP was set up by the US Treasury Department shortly after the terrorist attacks of September 11, 2001. Since then, the TFTP has generated significant intelligence that has been beneficial to both US and EU states in the fight against terrorism.

There is an agreement in place enabling EU citizens to make subject access requests (SARs) via their national data protection authorities for information held by the US Treasury Department. For UK citizens, this means that each request can be made via the ICO. The ICO facilitates the request-making procedure.

3.3.6 The European Union (EU) Information Commissioners

Each European state has in place an official body equivalent to the ICO. While the details vary from state to state, all of these bodies are subject to a common standard set out in EU data protection laws.

Examples of such bodies include:

*   **Germany** – The Federal Commissioner for Data Protection and Freedom of Information
*   **Ireland** – The Office of the Information Commissioner (Oifig an Choimisinéara Faisnéise)
*   **Switzerland** – The Federal Data Protection and Information Commissioner.

3.4 Obligations of Financial Services Firms to the Information Commissioner

In addition to adhering to the general terms of the Acts that fall within the remit of the ICO and the requirement to register with the ICO as a data controller, financial services firms have three further responsibilities, defined by the ICO in respect of data protection:

*   reporting data breaches
*   filing defaults with credit reference agencies
*   credit agreements and post-agreement data sharing.

3.4.1 Reporting Data Breaches

Although there is no legal obligation on data controllers to report breaches of security under the DPA, the ICO states that it believes that serious breaches should be reported to the ICO by the affected data controller.

3.4.2 Filing Defaults with Credit Reference Agencies

The ICO lists the following requirements in relation to the recording of information with credit reference agencies by lenders:

*   Data that is reported on a credit file must be fair, accurate, consistent, complete and up to date.
*   Should a payment not be made as expected, information to reflect this will be recorded on the borrower's credit file.

- If a borrower offers or makes a reduced payment, how it is reported will depend on whether it is agreed with the lender.
- If a borrower falls into arrears on their account, or they do not keep to the revised terms of an arrangement, a default may be recorded to show that the relationship has broken down.
- When an account is closed, the record should properly reflect the closing payment status of the account and any agreement between the parties.

3.4.3 Credit Agreements and Data Sharing Post-agreement

The ICO reports that a number of individuals have claimed in the past that information relating to accounts they have held with credit providers should no longer be held by credit reference agencies. The complaints maintained that the agencies only had permission to hold account information for the duration of a credit agreement and that once the agreement ended, so did the consent to process information about it.

The Information Commissioner's view on the matter was that the complainants' argument was based on the assumption that the credit reference agencies needed consent to process account information. This is not the case as the first data protection principle requires that as well as processing information fairly and lawfully, organisations must satisfy one of the conditions in Schedule 2 of the DPA.

The ICO's view in relation to the sharing of account data with credit reference agencies for the duration of a contract and six years beyond was:

The processing is necessary for the purposes of legitimate interests pursued by the data controller or by the third party or parties to whom the data are disclosed, except where the processing is unwarranted in any particular case because of prejudice to the rights and freedoms or legitimate interests of the data subject.

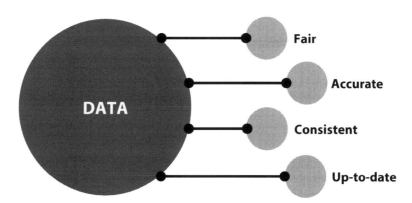

Figure 14: The ICO; data reported must be...

The ICO takes a wide view of legitimate interests and expressed the view that it is in the interests of other creditors to make informed lending decisions. The ICO pointed out that it is important to note that the fact that the processing may be seen by some to prejudice a particular individual (for example, someone with an adverse entry on his credit reference file may not be able to obtain credit facilities) does not necessarily render the whole processing operation prejudicial to all individuals.

The ICO went on to add that the fifth data protection principle requires that information processed for any purpose or purposes shall not be kept for longer than is necessary for that purpose or those purposes. The Commissioner pointed out that the DPA does not prescribe the period for which information is retained by credit reference agencies.

However, the ICO also noted that the *Crowther Report on Consumer Credit* (1971) expressed support for the view that a statutory time limit should be considered and suggested a period of six years should be adopted. At the time this practice was already common to some of the major credit reference agencies.

In conclusion, the ICO stated that the story of this historical information would appear to be relevant to the purpose of credit referencing and by holding this information the agencies would not appear to be in breach of the fifth principle.

3.5 The Financial Conduct Authority (FCA)

The primary goal of the Financial Conduct Authority (FCA) is to ensure that financial markets work well and that consumers consequently get a fair deal. This means ensuring that:

- the financial industry is run with integrity
- firms provide consumers with appropriate products and services
- consumers can be sure that firms are behaving in such a way that they have their best interests at heart.

To do this, the FCA regulates the conduct of over 50,000 businesses; for many of these businesses the organisation also considers whether they meet prudential standards that reduce the potential harm to the industry and consumers if they fail.

The FCA is funded entirely by the firms that it regulates, through a fee-charging structure. How much regulated firms pay is determined by what type of business they are and what activities they carry out.

The FCA is accountable to the Treasury (which is responsible for the UK's financial system) and to Parliament. However, it is an independent body and it does not receive any funding from the government.

3.5.1 The Prudential Regulation Authority (PRA)

The Prudential Regulation Authority (PRA) was created as a part of the Bank of England by the Financial Services Act 2012. It is responsible for the prudential regulation and supervision of approximately 1,700 banks, building societies, credit unions, insurers and major investment firms.

The PRA's objectives are set out in the Financial Services and Markets Act (FSMA) 2000. The PRA has three statutory objectives:

- A general objective to promote the safety and soundness of the firms that it regulates.
- An objective specific to insurance firms, to contribute to the securing of an appropriate degree of protection for those who are or may become insurance policyholders.
- A secondary objective to facilitate effective competition.

The PRA advances its objectives using two key tools:

- **regulation** – setting standards and policies that it expects firms to meet
- **supervision** – assessing the risks that firms pose to its objectives and, where necessary, takes action to reduce them.

The PRA's approach to using regulation and supervision has three characteristics:

- **Judgement based** – the PRA uses judgement in determining whether financial firms are safe and sound, whether insurers provide appropriate protection for policyholders and whether firms continue to meet the threshold conditions.
- **Forward looking** – the PRA assesses firms not just against current risks, but also against those that could plausibly arise in the future. Where the PRA judges it necessary to intervene, it generally aims to do so at an early stage.
- **Focused** – the PRA focuses on those issues and firms that pose the greatest risk to the stability of the UK financial system and policyholders. A stable financial system is one in which firms continue to provide critical financial services – a precondition for a healthy and successful economy.

The PRA states that it does not seek to operate a zero-failure regime. Rather, it seeks to ensure that a financial firm which fails does so in a way that avoids significant disruption to the supply of critical financial services.

3.5.2 CBEST

CBEST is a testing framework introduced by the Bank of England in 2014 to help large financial services institutions (and relevant regulators) understand the types of cyber-attack that threaten UK financial stability. It is also designed to assess the UK's level of vulnerability to cyber-attacks and the effectiveness of the detection and response measures already in place. CBEST reflects a shift in focus from preventing attacks entirely to improving an organisation's resilience and its ability to continue operating during an attack and to recover following an attack.

CBEST uses a common framework that is designed to deliver a controlled, bespoke, intelligence-led (meaning that it channels intelligence directly from government and commercial intelligence providers) penetration test against critical systems; those that are essential to the well-being of an institution and to that of the UK financial system as a whole. These tests are intended to mimic the tactics, techniques and procedures of genuine threat actors, although they can only, at best, reflect known past techniques with any accuracy. Future scenarios will always be speculative.

All firms that undertake CBEST are required to produce a set of key performance indicators (KPIs), which cover both threat intelligence and penetration testing. These KPIs are used to provide a cyber-security assessment to the firm once its CBEST programme is complete. The Bank of England's Sector Cyber Team also uses these KPIs to improve its own understanding of the financial sector's overall cyber-security position.

End of Chapter Questions

Think of an answer for each question and refer to the appropriate section for confirmation

1.   Name three of the five main areas of focus of the NCA.
     Answer reference: Section 1.2

2.   List the three activities of an organised crime group.
     Answer reference: Section 1.2.1

3.   Describe the executive powers held by Europol.
     Answer reference: Section 1.6.2

4.   List the four parallel crime-fighting strands promoted by the Hague Programme of 2004.
     Answer reference: Section 1.6.5

5.   Name one of the ISO standards dealing with ICT or InfoSec.
     Answer reference: Section 2.1.1

6.   List five of the 10 Steps to cyber-security promulgated by GCHQ.
     Answer reference: Section 2.7

7.   Name two of the acts and regulations dealt with by the UK Information Commissioner's Office.
     Answer reference: Section 3.2.1

8.   What were the two main drivers behind the introduction of SIS II?
     Answer reference: Section 3.3.2

9.   What is Eurodac?
     Answer reference: Section 3.3.4

10. What is the main cyber or information security responsibility financial firms have towards the ICO?
     Answer reference: Section 3.4

Chapter Four

Cybercrime and the Financial Services Industry

1. Recognising the Threat   143

2. Types of Threat Actor   147

3. Known Vulnerabilities   153

4. Cybercrime Detection   165

This syllabus area will provide approximately 7 of the 50 examination questions

I needed a password eight characters long so I picked Snow White and the Seven Dwarves. Nick Helm

1.   Recognising the Threat

The financial services sector is a very popular target of cyber-attacks for at least three reasons:

- It is where money is stored and handled.
- Its operations and policies are sometimes controversial and can stir up a great deal of public anger at certain periods.
- It is one of the **critical national infrastructure (CNI)** components and is therefore a target of any individual or state hostile to the hosting or home nation.

Learning Objective

4.1.1   Understand the importance of financial services as a component of critical national infrastructure: threats and impacts at national level; managing cyber-dependencies; national cyber-security culture

1.1   Threat Intelligence

Threat intelligence is an essential activity for any organisation that faces potential threats against its network and systems. Technological tools provide only one part of the solution. A three-part combination of techniques is required:

- threat intelligence
- risk management
- technical countermeasures.

This three-step approach serves to reveal not only who is being targeted but also how, when, why and possibly by whom.

Understanding the threat is a critical precursor to the development of an effective defence, as organisations will not merely expect to be attacked; they will also understand what that attack might look like.

As we saw in chapter 1, today's attackers use toolkits, not only to exploit older vulnerabilities but also to take advantage of new zero-day opportunities. Good threat intelligence should support the creation of a prioritised list of suspicious incidents by correlating all available information from across the enterprise. This can be done using a sequence of steps comprising a threat-intelligence cycle:

- **Collection** – data about potential threats is sourced.
- **Collation** – the data collected in Step 1 is organised and structured to support analysis.

- **Interpretation** – the structured data is subjected to analysis and interpretation by intelligence analysts properly trained for the task.
- **Dissemination** – the resulting intelligence product is shared with those who have a need to know, in a timely fashion.

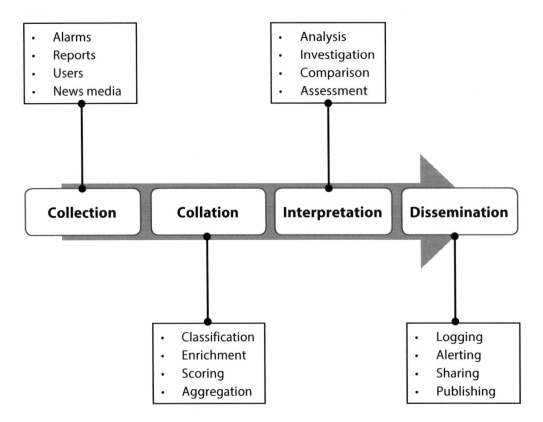

Figure 15: The Threat Intelligence Process

1.1.1   The Current Threat: Spear-Phishing

Attackers are becoming increasingly skilled at breaching networks by using highly sophisticated and cleverly targeted spear-phishing attacks. One common example is known as CEO fraud. This involves the attacker setting up a fake Gmail, Outlook or other email account using the name of a genuine company chief executive officer (CEO) and then emailing employees at the company to request sensitive data, such as customer contact lists. The UK suffered a rash of such attacks in late 2015 and early 2016 with many organisations falling victim.

Attackers have also perfected the so-called watering hole attack technique, making each attack more selective by infecting legitimate websites used by their targets, and then monitoring the visitors to the infected sites. In this way they can target only individuals or companies they have preselected. This is akin to a lion hiding near a real watering hole, waiting for antelope to come and drink.

1.1.2   The Current Threat: Trojan Software Updates

Further stretching many organisations' capacity to defend themselves is the appearance of Trojan software updates. Attackers identify common software programs used by targeted organisations. They then hide their malware inside fake software updates for those legitimate programs, which they publish online and broadcast via spam messages. The attackers then wait for their targets to download and install the Trojan software hidden within the fake updates, effectively waiting for the victims to infect themselves, thus providing avenues for further exploits.

1.1.3   Threats and Impacts at National Level

The majority of business or governmental sectors are verticals. While there are important dependencies between particular sectors, few have truly horizontal effects; ie, effects that have an impact on all other sectors. The primary exceptions to this rule are the nine critical national infrastructures (CNIs), defined in the UK as:

- communications (including internet)
- emergency services
- energy
- financial services
- food
- government
- health
- transport
- water.

Lose the ability to operate in any of these nine sectors and the effects on all others will be instantaneous and catastrophic.

For this reason, in addition to regarding operational threats as having potentially strategic implications when thinking exclusively about cyber-security, security management must also appreciate the cross-sector horizontal implications of data and communications security failures for all other sectors of the economy. The information communications and technology space is not merely another vertical; it is of strategic importance in its own right and it is relevant to everyone, everywhere, even if they are not users of computers and the internet.

1.1.4   Managing Cyber Dependencies

Cyber-security should now become an essential part of any organisation's risk strategy. While it will always be impossible to know everything about the threat, increasingly thorough risk assessments and more effective and agile response mechanisms can reduce the chances of cyber-disaster and will increase overall resilience to cyber-attacks.

There is a real need to address organisational imbalances in the area of cyber-risk management and to develop a more comprehensive understanding of cyber-security risks at senior management levels. Senior management must become more aware of the type and range of cyber-dependencies within their organisations and the potential financial and reputational impact of a major cyber-incident. They should be equipped with a degree of awareness that allows them to ask sensible questions of those providing technical services, security and risk management within their organisations.

Clear plans are needed and adequate resources must be allocated for disaster recovery. Cyber-security must not be allowed to fall victim to the ever-present desire to cut costs and increase efficiencies.

CNI organisations also need to participate in extensive horizon scanning designed to identify future threats and to develop long-term responses to the potential cyber-risks facing the organisation and wider society. In particular, these exercises need to focus on the impact of emerging technologies. Examples of the domains deserving our attention include:

- nanotechnology
- biocomputing
- quantum computing
- wearable technology
- embedded technology
- robotics.

On the wearable technology front, several recent incidents of exam fraud in Sweden, Thailand and China illustrate the nature of the evolving threat. In each case, fraudsters sent students into exam halls wearing glasses with tiny WiFi-connected cameras embedded in the frames. These students filmed the exam papers and the images were transmitted to their accomplices, who were setup nearby.

The fraud team then researched the answer to each question online and rapidly sent the correct answers back to other students in the hall, via their smart watches; all phones had been taken away from students, but the watches had not. Students had reportedly paid up to £15,000 each for this support.

In the case of China, drones equipped with signal intercept devices are now being flown over some exam halls in an effort to stop this kind of fraud. However, once technology becomes embedded within the human body, as many commentators anticipate it will be, the implications not only for exam bodies, but also for financial firms and markets are clear.

Training and development of all categories of staff at all levels in basic cyber-security threat awareness and countermeasures must become an integral part of risk-mitigation strategies.

1.1.5 National Cyber-Security Culture

The development of a national cyber-security culture is perhaps the most important facet of our collective defence mechanism. However, greater organisational and public awareness is urgently needed if we are to shape and promulgate such a culture.

There are many examples of best practice available, but these are not standardised, and practices differ across the public and private sector. Government and the financial services industry, along with other industries, must now work collaboratively to develop common models of best practice and language.

Incorporating cyber-risk into existing risk management processes is also essential. Cyber-security is merely another facet of risk, not a separate business silo. It needs to become a fixed item on the risk management agenda rather than being seen as remote, complex and the stuff of science fiction.

Chatham House opines that national cyber-risk awareness could be achieved by way of six factors:

1. Detailed, specific information communication and outreach strategies to achieve consistency in managing cyber-risks as part of a systematic approach to developing a culture of awareness. These should be targeted at, and tailored for, both board-level members and technology experts and disseminated across organisations to enhance overall awareness.
2. Internal strategic communications regarding cyber-threats should be transmitted across an organisation with a clear sense of decision-making hierarchies (or chains of command), responsibility and accountability.
3. Government will have to communicate with senior private sector management in language the latter can understand. The issue of cyber-risks needs to be made accessible to those who are neither familiar with technology nor highly IT literate.
4. Cyber-terminology should be clear and the language proportionate to the threat. It should also encourage a clear distinction to be made between IT mishaps and genuine cyber-attacks.
5. As part of communication and outreach efforts it would be useful to have a centre of intelligence sharing such as the Virtual Global Taskforce (which is used to coordinate approaches to cybercrime among financial institutions) for those who need to be informed. This would enable decisions to be made and information disseminated both vertically and horizontally between affected organisations.
6. Greater public awareness would help acclimatise a wider audience to cyber-security issues and encourage individual precautions and security measures. Public messaging must recognise the existence of disparities and varying levels of awareness.

2. Types of Threat Actor

Learning Objective

4.1.2   Understand how financial services firms are exposed to various categories of cybercriminal: employees and contractors; 'hacktivists' or single-issue extremists; hackers and script kiddies; fraudsters; nation states; organised crime networks; malware developers; software developers; social engineers

2.1   Classes of Cyber-Threat Source

There are at least four main classes of cyber-threat source and they have very particular characteristics:

*   Disasters:
    *   natural disasters
    *   man-made disasters.
*   Failures:
    *   beyond the control of organisations
    *   of controlled resources.
*   Human errors:
    *   of omission
    *   of commission.

- Attacks:
  - cyber-attacks
  - physical attacks
  - social engineering attacks
  - attacks on brand or reputation, including so-called doxing attacks.

When considering cybercrime and security, we focus on the last set (attacks) and on the threat actors behind them, of which there are again several types. There are generally at least two phases to any cyber-attack:

- **Access** – how did the attackers get in?
- **Exploitation** – how did the attackers use their access once they had gained it?

Access techniques are shared, which is to say that any attacker may select any access technique, according to the situation and their own levels of skill. However, exploitation methods are many and varied. They are determined not only by skill but also by the motivations of the attacker. Different types of attacker can have very different motivations and this will affect how an organisation needs to deal with the effects of an attack.

A well-constructed cyber-security plan must address the prevention of access and the management of various forms of exploitation as distinct issues. In addition to protecting the perimeter, the plan must address scenarios in which the attacker is persistent. As discussed in section 4.10 of chapter 1, this refers to a situation in which the attacker is still active within the system even after he has been detected.

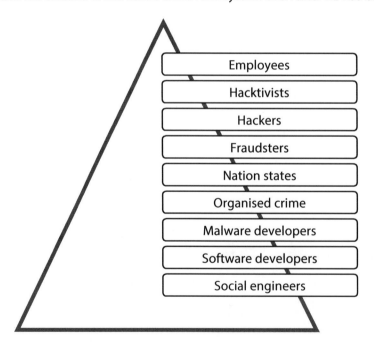

Figure 16: The Main Classes of Cyber-Attacker

2.1.1 Hackers

Penetrations, or hacking attacks, are access techniques and the manner in which they are then exploited can vary widely, for example via lateral movement, committing fraud or stealing data. Attackers are human and they live, breathe and think just like you do. While you are dealing with a cyber-security penetration, there is every chance that the hacker is watching you operate, responding to your moves, wiping evidence of the attack and continuing to exfiltrate data as you attempt to plug the leak.

Hacking is a disputed term that is used to refer to several different types of activity and individual. Perhaps the best description is:

A person with expert computing skills, who attempts to access a computer system without authorisation, by circumventing or cracking its security.

Loosely speaking, there are five main classes of hacker:

- Traditional hackers who like to tinker with technology for fun or kudos.
- Ethical hackers who test systems on behalf of the systems' owners.
- Hacktivists who are hacking in pursuit of a political or social goal.
- Criminal hackers who hack for financial gain, to cause harm or for other similar motives.
- Agents of the state, or in the employ of corporations, non-state actors or organised crime networks, otherwise known as spies.

Criminal hackers are more correctly termed crackers, but the media generally fails to make this distinction. However, technical people will sometimes state that a hacker is simply a particularly skilled computer expert. Hackers/crackers may be acting independently or they may have been recruited by one of the groups listed above. Several states, including the UK, USA, China, Russia, North Korea and Israel, directly employ large numbers of expert hackers, although most of these are unlikely to have criminal backgrounds; they are merely highly skilled.

Those hackers not driven by a desire for financial gain are commonly thought to be motivated by several factors:

- **Challenge** – most hackers are proud of their technical skills and derive immense satisfaction merely from defeating the efforts of teams of corporate or government programmers to create secure systems.
- **Status within the hacking community** – while some hackers shun the limelight, many want to be recognised within the hacking community.
- **Freedom of information or software** – a large proportion of hackers have ideological roots in the free software movement and hold a sincere belief in the principle of freedom of information, while abhorring the sale of software for profit. They strongly resent corporate and state efforts to secure data and limit access to information that many feel should be in the public domain.

Some hackers have ideological motivations, or they may be single-issue extremists who are focused entirely on one particular pet peeve. We commonly refer to politically motivated hackers as hacktivists.

Examples of some activist and single-issue extremist organisations that use cyber-attack techniques extensively, include:

- Anonymous
- the Syrian Electronic Army
- some animal rights organisations.

2.1.2 Script Kiddies

Script kiddie is a pejorative term describing supposedly young (although in fact they can be any age) and less skilled persons who execute software scripts, or use programs previously created by expert hackers, to attack computer systems and websites.

Script kiddies often obtain their hacking programs from internet sites and are often unaware of who the program's creator was or what the full implications of their actions may be. As a result, script kiddies represent one useful channel for malware or attacks that can be exploited by organised hackers, thus keeping the actual attacker one step removed from the crime.

While reliable statistics are rare, experts estimate that a majority of malware attacks (excluding Adware and Spyware) are channelled via script kiddies. There are believed to be relatively few truly expert criminal hackers in cyber-space and script kiddies are the active foot soldiers who are responsible for much of the malware problem.

2.1.3 Fraudsters

Financial fraudsters are thieves who commit fraud (dishonestly making a false representation or failing to disclose information). In cyber-security terms, examples include people who hack into a bank's systems in order to divert funds to their own accounts or someone who steals data by using another person's logon details and then sells that data to a competitor.

Opportunistic cyber-fraudsters are otherwise honest people who, when confronted with an opportunity to profit from crime, choose to do so. Depending on our personal circumstances, values, the nature of the opportunity and the risks of being caught, many of us are potential opportunists.

Employees may be motivated to commit opportunistic cybercrimes or to facilitate their commission by third parties for any number of reasons. Criminal greed and corruption are often cited, although the role of modern social aspirations should not be discounted. The concealment of trading or accounting errors is a common driver for many forms of high-tech fraud and this may extend to the commission of some forms of cybercrime. Revenge can also be a driver for cybercrime.

2.1.4 Nation States

State sponsors tend to be less driven by short-term business cases and are more interested in developing and refining their cyber-warfare capabilities over the long term, although we are now entering an era in which execution may eclipse planning and reconnaissance as the primary goal.

- **Cyber-warfare capacity** – many state sponsors appear to be still testing and refining their cyber-warfare capabilities and a minority are clearly very far advanced in this arena. Much of what happens today on the internet, in terms of state-sponsored attacks, is probably part of that testing process.
- **Mapping of targets** – intelligence in war has always been a leading requirement for victory and this was never truer than in the cyber-warfare sphere. The internet is more complex to map than physical geography and it also shifts and evolves constantly, with dramatic growth expected to continue for some years until the bulk of the world's population is online. Therefore, the task of locating, accessing and assessing targets for cyber-attacks is a mammoth one. Once mapped, every target will need to be constantly reassessed for changes in technology or security mechanisms.
- **Secret data** – states want secret data of several types, including military, economic, political, commercial and personal. This data is needed in order for them to assess the intentions and capabilities of potential opponents, identify their strengths and weaknesses, advance the business goals of their own national corporations and target key individuals.
- **Deniability** – finally, states require deniability in peacetime, for diplomatic and political reasons. Therefore, we will continue to see fledgling cyber-attacks and penetrations being carried out by non-state actors, some of whom will doubtless be acting with official sanction.

2.1.5 Organised Crime Networks

Organised crime is now turning to the internet as a domain in which a great deal of crime activity can and is being perpetrated. Today's cyber-attacks are therefore not solely the preserve of governments and hackers. Organised crime networks use the same techniques to address their own particular requirements:

- **Criminal gain** – theft of data for resale, to facilitate identity fraud or to provide access to credit card or bank account details are just a few of the ways in which criminals exploit the internet.
- **Leverage and intelligence** – cyber-attacks can provide a criminal with a wealth of information about a target individual or location. Web browsing habits, personal details, email content, social networking contacts and messages can all be used to blackmail a person in a key position or as intelligence during the planning stage of a criminal act.
- **Concealment** – spoofing and other such techniques can be used by criminals to avoid surveillance during the planning phase and to make police investigations difficult post-event. Concealment may also involve the concealment of sources of funds.

2.1.6 Malware Developers

Malware creators may be acting independently or they may have been recruited by another party or organisation. There are three common motives of those who create and disseminate computer malware:

- **Demonstrating vulnerabilities** – highlighting vulnerabilities in computing systems and networks, or in the training of users and administrators, for the sole purpose of encouraging administrators to up their game.
- **Accessing information** – using malware attacks to access key data, potentially in order to sell it.
- **Generating revenue** – by fraudulently directing traffic to a commercial site that receives payments based on traffic volumes, thus inflating revenue in a fraudulent manner, or providing DoS attack capabilities for money.

As we saw in chapter 1, the use of sophisticated malnets to spread malware is becoming a widespread problem.

2.1.7   Software Developers

Software developers may also be a source of cyber-attacks. With the increasing popularity of the app model (there are now over 1 million apps in each of the major stores), the potential for software developers to include malicious code, in the form of Trojan malware, has never been greater.

It is estimated that no less than 17% of Android apps hosted on websites other than the App Store itself are malicious.

2.1.8   Social Engineers

Social engineering is the art of manipulating people to:

- perform unplanned actions
- refrain from planned actions.

In cyber-security terms, social engineering is a human issue that exploits human failings and makes people a vehicle for crime. Most financial firms are familiar with social engineering as a tool used by criminals to trick gullible people out of their savings. In fact, social engineering has a rich history and is widely used by criminals, con artists, advertisers, marketers, sales people, politicians and penetration testers. When used by criminals, it is regularly employed to get confidential information, such as:

- personal information
- bank account details
- business information
- usernames and passwords.

Social engineering may also be used face-to-face to negotiate access to restricted areas. Social engineering is one of the biggest cyber-security threats we face because it exploits human weaknesses or naivety in ways that mean it cannot easily be designed out in the way that software flaws can. Increasingly, social engineers are turning to social media sites like Facebook and LinkedIn to identify targets and to launch social engineering attacks. As a result, social media is now emerging as one of the most important cyber-security vulnerabilities.

3.   Known Vulnerabilities

Learning Objective

4.2.1   Know typical classes of cybercrime vulnerability affecting networks

4.2.2   Know the typical classes of cybercrime vulnerability of connected devices

4.2.3   Know the typical classes of cybercrime vulnerability of common applications (apps) and browsers

4.2.4   Know the typical cybercrime vulnerabilities of database systems

4.3.5   Know how penetration testing and vulnerability assessment methodologies are employed to detect cyber-attacks

4.3.6   Know how artificial intelligence is used to detect cyber-attacks and vulnerabilities, its limits and its role in financial services, as well as the resulting cyber-security risks

3.1   Network, Connected Device and Application Vulnerabilities

Vulnerabilities are often discovered by using a vulnerability scanner. This is a technique that analyses a computer system using a list of known vulnerabilities, such as open ports, insecure software configurations and the susceptibility of the operating system and applications to malware infections.

The default settings of a computer system can sometimes reveal useful information about the software that it runs and how these programs are configured. Systems connected to the internet, or to another network, may broadcast a range of network protocols and communications channels in order to connect with other devices. These broadcasts may signal vulnerabilities that can be exploited if they are not removed or deactivated.

An attacker will point network scanning tools at a range of IP addresses and a network in an attempt to identify any of the following in relation to connected devices:

- open ports
- open services
- default settings
- vulnerable applications and operating systems
- the make and model of connected network equipment.

Unknown vulnerabilities, such as zero-day attack flaws, are often found using automated testing, which can identify certain kinds of vulnerabilities such as a buffer overflow exploit.

Attackers exploit one of two categories of attack capability when targeting networks:

- **commodity capabilities**
- **bespoke capabilities**.

3.1.1   Commodity Capabilities

A commodity capability refers to easy-to-use tools and techniques available off-the-shelf via the internet. These include tools and applications developed for use by security experts (eg, penetration testers).

Penetration testing applications and hardware can also be used by attackers. Some of these tools are designed to scan for well-known vulnerabilities in network ports, operating systems and applications. Poison Ivy is a good example of a popular commodity tool; it is readily available for use remotely and has been widely used for several years.

3.1.2   Bespoke Capabilities

A bespoke capability is one that is developed for a specific purpose, for example to attack a particular target. Bespoke tools require more specialist user knowledge.

Examples of bespoke tools include malicious code that takes advantage of software vulnerabilities (or flaws) that are not yet known to vendors or anti-malware companies – eg, the infamous zero-day vulnerabilities. Alternatively, a bespoke tool might target an undocumented software feature or poorly designed application. Internally developed applications and others built by small external software houses often contain such flaws.

Bespoke capabilities usually morph to become commodity capabilities once their use has been discovered and information about the incident has been broadcast online. This often happens very quickly.

Similarly, there are two primary categories of attack, each of which might make use of either commodity or bespoke capabilities:

*   untargeted attacks
*   targeted attacks.

Untargeted Attacks

In an untargeted attack, the attacker will indiscriminately target as many devices, network services or users as possible. Their primary objective is to breach any target or to infect as many targets as possible. To achieve this, attackers use techniques that take advantage of the open nature of the internet:

*   **Phishing** – sending unsolicited electronic messages of various types to large numbers of people asking for personal sensitive information (including bank details or data that can be used for identity theft) or encouraging them to visit a fake website.
*   **Water holing** – setting up a fake website or compromising a legitimate one in order to exploit innocent users who visit the trusted page. This is often done in the context of a wider malnet attack.
*   **Ransomware** – often takes the form of disk-encrypting extortion malware.
*   **Scanning** – inspecting or attacking devices across the internet by exploiting network vulnerabilities.

Targeted Attacks

In a targeted attack, an organisation or individual is singled out because the attacker has a specific interest in them or has been paid to target them. The groundwork for such an attack often takes months as attackers seek to find the best route to deliver their exploit directly to the targeted systems or users.

A targeted attack is often more damaging than an untargeted attack because it has been specifically tailored to attack selected systems, processes or people, based on prior knowledge and intelligence. Targeted attack techniques often include:

- **Spear phishing** – sending unsolicited electronic messages of various types to targeted individuals that either contain an attachment with malicious software embedded within it or a link to a malicious website that serves up malware when visited.
- **Deploying a botnet** – designed to deliver a DDoS (distributed denial-of-service) attack.
- **Subverting the supply chain** – designed to attack equipment or software being delivered to the organisation.

3.2 Common Cyber-Attack Stages and Patterns

Whether an attack is targeted or untargeted, or whether the attacker is using commodity or bespoke tools, cyber-attacks tend to have certain features in common. A sophisticated attack, when carried out by a persistent adversary, may consist of repeated stages as the attacker goes through a series of iterative steps in his attempt to break into the victim's system.

Attackers carefully probe a target's defences for vulnerabilities that, if discovered, will willingly give them access or allow them to deny services.

GCHQ lists the four main stages present in most cyber-attacks as follows:

- **Survey** – discovering, investigating and analysing available information about the target in order to identify potential vulnerabilities.
- **Delivery** – getting to the point in a system where a vulnerability can be exploited.
- **Breach** – exploiting the vulnerability or vulnerabilities to gain some form of unauthorised access.
- **Effect** – carrying out exploitation activities within a compromised system to achieve the attacker's goal.

3.2.1 Survey

Attackers will use any means available to find technical, procedural or physical vulnerabilities which they can attempt to exploit, including the use of **open-source** information such as LinkedIn and Facebook, other social media sources and domain name management/search services that list the names and contact details of domain name registrants.

Attackers also employ commodity toolkits and techniques, as well as network scanning tools to collect and assess any information about an organisation's computers, security systems and personnel.

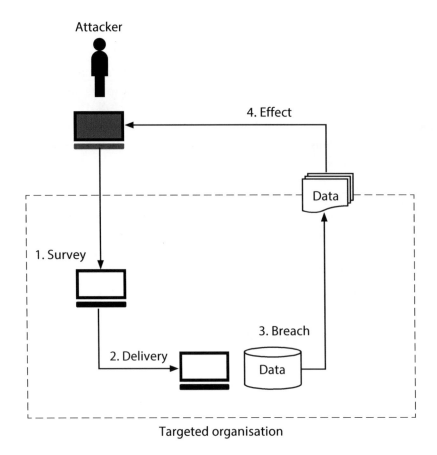

Figure 17: Common Stages of a Cyber-Attack

User errors reveal information that can be used in attacks. Common user errors include:

* releasing information about the organisation's network on a technical support forum
* neglecting to remove hidden properties from documents such as author, software version and file save locations.

In addition, attackers frequently use social engineering (often via social media) to exploit user naivety and goodwill to elicit further, less openly available information.

Armed with this initial intelligence, attackers then make use of commodity tools and techniques to probe the targeted system for any exploitable vulnerabilities that may provide opportunities for attackers to gain access to these systems.

Vulnerabilities typically fall into one of three categories:

* flaws
* features
* user errors.

Flaws

A flaw is an unintended feature or piece of functionality in a system or application, usually resulting either from a design and development error or an error made during implementation of the product. Flaws are often also introduced when products are updated with faulty patches or updated incorrectly. Conversely, many flaws persist because of a failure to update systems with new versions of software.

Flaws often go undetected for significant periods of time. The majority of common attacks seen today exploit these persistent vulnerabilities, and each year thousands of new vulnerabilities are detected and logged in various cyber-security databases around the world.

Features

A feature is an intended piece of functionality which can be misused by an attacker to breach a system. Features may improve the user's experience, help diagnose problems or improve efficiency and management control, but they can sometimes be exploited by an attacker too.

User Errors

A computer or system that has been carefully designed and implemented can minimise the vulnerabilities of exposure to the internet. Unfortunately, such efforts can be easily undone, for example by an inexperienced system administrator who enables vulnerable features, fails to fix a known flaw, or leaves default passwords unchanged.

More generally, users can be a significant source of vulnerabilities. They make mistakes, such as choosing a common or easily guessed password or leaving their laptop or mobile phone unattended. Even the most cyber-aware users can be fooled into giving away their password, installing malware or divulging information that may be useful to an attacker (for example, details of who holds a particular role within an organisation and their schedule). These details allow an attacker to target and time an attack appropriately.

3.2.2 Delivery

During the delivery stage, the attacker will seek a position from which they can exploit a vulnerability that they have earlier identified, or that they think might potentially exist, given the nature of the system. Examples include:

- attempting to access an organisation's online services
- sending an email containing a link to a malicious website or an attachment which contains malicious code
- giving an infected USB stick away at a trade fair or by leaving it on the ground in an organisation's car park
- creating a false website in the hope that a target will visit the site and pick up the infections hidden there. The site will often be designed to mirror the interests a target reveals via his social media activities.

It can be seen that a crucial decision for any attacker is the best delivery path for malicious software or commands that will enable them to breach their target's defences. In the case of a denial-of-service attack, however, it may be sufficient for the attacker to make multiple connections to a computer in order to prevent others from accessing it.

3.2.3   Breach

The harm suffered by the victim of such an attack will depend on the nature of the vulnerability, the assets exposed, the duration of the breach and the exploitation method used by the attacker. Typically, attacks may allow attackers to:

- make changes that affect a system's operations
- gain access to online accounts or sensitive information
- achieve full control of an infected computer, tablet or smartphone.

Having achieved any of these outcomes, an attacker can then exploit their access to carry out a wide range of crimes or malicious activities.

3.2.4   Effect

Depending on their motivations, attackers may explore compromised systems looking for vulnerabilities or sensitive data, or expand their access and establish a persistent presence across multiple platforms (a process sometimes called consolidation). Think of the attack as a series of cancerous nodes in a body that can spread to other parts over time if not detected quickly.

Taking over a user's account might facilitate a persistent presence, but taking over a system administrator's account is the ultimate achievement for an attacker. With administration access to just one system, an attacker can often install automated scanning tools in order to discover more about the network and take control of other systems. This process is called lateral movement. While doing this attackers will take care not to trigger any monitoring processes and they may even be able to disable them using their administrator privileges.

Determined attackers, if not detected, continue this process until they have achieved their end goals, which can include using the resources of the infected system to launch further attacks on others or as drop sites for storing stolen data taken from elsewhere. Depending on their objectives, the activities of attackers may vary:

- Retrieving information they would otherwise not be able to access, such as intellectual property or commercially sensitive information.
- Making changes to systems, data or applications for their own benefit, such as triggering payments into a bank account they control.
- Disrupting normal business operations or conducting crypto-extortion attacks.

After achieving his objectives, the attacker will often exit the compromised system or network, carefully removing any evidence of his presence by uninstalling all malicious applications, removing any fraudulent user accounts and deleting parts of the registry.

An attacker will sometimes create a hidden access route for future use, known as a backdoor. This can also be given or sold to others. On the other hand, some attackers will want to seriously damage a system or make as much 'noise' as possible to advertise their success and cause reputational harm.

3.3 Breaking the Attack Pattern

Only the most highly skilled and motivated attackers have the persistence to carry out multiple stage attacks but they will frequently do this using cheap, easy-to-use commodity tools and techniques. Putting in place security controls and processes that can counter these techniques will go some way to making an organisation harder to target. Unless an organisation is being deliberately singled out by attackers, they will often move on to look for a more likely prospect.

Adopting a defence-in-depth approach to risk mitigation, taking into account the full range of potential attacks, provides more resilience, even in the face of attacks that use bespoke tools and techniques.

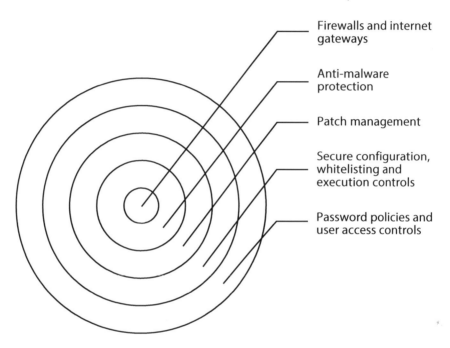

Firewalls and internet gateways

Anti-malware protection

Patch management

Secure configuration, whitelisting and execution controls

Password policies and user access controls

Figure 18: Basic Cyber-Security

There are proven ways to assure good cyber-housekeeping and reduce exposure to the most common types of cyber-attack:

- **Boundary firewalls and internet gateways** – establish network perimeter defences, particularly web proxy, web filtering, content checking and firewall policies to detect and block executable downloads, block access to known malicious domains and prevent users' computers from communicating directly with the internet.
- **Anti-malware protection** – establish and maintain malware defences to detect and respond to known attack code.
- **Patch management** – patch known vulnerabilities with the latest version of the software to prevent attacks which exploit software bugs.
- **Whitelisting and execution controls** – prevent unknown software from being able to run or self-install, including *AutoRun* features on USB and CD drives.
- **Secure configuration** – restrict the functionality of every device, operating system and application to the minimum needed for business to function.

- **Password policy** – ensure that an appropriate password policy is in place and test to confirm that it is being adhered to.
- **User access control** – this should include limiting normal users' execution permissions and enforcing the **principle of least privilege** – applying only those privileges to a user account that are essential to that user's role and duties.

Correcting vulnerabilities in any of these vital areas may involve the installation of a patch, a change in network security policy, reconfiguration of security systems (such as a firewall) or educating users about social engineering and other threats. The process of detecting and correcting vulnerabilities is known as **vulnerability management**.

3.4   Vulnerability Management

Vulnerability management is defined as *the cyclical practice of identifying, classifying, remediating, and mitigating vulnerabilities in software and firmware*. Vulnerability management is therefore an essential aspect of cyber-security.

Vulnerability management is delivered in several ways:

1. **Scan the network regularly for vulnerabilities**
   A vulnerability assessment scans your security environment across network devices, operating systems, applications, databases and web applications on a regular basis to check for vulnerabilities.

   Scanning your network regularly helps to identify and handle known security issues. It can, for example, identify an existing server that is exposed to a known vulnerability or spot a new device connected to a network without authorisation. In such situations, scanning helps to locate rogue devices that might in turn endanger overall network security.

2. **Prioritise and test patches and updates**
   When administrators are deploying a patch update, it is important that they pre-test the patch before it is applied across the network. This can be time-consuming, so it is important to prioritise those vulnerabilities that need to be fixed first, based on their severity.

   Prioritising and testing patch updates can often be more easily accomplished by employing patch management software, which has the ability to research, script, package and test patches for common third-party applications, as well as to obtain ready-to-deploy patches from trusted sites. One advantage of such systems is that they are not susceptible to being socially engineered into downloading Trojan updates.

3. **Stay up-to-date with patches**
   Timely patches help to correct any security and functionality problems in endpoint applications. Networks therefore need to stay up-to-date on their software patches in order to stay protected from the latest security threats and the dreaded Zero-Day exploit risk as unpatched applications are the favoured entry points for security attacks.

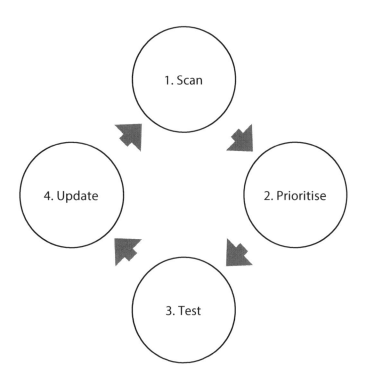

Figure 19: The Essence of Vulnerability Management

Anyone who has legitimate access to systems as an employee or a contractor should also be considered an important part of a holistic cyber-security regime. A rogue insider might use their normal access rights to compromise information, take advantage of unlocked computers or guess passwords. They often use social engineering techniques to gain further access. They may even have the technical skills to use commodity tools and techniques to become a hacker within the system, with the risk of greater damage and information exposure.

Without appropriate training, insiders can also accidentally compromise systems or the information they hold and particular care must be taken when evaluating all aspects of the insider threat.

3.5   Database System Vulnerabilities

Electronic databases are central to most modern business operations. Their uses are varied, but most databases constitute a collection of information that is organised so that it can be efficiently accessed, managed and edited. Databases are often classified according to their organisational approach. The most common of these approaches is the relational database, which uses a tabular layout that can be organised and accessed in a number of different ways, depending on user needs and the nature of the data it holds.

The top ten security issues commonly experienced by database managers are as follows:

1. **Weak or default usernames or passwords** – removing default or weak login credentials is an important first step for eliminating security holes in any database. Hackers maintain tables of common default account names and passwords and use them to attempt unauthorised access to sensitive data.

2. **Code injection attacks** – if poorly configured, a database platform may fail to block harmful inputs, for example via a web login page. Attackers are able to execute code injections, eventually allowing them to elevate privileges and gain access to a wide spectrum of features and data.

3. **Excessive user and group privileges** – rather than assigning separate privilege types to each user individually, users should all become part of a set group or role. The rights of those roles can then be managed collectively, ensuring that no user accumulates excessive levels of access.

4. **Unnecessary database features** – every database installation comes with a range of add-ons that are not always required by the organisation, but which can give users great power if they are enabled. Enterprises need to look for those packages they do not require and disable or uninstall them. This not only reduces risks of zero-day attacks; it also simplifies patch management.

5. **Broken configuration management** – many databases have a plethora of configuration choices available to administrators that allow them to fine-tune database performance and enhance functionality. Organisations need to conduct periodic database configuration audits in order to detect unsafe configurations.

6. **Buffer overflows** – these vulnerabilities are exploited by flooding input sources with far more characters than an application was expecting. The way some older software versions respond to such overflows allows hackers to insert malicious code that circumvents security. Vendors have largely addressed these flaws, but if systems are not patched they will remain vulnerable.

7. **Privilege escalation** – databases often contain vulnerabilities that allow attackers to escalate privileges within a hacked account and thus obtain system administrator rights. Updates and patching are the main defence against these flaws, which may not be obvious to system administrators. Regular audits to establish the patch level of sensitive systems are an essential control.

8. **Denial-of-service attacks** – attackers can use database vulnerabilities to take database servers offline by sending a flood of traffic to the system. Most such vulnerabilities are well-known, but unpatched servers still fall victim to this kind of attack on a regular basis.

9. **Data segmentation failures** – one very common vulnerability arises when sensitive data that is not actually required by database users is nevertheless stored in the database. There have been dozens of high profile cases in recent years in which data protection failed because sensitive personal or financial data was stored in a database that could be easily hacked from the web. Data of this kind should be separated from other data and only stored where it is genuinely needed – in other words, segmented.

10. **Unencrypted sensitive data at rest and in motion** – not only should sensitive data be segmented, organisations should never store sensitive data in readable form within a database table. The data should be encrypted, along with all connections to the database, to ensure that the data is secure from interception, both while it is at rest in the database and when it is in motion across the network.

3.6   Types of Penetration Test

A good penetration test will evaluate realistic technical exploits and describe plausible impacts. This allows both testers and those tested to propose practical solutions to proven vulnerabilities. There are several types of penetration test, each requiring a different set of skills, tools and techniques:

- **Network penetrations** – test the security of information systems, email servers and databases.
- **Web-facing application tests** – test the security of eCommerce, websites and other web-facing applications and services.
- **Wi-Fi network penetrations** – test wireless network access controls.

- **Social media penetrations** – test corporate and employee social media risk awareness.
- **Social engineering tests** – test employee resistance to face-to-face data extraction.

These test types are often combined in various ways during the course of any audit project.

3.6.1   Informed Versus Uninformed Tests

Tests may be either informed or uninformed. An informed test involves the testers being given details of the client's security arrangements in order that these may be stress tested. In an uninformed test, the testers have to approach the target blind and must find their own way around the systems and controls.

3.6.2   Artificial Intelligence (AI)

Artificial intelligence is a major area of growth and one that receives a great deal of attention from the media. It is already a part of our lives, involved in everything from driverless cars to Siri, Alexa, share trading and many financial services applications.

There are two forms of AI:

- **Narrow AI** – AI that focuses on a specific set of tasks, such as buying and selling shares. This form of AI is already in widespread use.
- **General AI** – AI that can mimic human thought and communication so effectively that it can pass the Turing Test and fool humans into believing that they are conversing with a real person.

3.6.3   How AI Is Used to Detect Cyber-Attacks and Vulnerabilities

Most AI systems are trained using very large amounts of historical data, such as data containing good transactions and fraudulent transactions, or information on cyber-attacks, as previously determined by human users or firewalls. By applying complex algorithms, often in an architecture known as a neural network, the AI engine will slowly be fine-tuned until it can detect fraud, or other anomalies, in the test data to the same degree of accuracy as human users have done previously, or better.

Once the AI engine has reached this point, it will be fed new data in which the fraudulent events or attacks have not yet been analysed. The AI will conduct the analysis in place of humans or traditional rules-based applications.

3.6.4   The Limits of AI

Narrow AI faces several challenges; here are the top two:

- It cannot make the kind of moral, ethical or intuitive judgements that humans are capable of. It is unable to think laterally.
- Its dependency on good training data is absolute. If the data is flawed, or if the underlying pattern of fraud and attacks changes, the AI system can struggle to adjust.

3.6.5   AI's Evolving Role in Financial Services

Despite these challenges, AI has an evolving role in financial services, in areas ranging from call handling to lending and fraud control. Because AI systems are deep-learning systems, based on computer technology that is becoming ever more powerful, it is likely that they will continue to improve until they become the primary tool for decision making across almost all areas.

What remains to be seen is whether AI will evolve to become a very smart assistant to human decision makers, or if it will be given overall control.

3.6.6   Cyber Security Risks Relating to AI

There are many ethical and philosophical risks in the AI picture, not least the well-established challenge of coding in human prejudices via the design of the AI or the selection of 'good' and 'bad' data. Once in place, such prejudices will be extremely hard to remove, or even to identify.

On the cyber-security front, the risks are likely to be more straight-forward:

- Inaccurate decision-making based on bad data, leading to fraud or security breaches.
- Poor coding of AI systems by software developers.
- Attacks on AI systems; for example, flooding an AI system with work to take it offline.
- Hacking of AI systems to change the way decisions are made.
- Theft of data from vast AI databases.

In cyber-security terms, AI changes very little. AI systems are a tool and a target, and they need to be managed as such, while being protected from attack just like any other IT resource.

4. Cybercrime Detection

Learning Objective

4.3.1   Know how firewalls are used to detect cyber-attacks and vulnerabilities

4.3.2   Know how intrusion detection systems (IDS) are used to detect cyber-attacks and vulnerabilities

4.3.3   Know how anti-malware applications are used to detect cyber-attacks and vulnerabilities

4.3.4   Know how logging and reporting applications are used to detect cyber-attacks and vulnerabilities

4.3.7   Understand how other common data sources can be utilised to identify evidence of cybercrime, including: customer complaints; suspicious transactions; internet and website usage patterns; customer device profiles; employee turnover statistics.

4.1 Firewalls

A firewall can be either a hardware or software construct. It sits between an internal and external network, such as the internet, and enforces access control policies that allow or deny admission to a network or computer system.

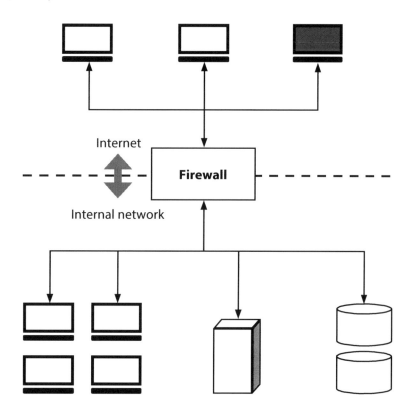

Figure 20: Internet Firewalls

A hardware firewall can normally be found at the **gateway** of a network or it may also be located at a host (device) access point as a software firewall, such as the firewall you probably have running on your laptop. A **router** can also be configured to act as a firewall.

The organisation's access control policy can be used by the user or administrator as a basis for configuring each firewall to enable data flows to be permitted or disallowed through the network.

There are generally two types of firewalls:

• application proxy firewalls
• packet filtering firewalls.

The basic technical functions of a firewall are as follows:

• packet filtering
• network address translation (NAT)
• application proxy
• monitoring and logging.

Firewalls are a very important component of computer security as they can inhibit malicious software, such as worms or Trojans, from accessing a computer system or network and gaining unauthorised access to data.

As the name suggests, a firewall can be viewed as an obstruction between a computer system and the internet. However, a firewall in no way resembles an anti-virus system as this is an entirely separate entity.

In an ethernet local area network (LAN) example, a **demilitarised zone (DMZ)**, or perimeter network, can be added to a firewall to provide extra security. A DMZ is a physical or logical subnetwork that contains and exposes an organisation's external-facing services to a larger and untrusted network, eg, the internet.

Firewalls have certain limitations and they typically cannot protect a system where:

• the attack has originated internally
• there are poorly trained network administrators who fail to configure or update the firewall
• there are social engineering attacks against users
• viruses and Trojans have been downloaded by users or introduced via removable media.

4.2   Intrusion Prevention and Detection Systems

An intrusion prevention system (IPS) is a network security/threat prevention technology that examines network traffic flows to detect and prevent vulnerability exploits.

Intrusion detection systems (IDSs) are placed within a network to raise an alert when an attack evades firewalls and other controls. If the firewall is the burglar alarm linked to your doors and windows, the IDS represents your dog barking at a burglar who has entered your home. Various sophisticated analysis technologies and real-time intrusion detection techniques are applied by IDSs.

4.3 Anti-Malware Applications

An anti-malware application can often detect, prevent and rectify malware infections on a computing system or device.

Some commonly known anti-malware brands include:

- McAfee
- Norton
- AVG
- Kaspersky.

Anti-malware is far from flawless, as explained under zero day vulnerabilities in chapter 1, section 2.1.2. Networks, therefore use a combination of firewalls, IDSs, anti-malware and numerous other controls to create a complex, multi-tiered defence, in the hope that if one control fails to detect or prevent a security breach, another one will provide resistance.

4.4 Logging and Reporting

Logging and reporting involve the use of software applications to document data flows, activities, malware events and other evidence of potential cyber-attacks as well as recording and logging traffic flows.

Logging and reporting applications provide the user with accurate bandwidth, web usage data, email usage data, suspect events and VPN usage information. This information is then aggregated and used to produce reports that allow managers and administrators to statistically analyse the events that have taken place, or to investigate specific attacks after they have occurred.

Additional features such as accessing real-time data, as well as developing trending analysis using historical reports, facilitate the diagnosis of problems and identifying trends and threats. Audit trails are frequently used to document past events step by step. This provides the user with a fingerprint or profile that might help to identify the person behind any particular attack or security breach and also link them to other similar breaches. It is important to note that one-key vulnerability remains largely unaddressed; hackers or staff with the appropriate access, can edit or delete log files without being detected. In fact, it is standard hacking practice to delete all log files as a last step before exiting a system.

4.5 Customer Complaints

Customer experience (also known as customer service and incorporating customer complaint handling) is a key indicator of when things have gone wrong. Many cyber-attacks first manifest themselves as customer experience issues. Examples of common problems reported by users or customers include:

- quality of service issues
- spam
- Spyware or Adware.

4.5.1   Quality of Service (QoS)

Quality of service (QoS) commonly relates to the performance of a computer or telephony network, but it can refer to any type of service delivery. Network services require constant monitoring for error rates, bandwidth supplied, throughput, transmission delay, availability and jitter. All of these technical aspects underpin the satisfactory delivery services such as streaming media and online gaming, IP telephony (VOIP) and video conferencing, as well as many other voice and data services.

QoS metrics are used to express the needs or expectations and the requirements of the end user. Cyber-attacks can negatively affect some aspects of QoS, for example when a DoS attack floods a network with data packets and blocks customer access to websites. Therefore, QoS metrics, as well as actual customer complaints, can provide a rich source of alarm data for cyber-security teams.

4.5.2   Spam

Unsolicited electronic messages sent via the internet may support **phishing** attacks, malware and unwanted advertising. These types of messages are normally sent in bulk to users with the intention of finding a potential victim.

User or customer complaints about spam can be the first indicator that an attack is underway. Alerts of this nature allow the organisation to warn employees and clients to be wary and they may also provide clues about what types of attack are pending; for example, malware or fraud based on phishing ploys.

4.5.3   Spyware and Adware

As we saw in chapter 1, this is software that performs particular actions without user consent and is normally designed to steal data or monitor user activities. Spyware often uses advertising to encourage users to visit infected web pages. It may make changes to computer configurations and, more importantly, it often collects sensitive information without the user knowing.

User complaints about system performance, the unexpected addition of features to their browsers, unsolicited pop-ups and ads, or changes to their browser's toolbar, default home page and search engine page can all be indicators of a spyware attack.

4.6   Suspicious Transactions and Cybercrime

This terminology commonly refers to financial transactions that give a financial organisation reason to suspect that an offence (money laundering, sanctions avoidance or funding of terrorism) has taken place. Regulated firms are required to submit suspicious transaction reports (STRs) when such cases are observed.

The evolution of online services has created a plethora of unregulated payment options that criminals use, or can potentially use, to avoid this form of monitoring. Some of the prime examples include payment in Bitcoin, the use of game money from sites such as World of Warcraft or Eve Online, and the use of emerging payment facilities provided by the likes of Facebook.

168

Another technique used both for laundering funds and for funding organised crime has been the excessive topping up of pre-paid mobile phone SIM cards with thousands of pounds in cash. The cards are then sent by post or handed to another party who can then sell them on the street or use them to sell calls to expensive destinations and premium rate service (PRS) numbers in order to recover the value. Increasingly, networks are also allowing balance transfers and payments to be made between SIM card users, as well as purchases of goods and services, all of which creates new opportunities for financial crime.

4.7   Internet and Website Usage Patterns

Web server log storage enables a website administrator to access information on web usage patterns from site visitors and to track their visits click-by-click. The log files are pre-processed and changed to the required format to enable web usage data mining methods to be performed. Analysis of the web usage pattern is carried out using specialist commercial tools and involves identifying browsing patterns derived from users' navigation of a given website.

The types of data analysed per visit include:

- IP address
- IP address geolocation
- user ID
- company ID
- search terms
- pages visited
- links clicked
- likes
- other websites passing traffic to the webpage (traffic referrers).

For example, it might be observed from analysis of a website's data set that fraudsters tend to go directly to a product page and then to the checkout without passing through the home page and without looking at alternative products or special offers. This knowledge can allow an organisation to add controls that detect such visits before payment is accepted, thus reducing fraud levels.

4.8   Customer Device Profiles

Many websites also capture information about each visitor's device, such as:

- device make
- device type
- MAC address
- Operating System (OS) type
- OS version
- language
- keyboard layout
- browser type
- browser version.

All of this data can be used to create a device profile. When used in conjunction with the web visit profile and suspicious transaction reporting or fraud alerting, this represents an increasingly powerful class of control.

4.9   Employee Turnover Statistics

The final act of most employees is to leave an organisation. High employee turnover rates can be expensive and they are often an important indicator of wider problems within an organisation, including poor management. This can expose an organisation to increased losses through fraud, including cyber-enabled fraud, due to:

- a decline in employee quality as there is pressure to recruit new staff quickly
- poor oversight and governance
- inadequate segregation of duties resulting from staff shortages
- increased temptation to commit offences resulting from general employee dissatisfaction and a belief that supervision is weak.

As with most things cyber, at the end of the day, it is the quality, support and training of people that provides the best defence.

End of Chapter Questions

Think of an answer for each question and refer to the appropriate section for confirmation

1. What are the four main steps in the threat intelligence cycle?
    Answer reference: Section 1.1

2. What is a watering hole attack?
    Answer reference: Section 1.1.1

3. List four of the elements of CNI.
    Answer reference: Section 1.1.3

4. List three of the emerging technologies that CNI organisations should be concerned about.
    Answer reference: Section 1.1.4

5. Name two of the steps recommended by Chatham House to create a national cyber-security culture.
    Answer reference: Section 1.1.5

6. List two of the four key cyber-threat sources.
    Answer reference: Section 2.1

7. Name any three cybercrime threat actors.
    Answer reference: Section 2.1

8. What is a commodity capability in cyber-security terms?
    Answer reference: Section 3.1.1

9. What are the three most common effects of most cyber-attacks?
    Answer reference: Section 3.2.4

10. List four basic cyber-security measures that help to prevent attacks.
    Answer reference: Section 3.3

11. List four types of penetration test.
    Answer reference: Section 3.6

Chapter Five
Combating Cybercrime

1. **Proactive Governance**   175

2. **Risk Management**   200

3. **Stress Testing**   207

4. **Incident Response**   213

5. **Business Continuity and Disaster Recovery Planning (DRP)**   216

6. **Password Security**   219

7. **Encryption**   221

This syllabus area will provide approximately 10 of the 50 examination questions

More people are killed every year by pigs than by sharks, which shows you how good we are at evaluating risk. Bruce Schneier

1. Proactive Governance

Learning Objective

5.1.1   Understand the goals of information security governance: scope and charter; organisational and third-party relationships; key cyber-security and information security risk metrics

5.1.2   Understand the information security framework: strategy; risk management processes; business impact assessments; policies and procedures; compliance; audit methodologies; testing and validation; training and awareness

5.1.3   Know commonly accepted cyber-security control frameworks: control categories; baseline controls; strengths and methods; components and architecture; inventory management and control (configuration management databases); user profiles and privileges management and reviews; key metrics; reporting exceptions

5.1.4   Know effective due diligence techniques for: customers; employees; service providers

5.1.5   Understand the impact of culture on cyber-security for international business

Information has been defined as data endowed with meaning. In the context of ICT, this meaning generally arises from some form of data processing activity, although it may be inherent within the raw data files themselves.

In chapter 4, we saw how information systems have become a key part of our critical national infrastructure (CNI). In the developed world, about 80% of all such CNI now resides in the private sector. Therefore, cyber-threats to private firms often have strategic national impacts. At the same time, in order to keep up with the rapidly accelerating pace of change, many public sector resources have now passed on the burden of protecting sensitive information assets to the private sector.

To achieve this task, the management of information and cyber-security needs to be elevated to the level of a management board governance responsibility, as have most other areas of strategic risk within firms. This governance practice also needs to become proactive because risks in the cyber-era evolve very rapidly and have devastating effects.

Effective cyber-security governance will demand an increasingly switched-on, flexible and informed response. Running 21st century firms with 20th century approaches to governance is an unsustainable model.

CHARTERED INSTITUTE FOR
SECURITIES & INVESTMENT

1.1   Information Security Governance

Information security governance is a set of responsibilities and practices designed to manage risk through the appropriate use of resources. Governance is exercised by the board and executive management within a firm, who provide strategic direction and are accountable for its effective implementation.

A cyber or **information security control** is a countermeasure designed to secure an information or computing asset. It is commonly defined as an action, process, technology, device or system that serves to prevent or mitigate the effects of a cyber-attack against a computer, server, network or other device.

Information security governance has proven value in several respects:

- Minimising the risk of legal liability by providing clear evidence of due diligence and regulatory compliance.
- Assuring compliance with company policies.
- Keeping risks below a defined and acceptable level.
- Providing a rational framework for allocating limited resources based on risk assessments: the risk-based approach.
- Helping to ensure that decision-making is based on accurate information.
- Supporting efficient and effective risk management processes.
- Allowing rapid and effective incident response and **business continuity** management.
- Ensuring that third-party providers are adhering to the same or equivalent standards.
- Reducing the risk of reputational harm.
- Supporting faster and more secure financial transactions.
- Providing accountability for the safeguarding of information.
- Ensuring cost-effective allocation and management of ICT resources.

A number of countermeasures exist that can be effectively implemented in order to combat cybercrime and increase security.

There are numerous technical controls that can be deployed to harden systems against attack. Firewalls, network- and device-based controls are the first line of defence in securing a computer network by setting access control lists (ACLs) that determine the services and traffic that can pass through each control point.

Anti-malware programs are used to prevent the introduction and spread of malicious code. Most computer malware infections have similar characteristics and this allows signature-based detection. Heuristic techniques, such as file analysis and file emulation, are also used to identify and remove malicious programs. Malware definitions need to be regularly updated and operating system hotfixes, service packs and patches must also be applied regularly.

Cryptography is frequently employed to encrypt and mask information, either in storage or transit. Tunneling, for example, will take data packets and encapsulate them in an encrypted stream to ensure data security during transmission. Encryption can also be employed at file level to protect information in storage, for example, on a hard drive.

Physical deterrents such as locks, card access keys and biometric devices are used to prevent criminals from gaining physical access to a machine on a network. Strong password protection, both for access to a computer system and the computer's binary operating system (BIOS), are also effective countermeasures against cybercriminals with physical access to a machine.

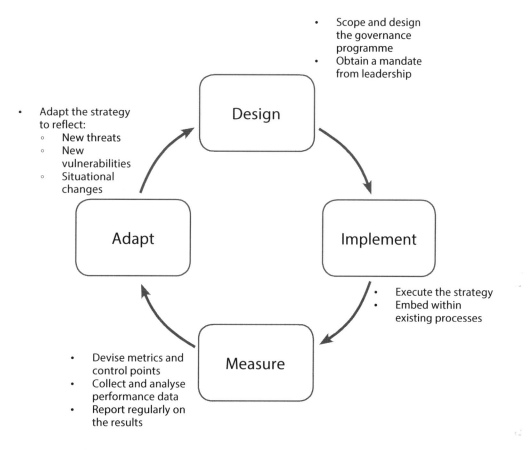

Figure 21: The Fundamentals of Cyber-Security Governance

1.2   The Goals of Information Security Governance

Effective governance in any sector starts with an informed leader who provides a mandate for operations and controls, as well as the requisite budget. Security and risk management teams that present overtly technical descriptions of risks and impacts to senior management generally fail to secure the support they seek. There is a stark divide between those with technical knowledge and those without. Many who possess such technical knowledge show themselves incapable of appreciating the gulf that separates them from the remainder of the population and, even when they simplify their explanations, what remains continues to be undecipherable to most audiences.

The starting point for communicating the need for good ICT security governance, therefore, is not a technical one but a business one. We must all learn to use the language that is best understood by decision makers and budget holders, and frame discussions about security and risk in business terms. Costs, margins, profits, losses and reputation are the first five headings that should appear on any risk management or security report, proposal or presentation slide pack. Compliance and penalties come next. Technical phrases should be used sparingly and only when absolutely essential.

1.2.1   Scope and Charter

Information security governance policies cover the entire spectrum of data processing and information management, including spoken, written, printed, electronic and any other form of data regardless of its state – in transportation, transmission, use or storage – and during or after its supposed destruction.

Information security governance is, therefore, a broader concept than simple IT security. Whereas IT security focuses on data held in corporate computer systems, information security governance extends to comments made in the lift, during an interview with journalists or on the telephone and via social media.

In order to conduct effective information security governance, organisations should carry out the following tasks:

- Conduct annual information security reviews.
- Conduct periodic risk assessments.
- Maintain up-to-date inventories of all information and technical assets.
- Implement risk-based policies and procedures.
- Develop and keep an up-to-date information security plan that addresses the security of networks, facilities, systems and information itself.
- Recognise and reinforce the perception of information security as an integral part of system and process lifecycles throughout the organisation.
- Provide information security awareness training and education to all employees at all levels and extend this down to cover subcontractors and third parties who may handle information for which the organisation is responsible.
- Execute programs to correct vulnerabilities, improve security and assign responsibilities.
- Develop an incident response plan and establish and test continuity plans.
- Evaluate the need to demonstrate compliance adherence to an accepted international standard and conduct an external compliance audit.

1.2.2   Organisational and Third-Party Roles and Relationships

Although organisational structures can vary, the following breakdown serves as a general guideline that should suit most organisations regardless of type:

- **Board of directors** – the board of directors provides strategic direction and a mandate for the operations of those tasked with responsibility for information security management. The board drives the development of policy, signs off on policy and is accountable for the effective implementation of information security across the organisation. Organisations that operate within the US, or that have US-based partners and subsidiaries, may be subject to regulations, such as the Sarbanes-Oxley Act of 2002, which require that every company listed on the US stock exchange maintains an audit committee with the required level of experience and demonstrable levels of competence. This committee is often made up of members of the company's board of directors and its responsibilities extend to auditing the organisation's internal controls, which include information security controls.
- **Executive management** – the executive management team is responsible for the actual implementation of information security government policies and processes. It provides the operational leadership and assigns the resources to the task. In the main, an executive management team will have a heavy dependence on an information security manager for the conduct of day-

to-day operations within the organisation. However, information security governance is a shared responsibility and every individual and team has a role to play.

- **Information security manager** – the information security manager coordinates the involvement of the executive management team in the process of information security governance. He or she must ensure that the executive team has clearly defined roles and responsibilities, often linked to KPIs for information security governance, and that those working within his or her span of control carry out their tasks efficiently and are adequately resourced.
- **Steering committee** – many organisations adopt a steering committee approach to information security governance. The steering committee will typically comprise senior attendees from every affected group within the organisation. Common areas of focus include:
  - the development of security strategy
  - the integration of security with other business unit activities and processes
  - determining specific actions required and measuring their progress in relation to particular security issues
  - maintaining focus on emerging risks, potential vulnerabilities and weaknesses and current practices and on any related compliance issues
  - reporting regularly to the board on the status of information security and highlighting any urgent risks that require board attention or awareness.
- **The chief information security officer (CISO)** – larger organisations now often have a dedicated CISO. Other organisations that do not have a specific individual with this title still have a person acting in that role. This may be the chief information officer (CIO), the chief financial officer (CFO) or the chief executive officer (CEO). The majority of CISOs report either to the management board or to the CEO. While there is no clearly defined role for this function that applies across all organisations, the primary focus of the CISO is defined by the title. In many situations an important part of their role centres on raising awareness of, and adherence to, information security standards and protocols.

1.2.3 Key Cyber-Security and Information Security Risk Metrics

The business of information security management is itself largely driven by data. Risks are assessed mathematically and expressed as a score which can be prioritised against other scores. Impacts are often computed financially in order to ensure that a business case can be developed for any actions taken to address a given risk. Vulnerabilities are measured in a similar way, as is the cost in both time and money of correcting them.

The adaptation of this business mindset towards the task of information security management has led to the development of a corresponding business model, the business model for information security (BMIS). This model is usually represented as a three-dimensional pyramid comprising four key elements and six dynamic interconnections.

The four key elements are:

1. **Organisation design and strategy** – the business goals and objectives to be achieved.
2. **People** – the human resources involved (staff, subcontractors, suppliers and customers).
3. **Processes** – the formal and informal mechanisms used to identify, measure, manage and otherwise control risk.
4. **Technology** – all of the tools, applications and technical infrastructure that support the processes required.

The six dynamic connections are:

1. **Governance** – the strategic guidance that sets the limits within which the organisation operates.
2. **Culture** – the behaviours, beliefs, assumptions, attitudes and work styles that characterise the conduct of information security management operations and define how things should be done. This is not a description of the actual culture, but rather a description of what is desired.
3. **Enablement and support** – the link between the technology element and the process element. This ensures that people are able to comply with required processes and rules because they are supported technically and compliance itself is not a hindrance to normal business operations.
4. **Emergence** – managing the process of change and the emergence of the unexpected through the use of feedback loops and business process re-engineering.
5. **Human factors** – ensuring that people understand and embrace information security policies and that they have the requisite skills to do so effectively.
6. **Architecture** – formal encapsulation of the people, processes, policies and technology that feature within any organisation's security strategy practices.

Table 5.1 provides a useful indication of an organisation's maturity level in terms of information security governance.

Table 5.1: High-level Information Security Governance Checklist

Control or business process	In place and effective?		Tentative action plan/next steps
	Yes	No	
Governance Framework Established			
Senior sponsor for cyber/InfoSec appointed			
GRC or Risk Committee active			
CISO or equivalent in place and trained			
Scope of risk management defined			
Assessment and Planning Conducted			
Information assets inventoried			
Threat assessment completed			
Vulnerability assessment completed			
Risk assessment completed			
Action plan in progress			
Disaster planning completed			
Policies and Practices in Place and Effective			
Cyber-security policy and plan			
Telecom security policy and plan			
BYOD policy and plan			

Control or business process	In place and effective?		Tentative action plan/next steps
InfoSec travel policy and plan			
Social media policy and plan			
Cloud services policy and plan			
Recruitment and vetting policy and plan			
IT procurement policy and plan			
Third-party due diligence policy			
Physical security policy and plan			
Incident response plan			
Equipment disposal policy and plan			
Policy management plan active			
Training and Awareness Programme in Place			
Basic cyber-security awareness programme for all employees			
Induction training includes cyber-risks and related policies			
Specific risk and security training for staff in key roles			
Testing, Audit and Monitoring Processes			
Network penetration testing			
Application penetration testing			
Social media penetration testing			
Physical site penetration testing			
Employee awareness assessments			
Cyber-security audit plan			
Cloud services audit plan			
Network surveillance plan			
Centralised logging system			
Logging and metering data quality assurance			
Alarm monitoring and response			

Many organisations face serious challenges when it comes to answering fundamental questions about information security. For example, could your organisation confidently answer the following questions?

- How secure is the organisation?
- What is the appropriate level of security?

- How do you benchmark adequate security levels?
- How do you define a cost-effective security response?
- How can you reliably quantify risk?
- Are you able to predict risks?
- Is security achieving its objectives?
- What security impacts are there on productivity?
- What would be the impact of a catastrophic data breach?
- What would be the impact of a prolonged loss of service?
- What impact will any proposed security solutions have on productivity?

If you are able to confidently answer all of these questions, then your organisation is clearly exceptional in terms of its information security maturity level. Unfortunately, very few organisations can make that claim today.

While security reviews, compliance audits and penetration tests can provide reliable snapshots of an organisation's security position at a given moment in time, they do not serve nearly as well when it comes to the day-to-day challenges of information security management. What is essential here is a reliable set of metrics.

Reliability is assured through adherence to a simple set of criteria:

- **Meaningful** – every metric must be understood by the recipients.
- **Accurate** – metrics must be reliable and reasonably accurate.
- **Cost-effective** – metrics must not be too expensive to acquire or maintain.
- **Repeatable** – each metric must be based on data that can be obtained reliably on an ongoing basis.
- **Predictive** – metrics must be indicative of outcomes. They have no value in and of themselves beyond indicating an impact or a likely future situation.
- **Actionable** – it should be clear to each recipient what action should be inspired by each metric.
- **Genuine** – metrics must be authentic and should not be random or subject to manipulation.
- **Comparable** – metrics must lend themselves to like-for-like comparison over time in order that changes and trends can be calculated or observed directly.

There are seven primary categories of information security governance metrics. These are:

1. Governance implementation metrics.
2. Strategic alignment metrics.
3. Risk management metrics.
4. Value delivery metrics.
5. Resource management metrics.
6. Performance metrics.
7. Assurance process integration metrics.

Risk management is the ultimate goal of information security. Although it is difficult to directly measure the effectiveness of risk management, there are indicators of a successful approach. Examples of important risk management metrics include:

- the completeness of the overall security strategy, expressed as a percentage
- the definition of specific controls of mitigation objectives for each identified risk, expressed as a percentage

- the percentage of key systems by a systemic and continuous risk management process
- the trending of risk assessment scores to indicate progress towards the required level of security
- trending reports on the impact of manifest risks and events, normally expressed as a financial value
- the completeness of an up-to-date inventory of all physical information assets
- the completeness of an up-to-date inventory of all data assets
- the percentage of business impact assessments conducted for all critical or sensitive systems
- the ratio of security incidents relating to known, registered risks and those relating to previously unidentified risks.

1.3   The Information Security Framework

The development of an appropriate information security framework for any organisation depends on those responsible having a firm grasp of:

- the nature and location of all data processing and information assets
- manifest and potential risks
- the criticality of given systems and network elements
- any security dependencies
- the responsibilities of teams and individuals for security and incident response continuity
- the logistical arrangements in place to support the information security management programme.

1.3.1   Strategy

To establish an information security framework, we first need to define what is meant by an information security strategy. We then need to develop a model for reporting the metrics that determine the extent to which the objectives of the strategy are being achieved.

Such a strategy should normally have at least six clearly defined outcomes:

- strategic alignment
- effective risk management
- value delivery
- resource optimisation
- performance measurement
- process assurance integration.

An additional essential component of a security strategy is a description of the future desired state. The desired state is a snapshot of all relevant conditions at a point in the future and describes the principles, policies and frameworks that should apply at that time if the security strategy has been properly implemented and adhered to.

The future desired state is normally described in a mix of qualitative and quantitative terms. Because the desired state encompasses such ideas as culture and values it is impossible to define it solely in quantitative terms.

1.3.2   Risk Management Processes

At its core, any risk assessment consists of three essential stages. The first step involves determining realistic or viable threats to information security. These threats are commonly broken down into the following categories:

- physical
- environmental
- technological.

Once this classification has been completed, the next stage is to determine the likelihood and probable magnitude or impact of each threat. In most instances, this will be achieved by examining previous events or by looking at the experiences of other similar organisations exposed to a similar threat environment. Both frequency and impacts are important. An incident with relatively low impact, but which occurs very often, may be just as significant and deserving of attention as a more impactful incident that occurs only rarely. This is why most banks will act to prevent minor thefts occurring but will do nothing to deal with the threat of a meteorite impact, even though the meteorite might cause catastrophic harm.

The next step in the risk assessment process is to assess the organisation's vulnerabilities exposure to the threats already identified. The issues that deserve the most urgent attention are those in which a threat occurs frequently, potentially has a very significant impact and is not countered by an adequate or effective set of controls or other protections.

As we will see in section 2 (Risk Management), a structured risk-based approach allows organisations to prioritise their responses to risks and provides a logical foundation which uses a business case approach to justify expenditures of time, effort and resources.

1.3.3   Insurance

Insurance is a common method of transferring risk from the organisation to the insurer. Risks insured are normally relatively rare categories of event, including so-called Acts of God such as flood, fire and hurricane, or relatively infrequent human activities such as major frauds and embezzlement, bank robberies and large-scale cyber-attacks.

There is today a burgeoning cybercrime insurance market which allows organisations of all sizes to insure themselves against the various impacts of a cybercrime event.

1.3.4   Business Impact Assessments (BIAs)

A **business impact assessment (BIA)** is a computation intended to quantify risk and provide a basis for prioritising the restoration of services after a major event, based on the three considerations of confidentiality, integrity and availability. It measures the consequences of losing the support of, or access to, any key resource (people, technology and data). In a cyber-security context, it relates primarily to information communications technology and the data held and processed by such systems.

The conduct of such an impact assessment is an essential first step towards developing a sensible information security strategy, classifying information assets appropriately and addressing the matter of business continuity in a realistic fashion. In the absence of a proper appreciation of the business impact of a given threat or set of threats, it is not possible to inform either strategy, controls or incident response correctly.

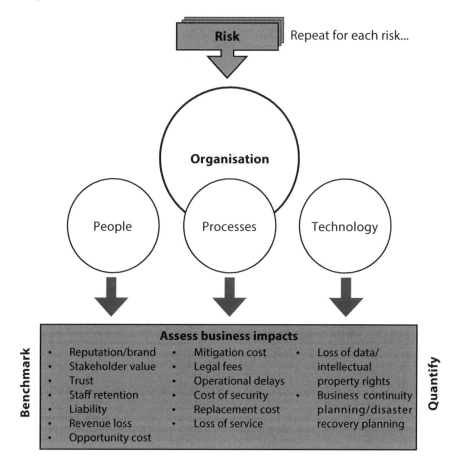

Figure 22: Business Impact Assessments

1.3.5 Policies

Carefully crafted and properly thought out policies are a key component of any information security governance programme. To be effective, policies must be signed off by the board and by executive management in order that they have weight and that they serve as a mandate for the operational teams that must implement them.

A good policy has the following key attributes:

- It should be an articulation of a well-defined strategy that captures intent, expectations and direction of management.
- It should state only one general mandate.
- It must be clear and easy to understand by all affected parties.
- It should rarely be more than a few sentences in length.
- Few organisations should expect to have more than 20 to 25 policies in place.

Above all else, it must always be borne in mind that a policy document is not a standard procedural guide. It is not intended to describe *how* things are to be done, but only what *should* be done and *why*.

1.3.6 Compliance

Organisations in the modern world are required to demonstrate compliance with various regulatory standards. The financial services sector is subject to several strict compliance standards.

Compliance is often a very effective tool for engaging senior managers and other departments in the information security arena. While they may often regard information security itself as a back office function, with little relevance to their own day-to-day operations, they will almost inevitably be well aware of the issues and sensitivities that arise from the failure to comply with various banking regulations. Instead of spending inordinate amounts of time attempting to educate colleagues on the technical aspects of information security, it often makes more sense to focus on the penalties that arise from a data breach or other information security failure.

1.3.7 Audit Methodologies

The conduct of audits is one of the most effective techniques used to identify deficiencies in information security, particularly from a controls and compliance perspective. There are two basic categories of audit:

- internal audits
- external audits.

In most large organisations, internal audits are conducted by an in-house audit department. It is common for such departments to include a specialist unit that specialises in cyber and information security. The key advantage held by internal auditors is their familiarity with the organisation's operational processes, systems and history, as well as its culture. However, in some instances, internal audit can be a disadvantage because a small internal audit IT practice may have limited resources.

External audits have historically been more closely linked to the operations of the finance department in most large organisations. However, the larger external audit houses have been building up their IT audit practices over many years. External auditors can bring extra capacity to the cyber and information security domain and may also be able to provide penetration testing services and consultancy designed to validate any controls implemented. On the downside, external auditors may lack the detailed in-house knowledge possessed by the internal audit team.

Audit reports themselves, even if they do not address matters directly related to cyber or information security, can still be of great interest to information security managers. Such reports often contain a great deal of confidential (even sensitive) financial data and this data needs to be protected. The reports may also highlight vulnerabilities relating to the security of information and systems that have not previously been brought to the attention of those responsible for information security.

Finally, an audit report can provide a wealth of indirect evidence about the culture of an organisation, the quality of its controls, and the extent to which its members are aware of and comply with various guidelines. This can provide key indicators that information security managers can use when developing their own plans and designing training and awareness packages.

1.3.8   Testing and Validation

In chapter 4, section 3.6 we looked at the topic of penetration testing. Any testing and validation of a cyber and information security strategy needs to address a core set of common issues, requirements and vulnerabilities. These include but are not limited to the following:

- The level of senior management support for the strategy.
- The extent to which the strategy is intrinsically linked with the organisation's goals.
- The completeness and consistency of security policies; these must be aligned with the strategy.
- The existence of clear, comprehensive and realistic procedures for all key operations.
- Clear assignment of responsibilities and properly documented descriptions of roles.
- The existence of a sensible organisation structure that clearly delineates authority and responsibility for information security without creating conflicts.
- A comprehensive and up-to-date register of physical and information assets.
- An up-to-date risk register listing all credible cyber and information security threats to the organisation and corresponding levels of risk.
- The presence of effective controls to counter each risk, based on a controls plan that reflects the relative risk scores.
- A workable programme of monitoring and reporting based on metrics collected from across the business.
- Functional and property incident and emergency response capabilities.
- Business continuity and disaster recovery plans.
- The inclusion of security sign-off during the change management process.
- The presence of an effective awareness and training programme for all users.
- Evidence of an acceptable security culture.
- Evidence that the business is fully aware of its responsibilities with respect to compliance and makes credible efforts to ensure said compliance and to demonstrate due diligence.
- The prompt resolution of compliance failures.
- Evidence of self-reporting of information security breaches, where this is required.

Audits may be conducted using a variety of techniques, including penetration testing, interviews and workshops. It is important to remember that an audit is not a hostile event; its purpose is to identify weaknesses in order that they can be corrected for the good of the organisation, not to catch people out and embarrass them.

1.3.9   Training and Awareness

Information security and cyber-security training and awareness cannot be delivered effectively as a one-off. What is required is an effective action plan that implements an ongoing programme. More importantly, this training must be interesting and interactive, because experience shows that a majority of employees in most organisations remain largely unaware of current security policies and practices, despite having attended training courses on the topic. Boring training is almost as bad as no training at all.

One key technique for delivering training that holds people's interest is to use storytelling that is relevant to the particular audience. For example, using a social engineering scenario to explain the risk of data breaches to customer services staff as a story about a remote database hack is unlikely to hold the interest of this particular group of people.

Audiences should be subdivided based on their roles, so that training messages that are of interest to them can be delivered. Training sessions should also be of short duration, because most people find the topic off-putting and are likely to enter the room already feeling they will not understand most of the material. It is therefore essential to build their confidence by delivering bite-sized pieces of training over an extended time period, rather than trying to educate them all in one go.

1.4   Commonly Accepted Cyber-Security Control Frameworks

1.4.1   Control Categories

There are essentially two classes of cyber-security control:

- general controls
- application controls.

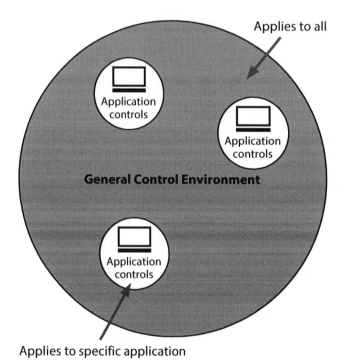

Figure 23: Classes of Control

General controls are those controls implemented to protect the infrastructure and operating environment as a whole. These controls support the entire organisation in a centralised manner. This terminology is used because in most cases infrastructure will be used across the organisation and shared by different individuals and teams.

Application controls are applied where there are instances of specific, non-centralised information processing activities, for example, in relation to a billing application that sits on a specific server and is used by a small team. This application might require a different level of control, or different approaches to control, than an email system that is shared by every employee.

Within each class there are five control categories:

1. **Preventative controls** that protect against a vulnerability and reduce its impact. Preventative controls inhibit attempts to violate security policy and include such controls as access control enforcement, encryption and authentication. Before the event, preventative controls are intended to prevent an incident from occurring, eg, by locking out unauthorised intruders.

2. **Detective controls** that discover an attack and trigger preventative controls. These controls warn of violations or attempted violations of security policy and include controls audit trails, intrusion detection methods and checksums. During the event, detective controls are intended to identify and characterise an incident in progress, eg, by sounding the intruder alarm and alerting the security guards or police.

3. **Corrective controls** that reduce the impact of an attack. They remediate vulnerabilities. Backup and restore procedures are one example of corrective controls – the incident has occurred, but a corrective control allows the organisation to recover. After the event, corrective controls are intended to limit the extent of any damage caused by the incident, eg, by recovering the organisation to normal working status as efficiently as possible.

4. **Compensatory controls** that reduce the likelihood of an attack. Compensatory controls compensate for the increased risk by adding controls that mitigate a risk, for example, by adding a challenge response component to weak access controls.

5. **Deterrent controls** that also reduce the likelihood of an attack. These controls provide warnings that can deter potential compromise.

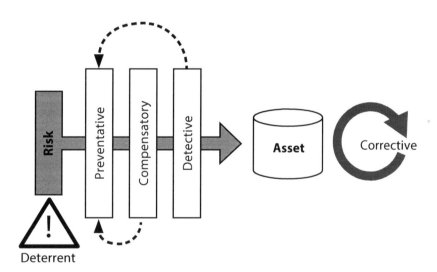

Figure 24: The Five Main Control Categories

1.4.2 Control Types

Security controls can also be categorised according to their type:

- **Physical controls** – fences, doors, locks and fire extinguishers.
- **Procedural (or administrative) controls** – incident response processes, management oversight, security awareness and training.
- **Technical (or logical) controls** – user authentication (login) and logical access controls, antivirus software, firewalls.
- **Legal and regulatory or compliance controls** – privacy laws, policies and clauses.

Physical controls monitor and control both the operational environment and the computing facilities housed within it. They also monitor and control access to and from facilities. Examples include doors, locks, heating and air conditioning, smoke and fire alarms, fire suppression systems, cameras, barricades, fencing, security guards and cable locks. The division of the work area into separate zones is also a form of physical control.

Procedural or administrative controls consist of written policies, procedures, standards and guidelines. These types of control provide a framework for administering the organisation, as well as managing people and resources. Formalised guidelines inform people about how the business is to be run and how day-to-day operations are to be conducted, extending into such topics as segmentation of duties. Administrative controls form the basis for the selection and implementation of appropriate logical and physical controls.

Technical and logical controls make use of software and data processing to monitor and control access to information and computing systems. Common examples are passwords and other forms of authentication, network and host-based firewalls, network intrusion detection systems, access control lists and data encryption.

1.4.3   The Principle of Least Privilege

One logical control that is often forgotten is the principle of least privilege. This requires that an individual (or a program) is not granted greater access privileges than are required to perform the task in question. For example, logging into Windows as an administrator merely in order to read email or surf the web would constitute a violation of the principle. Violations of this principle most commonly occur when a user collects additional access privileges over time, often without even realising it. This can happen when a user's duties change or when they are promoted to a new position or transferred to another department. The access privileges required by their new duties may be added to their existing access privileges, even though these may no longer be appropriate.

1.4.4   Security Classification of Information

One very important aspect of information security and risk management is the classification of information, usually on the basis of some kind of perceived value or sensitivity. Not all information is equal and so not all information requires the same degree of protection. This means that all information that is processed, stored and transported by any organisation must be assigned a security **classification**.

The building blocks of information classification schema are described below.

*   The definition of a set of information classification criteria (such as sensitivity, criticality to the business, regulatory stipulations and fraud risk).
*   The description of a process for classifying data.
*   The assignment of ownership and accountability for various types of data at different stages of processing and handling.
*   The development of a set of security guidelines relating to the storage and handling of each data class.
*   The constructing of inventories of data held by the organisation, broken down by class and location.

This last step allows for the conduct of vulnerability and business impact assessments.

The selection of information security classification labels depends on the nature of the organisation:

- In the business sector, labels such as 'public', 'sensitive', 'private and confidential' are often used, but precisely what they mean can vary.
- In the public sector, labels such as 'unclassified', 'confidential', 'secret' and 'top secret' are commonly used.

1.4.5   Components and Architecture

Modern cyber-security architectures must address the four top cyber-security challenges facing businesses today:

- **Prevent downtime** – the single biggest cost stemming from cyber-attacks is lost revenue owing to network and system downtime, which prevents employees from working or customers from buying. In the oil and gas sector, the cost of a major cyber-attack that causes 24 hours of downtime can run into millions of pounds. However, the costliest cybercrimes involve DDoS attacks, such as the campaign against US banking websites that began in 2012, or the use of malware to wipe 48,000 systems used by South Korean banks and broadcasters.
- **Safeguard the 'crown jewels'** – the goal of many APT attackers is to steal valuable intellectual property and such attacks can be devastating. Attacks against US defence contractors, blamed on China, reportedly resulted in information theft that undermined the combat readiness of new weapons systems, including the cutting edge F-35 Joint Strike Fighter.
- **Maintain reputation** – security breaches can also be a public relations nightmare. Hacktivists associated with Anonymous, for example, have publicised their causes by hacking into businesses – including Sony – and exposing millions of customer records, credit card numbers and sensitive emails. Meanwhile, breaches of LinkedIn and eHarmony only came to light when customer records surfaced on underground hacker forums, calling into question the cyber-security resilience of those trusted social media sites. In fact, when it comes to sensitive personal data, few sites hold more than the likes of Facebook and LinkedIn.
- **Protect critical infrastructure** – the vast majority of critical infrastructure systems – comprising the power, oil, water, telecoms, finance and transportation industries – are today privately owned. Most of these systems were formerly state assets, precisely because of their criticality to the operations of nation states. To make matters worse, the networked industrial control systems that support these industries are aging and often insecure and vulnerable. As a result, the US Congress has been debating laws that would require US businesses to demonstrate that their critical infrastructure systems are secure. Attacks against these systems are not theoretical, as the highly destructive Stuxnet and Saudi Aramco attacks revealed.

For maximum effectiveness, cyber-security programs should take the following steps:

- **Establish consistent architecture** – using a consistent security architecture across all devices and networks enables security policies to be written once, then enforced consistently with controls for every conceivable access scenario. Such scenarios include corporate user, contractor, managed or unmanaged BYOD, guest WiFi and more.
- **Control access** – know who and what's on your network, check the health of the devices on your network and then use access controls to ensure that only authorised personnel with secure devices are granted access to sensitive data.
- **Strengthen authentication** – require strong user and machine authentication for any accesses to your most valuable assets. For many businesses, the 'crown jewels' involve intellectual property – such as the secret formula for your product – and customer databases.

- **Encrypt data** – ensure that all sensitive data is encrypted both in transit and at rest. Encrypting stored data prevents data from being exposed and exempts organisations from issuing expensive data breach notifications. However, as demonstrated by ongoing breaches, many organisations have not yet understood this message.
- **Layer the defences** – by layering your security defences, you will not only repel attacks but will also better contain intrusions. According to the 2013 *Verizon Data Breach Investigations Report*, a phishing attack campaign that uses just six emails has an 80% chance of an included link or attachment being clicked on or opened by a recipient.
- **Automate security** – automated security controls provide rapid attack detection and response. Automation frees scarce information security resources from dealing with spam, malware and other nuisances, allowing them to focus on more high-value security activities, such as refining policies and remediating attacks. With the BYOD trend, as more employee-owned devices touch the corporate network, automation ensures that these devices keep sensitive information secure at all times.

The Australian Cyber Security Centre states that most of the targeted cyber-intrusions it responds to could be prevented by following eight core mitigation strategies in its guide[1], *Strategies to Mitigate Cyber Security Incidents*:

The Essential Eight strategies are:

- application whitelisting – to control the execution of unauthorised software
- patching applications – to remediate known security vulnerabilities
- configuring Microsoft Office macro settings – to block untrusted macros
- application hardening – to protect against vulnerable functionality
- restricting administrative privileges – to limit powerful access to systems
- patching operating systems – to remediate known security vulnerabilities
- multi-factor authentication – to protect against risky activities
- daily backups – to maintain the availability of critical data.

1.4.6   Inventory Management and Control

Creating an inventory of data assets helps to keep track of sensitive data resources and can be used to support the elimination of information security measures throughout the organisation.

The data inventory should record:

- what the data mean
- how the data are created
- where the data were obtained
- who owns each data item
- who has access, use and editing rights on an item-by-item basis
- who is responsible for managing the data
- how the data will or can be shared.

1   https://acsc.gov.au/infosec/mitigationstrategies.htm

192

The inventory can thus:

- record storage and back-up strategies
- keep track of versions
- record data quality control procedures.

Data management should be reviewed annually. The maintenance of an inventory also facilitates data sharing as it contains all the essential information required to enable future reuse and to make data archiving easy.

Data management might be supported by a purpose-built data management application or, in smaller organisations, by something as simple as an Excel spreadsheet. The emphasis here is not on the technology used, but rather on the existence of a well-managed process.

1.4.7   Segmentation and Encryption of Data

Data segmentation refers to the principle of storing data with different classifications and uses in an arrangement that ensures that:

- data can only be accessed, edited, deleted or viewed by those users and systems that have a legitimate need
- sensitive data is captured in a secure manner
- sensitive data is held separately from non-sensitive data
- different classes of data can be protected in different and appropriate ways.

Data classification and inventory are essential prerequisites for effective data segmentation; unless an organisation knows exactly what data it holds, and how sensitive or critical each class of data is, it cannot effectively segment it.

Proper segmentation of data can deliver cost savings. By storing sensitive data separately, it is possible to focus security expenditures on that data set, while setting lower levels of control for non-sensitive information.

One of the most effective methods of securing sensitive data is encryption. This is the use of cryptography (complex mathematical encoding) to transform usable information into a form that renders it unusable by anyone other than an authorised user.

Information that has been encrypted can be converted back into its original usable format (decrypted) by an authorised user (or by a clever hacker or security operative in some cases) who possesses the cryptographic key.

Cryptography is used in information security to protect sensitive information from disclosure while the information is:

- in transit electronically: if you use a VPN connection to access your organisation remotely, your session is encrypted
- in transit physically: for example, by encrypting files on a laptop's hard drive or by encrypting the entire drive
- in storage: for example, in a corporate database.

Cryptography provides information security with a range of other useful applications, including:

- improved authentication methods
- message digests
- digital signatures
- non-repudiation
- secure WiFi networks
- encrypted emails.

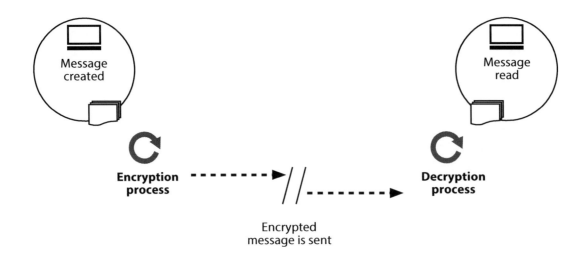

Figure 25: The Basic Process of Encryption

The use of encryption can introduce security problems when it is not implemented correctly. Hackers have even been known to use the encryption applications installed by an organisation on its servers to encrypt those very same devices, thus locking out the legitimate users. One useful security step is, therefore, to remove or otherwise secure the encryption applications themselves, because they are weapons that can be fired in both directions.

The length and strength of the encryption key is also an important consideration. A key that is weak or too short will produce weak encryption. Furthermore, the keys used for encryption and decryption must be protected from exposure, destruction or loss. The loss of a key could result in a self-inflicted crypto-attack and a hacker may well target the key itself, rather than the encrypted systems and data.

1.4.8   User Profiles and Privileges Management and Reviews

In general terms, **privilege management** involves the assignment, recording and review of specific user rights to individual users. Anyone using a PC or laptop will be subject to some level of privilege management; they will either log on as an administrator, a user, a child user or a guest user. Each type of account can do different things (such as installing new software or creating new user accounts) but only an administrator can do everything.

A single user might have more than one account with different privileges. For example, an administrator may well opt to log on as a basic user at most times, in order to read email or produce documents, only using their system admin login when necessary. This reduces the risk of their system admin account being hijacked by a hacker, malware or another user.

In larger networks, managing privileges across a wide range of devices and applications is more challenging and most big firms will use purpose-built privilege management software to add joiners, assign them to groups, define their specific roles and related privileges and deactivate, edit or remove movers and leavers.

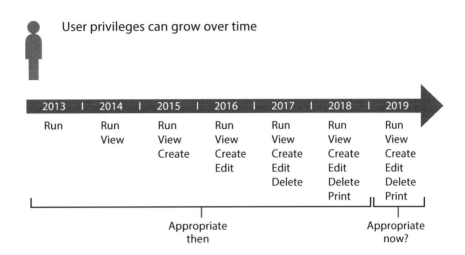

Figure 26: User Privilege Creep

Increasingly, larger organisations use centralised systems for privilege management. These involve the use of a single server and application to cover all users across all devices (hosts), network access points and applications.

The types of user group, role and privileges available are different in most organisations. They are a function of the regulatory environment, size, complexity, sensitivity of data, numbers of systems, applications and users, maturity of information security and the level and nature of perceived threats.

Regular reviews of privilege management (also known as privilege auditing) are essential, because most organisations are in a constant state of flux due to changes in personnel, systems, data and the regulatory and cyber-security environment. A reviewer should focus on the following:

- All users have the privileges necessary to perform their roles.
- No user has greater privilege levels than they legitimately require.
- Privileges are signed off by the managers responsible for the data being viewed or manipulated and/or by the application owner, before they are granted. For data classified as sensitive, additional sign-offs by security and senior management may be appropriate.
- Movers have their privileges reviewed and adjusted as soon as they enter a new role.
- Changes in operating procedures trigger reviews of all affected users and their privileges.
- Leavers have their privileges revoked, in accordance with the organisation's HR and information security policies, and those policies are in tune with each other.
- Any lapsed accounts (eg, belonging to contractors who are no longer active) are deactivated.

1.4.9   Access Control

Access to protected information must be limited to those who are authorised to access the information – those who have a genuine business or freedom of information need. The computer programs and the computers that process information must also be authorised to do so.

This requires that mechanisms be in place to control and log access to protected information. The sophistication of the access control mechanisms should be in keeping with the value of the information being protected: the more sensitive or valuable the information, the stronger the control mechanisms need to be.

The foundations on which access control mechanisms are built rest on the three pillars of identification, authentication and **authorisation**.

Identification

Identification is the confirmation of who someone is or what something is. For human users, this may take the form of a username, while for devices it might be a device identifier like an IP address or a MAC address.

Authentication

Authentication is the act of verifying a claim of identity. There are at least five different types of information that can be used for authentication:

- **Something you know** – things such as a PIN, a password or your mother's maiden name.
- **Something you have** – a driver's licence, a dongle or a magnetic swipe card.
- **Something you are** – biometrics, including palm prints, fingerprints, voiceprints and retina (eye) scans.
- **Somewhere you are** – a location or IP address.
- **Somewhere you are not** – a location or IP address.

Strong, multi-factor, authentication requires a user or device to provide more than one type of authentication information. This will typically involve two- or three-factor authentication. The username is the most common form of identification on computer systems today and the password is the most common form of authentication, but these systems are no longer truly effective in many situations. Username and password systems are therefore slowly being replaced with more sophisticated authentication mechanisms.

Authorisation

After a person, program or computer has successfully been identified and authenticated, it must be authorised to access specific tools and informational resources. The particular types of action are also authorised individually. Examples include:

- run
- view
- create
- edit
- delete
- print.

Authorisation to access information and other computing services begins with administrative policies and procedures.

- The policies **prescribe** what information and computing services can be accessed, by whom and under what conditions.
- The access control procedures are then configured to **enforce** these policies.

Different computing systems are equipped with different kinds of access control mechanisms and some may even offer a choice of these mechanisms. The access control mechanism offered by a system will be based upon one of three approaches to access control or it may be derived from a combination of all three approaches:

- non-discretionary
- discretionary
- mandatory.

The non-discretionary approach consolidates all access control under a centralised administration. The access to information and other resources is usually based on the individual's function (role) in the organisation or the tasks the individual must perform.

The discretionary approach gives the creator or owner of the information resource the ability to control access to those resources.

In the mandatory access control approach, access is granted or denied based upon the security classification assigned to the information resource.

To be effective, policies and other security controls must be enforceable and upheld. Effective policies ensure that people are held accountable for their actions. All failed and successful authentication attempts must be logged and all access to information must leave some type of audit trail.

1.5. Customers, Employees and Third-Party Service Providers

Different access control challenges arise based on the relationship between the organisation and the person accessing the systems or data.

1.5.1 Customers

Customers often require access to data pertaining to themselves, for example, their own bank account details. They also require the right to conduct transactions, within certain constraints, and to close or move their accounts.

1.5.2 Employees

Employees may need access to customers' data and accounts but, in most cases, they will not be given the ability to move funds, except in specific cases and subject to tight controls.

1.5.3 Service Providers

Service providers may require the same capabilities as employees or they may be engaged solely in system maintenance and support, in which case their capabilities will be limited.

All of the above requires careful planning and management, as well as frequent audits and testing.

1.5.4 The Impact of Culture on Cyber-Security for International Business

Employee behaviour can have a very significant impact on the state and quality of information security in any organisation. Information security culture (ISC) refers to the sum of the discrete patterns of behaviour taking place within an organisation that contribute to the protection of information of all kinds.

A well-constructed ISC can help to reduce risks in tangible ways. This is particularly important when it is remembered that perhaps 50% of all security breaches have an insider element, either in terms of deliberate acts or in terms of negligence and inadvertent disclosures.

ISC goes beyond conventional cyber-security controls; it has an ethical dimension too. In a sense, it provides the **environment** within which control can be effectively achieved and maintained. However, ISC is strongly influenced by both the wider organisational culture and by national culture, both of which can either enhance or inhibit it.

This final point is of particular relevance to global organisations, which can find it challenging to implement a single unified ISC worldwide. Many organisations have found it necessary to adapt to local organisational and national cultures. Changing cultures, particularly those that are alien to us, can prove to be an almost insurmountable challenge.

1.5.5 Organisational Culture

Creating or adapting a suitable organisational culture is an oxymoron; cultures evolve – they aren't manufactured. But in any organisation, leadership can make a dramatic difference to the corporate culture by doing the things that shape the environment of control. The actions of top management can influence everyone in the organisation to internalise the positive attitudes and behaviours that prevent cybercrime and fraud or make their detection more likely.

Some management actions that can improve the cultural environment are described below.

Setting the Right Tone

Even seemingly small rules exist for everyone in the organisation, including top management. They provide a consistent framework which people can depend upon when they are fairly and consistently applied. Senior managers must make it clear to all that they support these rules.

Leading by Example

If senior management does not follow procedures (for example by bringing their own devices to work when this is against the organisation's policies) other employees might feel resentful or they may even feel that these behaviours authorise them to ignore the rules as well.

Maintain Transparency

Transparency is one of the core requirements of trust and it must permeate every step managers take to create a strong information security culture. The rationale for each rule or control should be openly discussed and even debated with stakeholders. Good security does not arise as a result of edicts from above; it is created when everyone affected buys in to the programme.

'No Broken Windows'

In 1969, sociologist James Q. Wilson published an influential paper entitled *Broken Windows*. He made the observation that neighbourhoods where broken windows went unrepaired invited more serious breakdowns in social control, often leading to serious crime. People are affected by their environment and they act differently when they feel that standards are low.

In ISC terms, this suggests that a positive environment of control implies a zero-tolerance attitude toward fraud and cybercrime. Leadership must not tolerate it and they must make their intolerance clear across the whole organisation.

National Culture

ISC needs to be improved continuously. This is a never-ending cycle of evaluation and change or maintenance. There are four basic steps that need to be taken in order to manage ISC at a national level:

- **Evaluation** – identifies the awareness of information security on the part of citizens and analyses current security policies.
- **Strategic planning** – sets targets and defines responsibilities.
- **Operational planning** – defines the specific goals and measurement criteria for developing and delivering communication, gaining buy-in and implementing an effective, tailored security awareness and training programme that reaches all parts of the population.
- **Implementation** – applies the information security culture change by gaining commitment from leaders and influencers of all types, communicating and debating the issues with a wide range of stakeholders (parents, business owners, police forces, local government, corporate bodies) and ultimately gaining the commitment of as many people and organisations as possible.

The key point to bear in mind is that many people only commit to change when they see what's in it for them. This may be anything from self-respect to service, recognition or even job security. Messages that focus on the effect of cybercrime on normal people, rather than its effects on the profits of major firms, are often more effective. It should not be forgotten that some cyber-attacks, such as those orchestrated by Anonymous against the banks, often have a great deal of silent support from onlookers in the general population.

2. Risk Management

Learning Objective

5.2.1 Know the additional measures financial services firms can take to manage the risk of cybercrime originated or enabled by an employee: raising awareness; improving the management of privileges for joiners, movers and leavers; classifying and segmenting data; embedding ethical practice in relation to data security; implementing whistleblowing procedures

5.2.2 Know the implications of cybercrime for technological procurement: bespoke software development; standards of software development; supplier due diligence; hardware and software lifecycles, including disposal with respect to corporate social responsibility and the data protection principles

5.2.3 Know how to manage the risk of cybercrime throughout the employee lifecycle

2.1 Risk Management Definitions

Risk is the relationship between the likelihood that some threat will harm an information asset and the impact or effect that the incident could potentially engender. A threat is anything that might act independently to cause said harm; it could be anything from a tsunami to a hacker. For example, if a hurricane would probably demolish your house and hurricanes are frequent where you live, then the risk to your house (your asset) is high. On the other hand, if your house is fragile but hurricanes are extremely rare, then the risk to your prized asset is either moderate or low.

In order to fine-tune such an assessment, two additional factors are important:

- **Asset value** – if your house is worth millions, you might want to increase the risk score to reflect the impact of an adverse event.
- **Vulnerabilities** – if you have identified a number of controls that could protect you, but which are not implemented or working correctly (for example, if the coastal defences are broken near your home), then you might also want to increase the risk score.

The **value** of the information or computing asset you want to protect will therefore affect how you perceive risk. If you just received a brand new high-spec tablet for your birthday, you are likely to guard it far more carefully than if you are struggling to type on a ten-year-old laptop with a partially damaged screen. Likewise, the exposure of sensitive customer data will cause you more concern than information about your office lighting expenses.

A **vulnerability** is a weakness in control that can be exploited in order to cause harm to an information asset or to a piece of technology. For example, weak password controls constitute a common vulnerability. Even if the potential frequency and impact of a hacking attack remains unchanged, the discovery of a weak set of passwords should cause you to increase your risk score.

When a threat exploits a vulnerability to inflict harm, it has an impact. This could be anything from zero to catastrophic. In the context of information security, the impact might be a loss of availability, integrity and confidentiality, lost income, loss of real property, reputational harm or even loss of life.

It should be pointed out that it is not possible to identify all risks, nor is it possible to eliminate all risk. The remaining risk that cannot be identified or eliminated in a cost-effective way is called residual risk; it is the risk that remains after all reasonable steps have been taken to provide security. Even if you live in Fort Knox, there is always a residual risk that a massive earthquake will shake your building to pieces, unlikely as that may be.

2.1.1 Risk Assessments

A risk assessment is best conducted by a team of people who have knowledge of specific areas of the firm. Membership of the team may vary over time as different areas and classes of risk are assessed. The assessment may use a subjective, qualitative analysis based on informed opinion or, where reliable financial figures and historical data are available, the assessment may be only quantitative in nature.

Experience has demonstrated that the most vulnerable point in most information systems is the human user, operator, designer or other human actor. The ISO/IEC 27002:2005 Code of Practice for Information Security Management recommends that the following be examined during an information security or cyber-security risk assessment:

- security policy
- organisation of information security
- asset management
- human resources security
- physical and environmental security
- communications and operations management
- access control
- information systems acquisition, development and maintenance
- information security incident management
- business continuity management
- regulatory compliance.

In broad terms, the risk management process consists of the following:

- Identification of assets and estimating their value, including people, buildings, hardware, software, data (in all formats) and other supplies.
- Conduct of a threat assessment, to include acts of nature, acts of war, accidents and malicious acts originating from inside or outside the organisation.
- Conduct of a vulnerability assessment, to identify missing controls or weak controls, and for each vulnerability to calculate the **probability** that it will be exploited. This assessment encompasses policies, procedures, standards, training, physical security, logical security, technical security, governance and change management.
- Conduct of a business impact assessment to calculate the effect that each threat would have on each asset. This may make use of both qualitative analysis and quantitative analysis.
- Identification, selection and implementation of the appropriate controls to provide a proportional response. This takes into account the effects of each control on productivity and also the relative value of the asset: the cost effectiveness and **return on investment** of each control.

For any given risk, management can choose to accept the risk based upon the relative low value of the asset, the relative low frequency of occurrence and the relative low impact on the business, or to mitigate the risk by selecting and implementing appropriate control measures.

In some cases, a risk can be transferred to another business by buying insurance or outsourcing, or it may be avoided by a change in policy or business processes.

2.2 Managing the Risk of Insider Cybercrime Throughout the Employee Lifecycle

If you ask the question: *Which of the cybercrimes and cyber-enabled frauds affecting my business would be easier to commit from the inside?* The answer, unfortunately, is probably all of them!

Belief and faith in those that work for you is vital and is to be encouraged, but unquestioning or blinkered trust is not. Knowing your loyal staff and protecting them from the small minority of disloyal employees will reinforce that trust and ensure it is returned.

2.2.1 Motivations for Internal Attack

In the mid-1940s an eminent criminologist, Donald Cressey, devised the *Employee Fraud Triangle*, showing the three constituent parts of an employee fraud:

- rationalisation
- opportunity
- motivation.

How any individual might rationalise his future actions is naturally difficult to predict with confidence. However, motivation is often quite predictable but is rarely considered before the event. This may represent a missed opportunity to develop logical scenarios that plot the possible course of a range of internal crimes, as well as highlighting the markers that can be monitored in order to detect increased levels of risk. Indeed, a 20-year study, *Theft by Employees* by Hollinger and Clark (1983) and based on 12,000 employees, concluded that the most common reason employees committed crimes had little to do with opportunity and more to do with motivation.

Types of Motivation

No studies have examined the full breadth or depth of motivations for internal crime or their potential relevance in internal fraud/crime management, but there are probably three major classes of motivation (with some crossover):

- Greed.
- Need:
  - debts (self-inflicted)
  - debts (true necessity)
  - targets /survival/concealment of error/deficit
  - coercion/under threat/blackmail
  - addictions: alcohol, drugs, sex, gambling.

- Miscellaneous:
  - malice/revenge (existing)
  - malice/revenge (responsive)
  - competitive sabotage

- ◦ peer (or family) pressure/loyalty
- ◦ psychological problems
- ◦ excitement/challenge/entertainment/kudos/ego
- ◦ idealism/terrorism
- ◦ stupidity/naivety
- ◦ mole/cell (ie, planted within the organisation)
- ◦ industrial or state espionage
- ◦ altruism – the Robin Hood syndrome.

There are numerous cybercrime techniques that can be perpetrated against a target. Few of these techniques are specific to insider attacks but the following list highlights some common areas in which internal crimes often depend on some degree of staff involvement in the form of either collusion or neglect:

- account adjustments or theft from accounts
- sales commission adjustments
- processing duplicate or fake invoices from suppliers
- identity theft
- data breaches and insider trading offences.

These activities can be very serious when they are committed on a large scale but this normally involves an external element: the insider is facilitating somebody outside the organisation.

2.2.2 Technical Post Holders

Highly proficient technical post holders are probably the most sensitive class of employee. If they become miscreants, their capacity to steal funds or manipulate systems is potentially boundless and their ability to conceal their deeds for long periods of time exacerbates the danger. The simple reason for this is that they are often the only people within the business who understand the technology at a deep level. This means that they have access to the most sensitive classes of data, while at the same time nobody else within the organisation has the skills to monitor their activities to investigate suspected crimes effectively.

2.2.3 Threat Scoring

Threat scoring exercises identify threat types by role and measure their severity in detail by examining all elements of:

- role opportunity
- threat reality
- threat impact.

All role types (and role type families) across the organisation are identified with the assistance of the HR team. Volunteers are taken from each role type (or family) and they are then interviewed by risk management professionals. It should be clearly explained to each interviewee that the interview is an objective examination of the threat potential of their role and is not about them personally.

Once the interviewer has established exactly how their role is performed, how it relates to other roles and parts of the business and the controls to which it is subjected, the interviewee is invited to explore with the interviewer how an insider with malicious intent could pose a threat to the firm.

The roles are scored during this examination using the following criteria:

Role Opportunity

1. Level of authority
2. ability to supervise
3. level of supervision imposed
4. access to business element (eg, systems, network, client monies)
5. ability to change, divert or manipulate that element.

Threat Reality

6. Ease of attack
7. detection likelihood.

Threat Impact

8. Financial effect
9. business element impact
10. damage limitation/recovery possibility
11. client/investor confidence
12. market reputation.

Once the principal threat for each role has been determined, the 12 criteria listed above are scored individually to determine the overall threat score.

Making the connection between internal crime motives, threat scoring and related controls is the final step. It is important to bear in mind that attack techniques will vary as attackers respond to changes in the operating business processes, the technology in use within the business and the evolution of controls themselves.

2.2.4 Controls

Many of the controls that relate to reducing the risk of internal cybercrimes or crimes of facilitation are process-oriented rather than technical in nature.

Vetting (Pre-employment Security Screening)

This is the principal tool in the internal threat prevention armoury. Spotting risk factor indicators requires detailed **vetting** checks and, realistically, an organisation can normally only conduct that level of vetting on a small subset of critical or sensitive roles. This is why the threat-scoring activity is essential.

Vetting is a sensitive subject and it is important to understand the legal restrictions within your jurisdiction and your local HR policies. Where permitted, a hierarchical system of vetting could be introduced for those roles that represent high internal-threat potential and such roles should be subject to enhanced checks.

Any vetting scheme should be based on three key principles:

- **Voluntary** – all applicants and potential applicants must be made aware of the level of screening from the stage of post advertisement onwards and their consent must be obtained either by inclusion in the contract of employment or via a separate document. The subject may decline to offer such data or decline to obtain such data; in this case the future of the recruitment or promotion process in respect of this individual must be carefully considered.
- **Open/overt** – the subject is entitled to know of the existence and operation of the policy, the data sought and the sources used.
- **Proportionate** – the level and intensity of the screening will be directly proportional to the criticality of the role concerned and must be demonstrably proportionate, ie, by application of the appropriate threat-quotient level accorded and/or application of role access levels as described in the information classification treatment control described later.

Some standard checks that are often included, which again are subject to relevant local legal guidance, are:

- criminal record
- identity verification
- credit reference
- electoral roll
- residence
- document verification
- financial sanctions.

Some enhanced checks that are sometimes included are:

- Security interviews with successful candidate at commencement of screening.
- Telephone or face-to-face interviews with three candidate referees.
- Identity verification of referees.
- Financial analysis – the candidate is asked to supply a statement of all financial outgoings as well as six months' bank and credit/debit card statements. The analysis will attempt to identify any anomalies.
- Detailed searches on past and present directorships held and any disqualifications registered.
- Final security interview with the candidate – the candidate must be given an opportunity to explain any anomalies found.

2.2.5 The Role of Human Resources (HR)

An exit process (immediate removal of passwords, access control, recovery of equipment and removable media) for all leavers should also be part of the staff integrity process.

Many of the motivations we looked at in section 2.2.1 originate when staff morale is low and/or industrial relations break down. Not only does dishonesty tend to increase but the likelihood of honest staff reporting their concerns decreases. Thus, it is the job of the human resources (HR) department to ensure, along with line management, that difficult times are met with good treatment for staff and good times are enjoyed as well. Loyalty from the business, honesty and transparency are usually what staff want most.

2.3 The Implications of Cybercrime for Technological Procurement

The tactics of cybercriminals present the procurement function with a new set of challenges. In effect, any technological product or service, whether hardware or software, comes with an inherent set of risks:

- It can be deliberately infected at the point of production or manufacture.
- It might contain undetected vulnerabilities that facilitate attacks.
- It might be unreliable, leading to errors, data loss or even failures in the management of key systems.

2.3.1 Bespoke Software Development

Bespoke software development taking place within the firm or at third-party sites may have several advantages, not least that of having software developers engaged who are close to the effective business process and who are able to converse freely and easily with stakeholders. However, modern software is increasingly complex and the use of in-house teams or small software development houses can result in the development of code that lacks some of the more modern security controls.

Another risk arising from the development of bespoke software is the dependency of the results when a firm is reliant on a small group of internal or external developers. While this can be managed contractually, the risk does not necessarily go away and serious consideration should be given to the question of which drivers exist for supporting a decision to produce a bespoke solution.

Supplier due diligence is therefore essential. Firms must ensure that their hardware and software come from reliable sources and this is more easily achieved when recognised brands are used.

2.3.2 Change Management

Hardware and software lifecycles are becoming shorter and shorter as time progresses. Development and information projects that once would have taken years are now being pushed through in months, particularly when the applications or devices will be in the hands of consumers. The App Store model has raised consumer expectations dramatically and this puts pressure on both IT and procurement to move very quickly. Consequently, change management is increasingly important; it is during development, implementation and updating that the majority of security flaws are introduced.

2.3.3 Disposal

Equipment disposal is just as important as equipment procurement. Many people are unaware of the fact that simply deleting data from a hard drive does not in fact delete the data; it merely removes the road signs that point to that data.

Controlled disposal of old equipment is another essential aspect of cyber-security. There are numerous companies now providing such services and any regulated firm should have in place an effective equipment disposal policy. This will demonstrate the firm's commitment to corporate social responsibility, because old equipment contains numerous contaminants, as well as its adherence to data protection principles.

3. Stress Testing

Learning Objective

5.3.1   Understand the application of penetration testing to different types of vulnerabilities

5.3.2   Understand the correct application of prepared planning and dry-run modelling

5.3.3   Know how firms can measure, or predict, the impact of cyber-attack

In response to the massive volume of cyber-attacks that they face on a daily basis, UK banks now undergo periodic cyber-stress tests to benchmark their network security.

3.1   Security Testing Taxonomy

Cyber-security testing encompasses a wide range of activities. Step one in understanding the testing process involves learning to recognise the basic testing taxonomy. Common concepts for the delivery of security testing are described below.

3.1.1   Discovery

The purpose of this stage is to identify systems within scope and the services in use. It is not intended to discover vulnerabilities, but version detection may highlight deprecated versions of software/firmware and thus indicate potential vulnerabilities.

3.1.2   Vulnerability Scan

Following the discovery stage, this involves looking for known security issues by using automated tools to match conditions with known vulnerabilities. The reported risk level is set automatically by the tool, with no manual verification or interpretation by the test vendor.

3.1.3   Vulnerability Assessment

This uses discovery and vulnerability scanning to identify security vulnerabilities and places the findings into the context of the environment under test. An example would be removing common false positives from the report and deciding risk levels that should be applied to each report finding to improve business understanding and context.

3.1.4   Security Assessment

This builds on the vulnerability assessment by adding manual verification to confirm exposure, but does not include the exploitation of vulnerabilities to gain further access. Verification could be in the form of authorised access to a system to confirm system settings and involve examining logs, system responses, error messages and codes. A security assessment is intended to gain a broad coverage of the systems under test but not the depth of exposure that a specific vulnerability could lead to.

3.1.5　Penetration Test

A penetration test simulates an attack by a malicious party. Building on the stages described above, it involves exploitation of found vulnerabilities to gain further access. Using this approach will result in an understanding of the ability of an attacker to gain access to confidential information, affect data integrity or availability of a service and the respective impact of such access. Each test is approached using a consistent and complete methodology in a way that allows the tester to use their problem-solving abilities, the output from a range of tools and their own knowledge of networking and systems to find vulnerabilities that would/could not be identified by automated tools. This approach looks at the depth of attack as compared to the security assessment approach that looks at the broader coverage.

3.1.6　Security Audit

This is driven by an audit/risk function to look at a specific control or compliance issue. Characterised by a narrow scope, this type of engagement could make use of any of the earlier approaches discussed (vulnerability assessment, security assessment, penetration test).

3.1.7　Security Review

This is verification that industry or internal security standards have been applied to system components or products. It is typically completed through gap analysis and utilises build/code reviews or reviews of design documents and architecture diagrams. This activity does not utilise any of the earlier approaches (vulnerability assessment, security assessment, penetration test, security audit).

3.2　Security Testing for Financial Institutions

One of the primary cybercrime risks facing financial institutions is not a financial crime but rather the DDoS attack. In testing resilience to DDoS attacks, firms need to confirm that the following processes and controls are effective.

3.2.1　Scheduling

When session requests are made to a server, a piece of software called a scheduler determines which sessions will be processed and when. Historically, these decisions have been based on fairly simple rules such as first come, first served. More advanced scheduling factors in the risk score assigned to a packet in order to ensure that the server is not flooded with high-risk session requests.

3.2.2　Anomaly Detection

In simple terms, traffic patterns can be examined in a number of ways to detect anomalies that may be suspect.

3.2.3　Volumetric Analysis

This involves looking for evidence of lots of requests in a short time period.

3.2.4 Characteristics

This includes searching for high-risk IP addresses or ports in incoming packets.

3.2.5 Traffic Flow Pattern Analysis

This is used to identify changes or fluctuations in patterns of traffic flow that match known or suspected attack scenarios.

3.2.6 Server Load Analysis

During a DoS or DDoS attack, the target server's load counter will show a high amount of time delays to attend processes and a much larger than normal number of processes. Depending on the variety of the attack, access log and error log files may also grow abnormally. Each of these characteristics can be detected and reported to administrators in the form of alarms.

3.3 Penetration Testing as Applied to Different Vulnerabilities

The other key threats to information systems are social engineering, intrusions of various types, application exploits and malware. Penetration testing is designed to identify vulnerabilities in systems. It can support the risk assessment and validation processes and is one of the main tools used to combat cyber-security and cybercrime risks.

A good penetration test will convincingly simulate a credible attacker in order to identify genuine vulnerabilities. Testers must work by the medical standard of 'first, do no harm', but tests must evaluate realistic exploits and describe plausible impacts. An effective penetration test allows testers and those tested to devise practical solutions to proven vulnerabilities.

There are several types of penetration test, each addressing different types of vulnerability, and each type of test requires a different set of skills, tools and techniques:

- Physical site penetrations may require burglary or social engineering skills.
- Network penetrations require hacking skills.
- Social media penetrations or data extraction via online forums call for solid Web 2.0 skills.

3.3.1 Informed Versus Uninformed Tests

As we saw in chapter 4, penetration tests may be either informed or uninformed. An informed test involves the testers being given details of the client's security arrangements in order that these may be stress tested. In an uninformed test, the testers have to approach the target blind and must find their own way around the systems and controls. Informed tests are useful when particular known risks or recently added controls need to be validated. Uninformed tests serve to highlight new risks or likely avenues of attack.

The goal of both types of penetration tests is to ensure that the selected physical facilities, web-facing applications, networks and platforms are secure in terms of both technology and staff awareness in relation to unauthorised network access. This includes detection of and access to hidden Wi-Fi networks and on-site physical network attacks. Typically, evidence in the form of screen captures and packet capture is required in the event of a successful penetration.

3.3.2   Preparation and Planning for Penetration Testing

The majority of penetration tests adhere to a standard four-step methodology:

*   **Scoping** – to define the scope and approach of the test and to set markers for abort, test limits, authorisation and liability exceptions.
*   **Reconnaissance and vulnerability scanning** – to determine the systems and applications in use and identify any potential vulnerabilities or access points.
*   **Execution and verification** – to attempt actual penetrations and, if successful, verify by using the access gained to navigate to internal systems or execute other predetermined tasks.
*   **Reporting** – to gather evidence such as screenshots and packet captures and to produce a written description of the test and its results. This often includes a short bio or storyline of the test process.

This systematic testing process ensures that appropriate tests have been applied. The process is iterative and may involve retesting as new vulnerabilities are uncovered.

3.3.3   Social Media Penetration Testing

Social media penetration testing is increasingly used to assess the risk of data leakage and reputational harm via social media friend networks, public posts and network analysis. Testing commonly involves exploits to persuade employees into disclosing business, customer or personal data.

3.3.4   Testing Limitations and Caveats

The abort conditions for any test should be agreed with the sponsor in advance. This is often defined as the point at which it is certain that staff or systems are in the process of invoking security protocols or otherwise denying access in a firm and certain manner.

As a general rule, testers must not delete files or data during testing, nor deface webpages or edit and delete user accounts. New accounts might be added where needed (when possible) but any additions must be documented to allow the test subjects to remove them on completion of the test. Unless agreed in advance, testers should not use any form of DoS attack on the target network or systems. You also need to be aware that during testing it is possible for any given network device or record (eg, routers or files such as log files) to be affected and you should alert those requesting the test of this potential hazard.

Convention dictates that there are **Six Rs** to acceptable and ethical penetration testing. Tests must be:

*   **risk-based** – aligned with the client's risk appetite and their perceptions of risk
*   **realistic** – they must model credible attack scenarios
*   **reliable** – they must be executed by expert testers
*   **respectful** – of people, particularly users and security staff who may be embarrassed by the test result

- **responsible** – towards assets such as systems, data and the brand
- **reportable** – via screen captures, packet captures and data exfiltration, as appropriate.

To stay safe while testing, it is helpful to assess every step of your test plan and execution against each of these criteria as you go along.

3.3.5 Dry-Run Modelling

Dry-run modelling is an alternative to live penetration or stress testing. In a dry-run, the testers examine models that represent the organisation's information systems and data structures and develop attack scenarios which can then be assessed against the existing control framework.

This largely intellectual exercise facilitates the discussion and exploration of major threats and incidents that could not realistically be tested on the live network and systems without creating a serious risk.

3.3.6 The Desired Cyber-Security End State

At the end of the process, a secure, robust and reliable information technology system should exhibit:

- quick problem resolution
- reduced susceptibility to security attacks
- increased availability
- minimal legal exposure
- lower compliance risks
- preserved brand identity.

3.4 Measuring or Predicting the Impact of a Cyber-Attack

The impact of cyber-attacks on business, government and nation states is not merely financial. Of far greater import are the effects that attacks can have on trust and consumer confidence; their impact on the brand.

The total cost of any cyber-security breach is the product of direct losses plus indirect losses and the cost of security both prior to and following the event. Security implemented in response to a threat, therefore, can be thought of as part of the cost of a subsequent attack, whether that attack succeeds or fails.

Meanwhile, actual criminal revenue may only be a fraction of this sum. Consequently, estimates of costs provide no basis for computing criminal gains and estimates of criminal gains conversely provide no basis for calculating costs. The two values are decoupled and, in fact, the value of criminal gain is largely irrelevant when it comes to determining cyber-security strategy – the more logical approach is primarily risk- and cost-based.

It follows that cyber-security events cannot be regarded simply as digital bank robberies. In a traditional robbery, assuming that nobody is harmed, the cost of the robbery is equal to the amount of money stolen, plus some secondary indirect costs. As long as the bank has acted responsibly throughout and is perceived as a victim, the other costs are likely to be minimal. In fact, it is the insurers who will pay.

A digital attack on a bank, on the other hand, might not involve a robbery at all; it may well take the form of effectively locking the digital vault so that funds, while remaining secure, cannot be accessed by account holders. Nothing has been stolen but the indirect costs to the bank are huge.

In order to compute cybercrime costs, one must move away from considerations of criminal gain and focus on other factors.

The indirect financial costs of cybercrime break down further into several components:

- losses to acquisitive crime
- liability for third-party losses or claims
- regulatory penalties/fines
- equipment write-offs
- direct revenue losses, ie, through downtime or lost sales
- professional fees.

Secondary losses include the costs of investigative, legal and customer care or public relations activities.

Aside from fraud, one of the most significant areas of crime losses is blackmail, for example the electronic hijacking of systems. This is typified by the crypto-extortion attack in which critical data is encrypted by an attacker who will only decrypt it in exchange for a payment. Such cases often extend to the theft of equipment, such as laptops, which will only be returned in exchange for a reward.

3.5   Change Management

In a complex environment, even seemingly minor changes can have unexpected consequences. ICT change management is a process for directing and controlling alterations to the information processing environment: hardware, software and business processes. This covers changes to users' devices, the network itself, servers and software applications. The goal of change management is to reduce the risk introduced by change and assure stability and reliability.

Not all changes need to be managed. Some types of change are part of the normal routine of information processing and are achieved through predefined procedures. Examples include the creation of a new user account or the deployment of a new desktop computer. However, major tasks such as upgrading an email server can pose a much higher level of risk.

Change management is usually overseen by a change review board, composed of representatives from key business areas, risk, IT security, networking, systems administrators, database administration, applications development, desktop support and the help desk. The responsibility of the board is to ensure that the firm's formal change management procedures are followed.

The change management process normally involves the following steps:

1. **Request** – the change is requested and reviewed.
2. **Approval** – the change is approved and prioritised.
3. **Planning** – the scope and impact of the proposed change are assessed and the appropriate resources are allocated. An implementation plan, testing plan and a back-out plan are developed.

4. **Testing** – the change is tested in a safe test environment, possibly using the dry-run modelling approach.
5. **Scheduling** – the proposed implementation date is checked for potential conflicts with other scheduled changes or critical business activities.
6. **Communication** – information is given to others in order to give them an opportunity to remind the change review board about other changes or critical business activities that might have been overlooked when scheduling the change. The communication also serves to make the help desk and users aware that a change is about to occur.
7. **Implementation** – the changes are implemented.
8. **Documentation** – this includes the initial request for change, its approval, the priority assigned to it, the implementation, testing and back-out plans, the results of the change review board critique, the date/time the change was implemented, who implemented it and whether the change was implemented successfully, failed or postponed.
9. **Post change review** – the change review board holds a post-implementation review of all approved changes. It is particularly important to review failed and backed-out changes. The review board should try to understand the problems that were encountered and look for areas for improvement.

Change management procedures that are simple to follow and easy to use can greatly reduce the overall risks created when changes are made to the information-processing environment. Good change management procedures improve the overall quality and success of changes as they are implemented.

4.   Incident Response

Learning Objective

5.4.1   Know the role of a computer emergency response team (CERT) or computer security incident response team (CSIRT)

5.4.2   Understand the concept of recovery time objectives (RTO)

5.4.3   Know the components of an incident management procedure

5.4.4   Know how to develop an incident management response plan

4.1   Key Principles of Incident Response

Cyber-security incident management involves:

*   the detection and monitoring of security events on a computer or computer network
*   the execution of proper responses to those events.

4.1.1   Components of an Incident

An incident is an event attributable to a human root cause. This distinction is particularly important when the event is the product of malicious intent to do harm.

An event is an observable change to the normal behaviour of a system, environment, process, workflow or person. There are three types of events:

- **Normal** – does not affect critical components or require change controls prior to the implementation of a resolution.
- **Escalation** – affects critical production systems or requires the implementation of a resolution that must follow a change control process.
- **Emergency** – may affect the health or safety of human beings, breach the primary controls of critical systems, materially affect component performance or be deemed an emergency as a matter of policy.

4.1.2   Response Teams

A computer emergency response team (CERT) or computer security incident response team (CSIRT) manages the response process. They assess each escalated or emergency incident and make decisions regarding the proper course of action. The response team meets regularly to review status reports and to authorise specific remedies.

The investigation must determine both the circumstances and the impact of each incident. In addition, it should make recommendations that address root causes and ensure, if possible, that the particular incident is not repeated.

4.2   Recovery Time Objectives (RTO)

A **recovery time objective (RTO)** is an expression of the maximum tolerated period during which a device, system, network or application can be unavailable after a cyber-attack, technical failure or disaster occurs. The RTO will differ for each organisation and class of system.

The RTO is a function of the extent to which the interruption disrupts normal operations and the amount of revenue lost per unit of time as a result of the disaster. These factors in turn depend on the affected equipment and applications. An RTO is normally expressed in seconds, minutes, hours or days.

The actual cost of any downtime period depends on long-term and intangible effects, as well as on immediate, short-term or tangible factors. Once the RTO for an application has been defined, administrators can decide which disaster recovery technologies are best suited to the situation. For example, if the RTO for a given application is one hour, redundant data backup on external hard drives may be the best solution. If the RTO is five days, then offsite storage on a remote web server may be more practical.

4.3   The Components of an Incident Management Procedure

The primary goal of the incident management process is to restore normal service operation as quickly as possible and minimise the adverse impact on business operations, thus ensuring that the best possible levels of service quality and availability are maintained. Normal service operation is defined here as service operation within service level agreement (SLA) limits.

The objective of the process is to ensure that:

- incidents are properly logged
- incidents are properly routed
- incident status is accurately reported
- the queue of unresolved incidents is visible and reported
- incidents are properly prioritised and handled in the appropriate sequence
- resolution provided meets the requirements of the SLA for the customer.

4.3.1   Incident Management Response Plan of Action

There are a number of frequently used approaches to incident management planning. The basic incident response plan process flow contains five stages, as described below:

- **Prepare** – defines all the preparatory work that must be completed in order to create the capacity to effectively respond to each category of foreseeable incident. This includes the development of vision and mission, obtaining funding and support, evaluating incident-response capabilities and requirements and documenting the appropriate policies and procedures, as well as assigning responsibility.
- **Protect** – reduces the likelihood and impact of incidents by implementing countermeasures to protect key infrastructure and data assets proactively.
- **Detect** – organises the collection of data from multiple sources and the creation of alerts and reports intended to quickly detect anomalies indicative of a potential or ongoing incident.
- **Triage** – sorts, categorises, scores, prioritises and assigns incoming incident reports in order to ensure that the most serious incidents relating to the most critical systems and data, and with the greatest potential business impact, are addressed first.
- **Respond** – encompasses the steps required to resolve or mitigate each incident. This will typically break down into at least three categories of response – technical, managerial and legal. The managerial component includes public relations and human resources activities plus any other steps required to protect brand and reputation.

5. Business Continuity and Disaster Recovery Planning (DRP)

One of the most significant impacts arising from a cyber-security incident is the failure of the business to continue operating. Business continuity and disaster recovery planning (DRP) covers the processes required to mitigate this risk.

Learning Objective

5.5.1   Understand the concept of business recovery and disaster recovery planning (DRP)

5.5.2   Know the purpose of the FCA 'Business Continuity Management Practice Guide'

5.5.3   Know FCA requirements for business continuity (SYSC 13.8) and incident response

5.7.1   Know the fundamentals of encryption: substitution and transposition explained; a short history of encryption, from the Caesar Code to RSA; symmetric encryption explained; prime numbers, semi-primes, the factorisation challenge and asymmetric encryption demystified; ephemeral keys and modern encrypted messaging apps

---

Disaster recovery and business continuity are additional essential components of cyber-security planning and stress testing. The two domains are closely related but distinct, with separate planning processes designed to ensure that any organisation can deal with and recover from any disruptive or damaging event.

The type of event can range from severe weather or an earthquake to a major cyber-attack. Impacts on a business can include:

- loss or failure of resources (including people and technology)
- loss of data
- physical effects from external events such as vandalism or natural disasters.

5.1 Business Continuity Planning (BCP)

5.1.1 The Purpose of BCP

BCP addresses business continuity through events on all parts of the scale, from the very small to the very large and ensures that an organisation can continue providing services and remain profitable and efficient. BCP addresses power outages, data loss, communications loss (including phone and internet), illness and/or the loss of key personnel. Business continuity, therefore, is the mechanism by which an organisation continues to operate its critical business units, during planned or unplanned disruptions that affect normal business operations, by invoking planned and managed procedures.

In summary, the purpose of a business continuity plan is to:

- minimise interruption of normal operations
- limit disruption and damage

- minimise any financial impact
- establish alternative means of operation
- train personnel in emergency procedures
- provide smooth and rapid service restoration.

5.1.2   Developing a BCP

BCP includes directions on who decides when a crisis is underway and how employees and customers are informed. The planning process should involve managers from all parts of the organisation and regular rehearsals to test key parts of the plan are very important, in a similar way to fire drills.

Not only is business continuity about the business, it is also an IT system and process. Disasters or disruptions to business are a reality so, regardless of whether the disaster is natural or man-made, it affects normal life and, therefore, business. Hence, planning is important.

A BCP will address the following points:

- Which emergency response services or internal organisations should be contacted?
- What parts of the business and/or information systems should be recovered first?
- What are recovery time objectives on a system-by-system basis?
- What resources may be required in order to facilitate recovery?
- Where will the recovery operation be managed from, assuming that the main site is temporarily inaccessible or unusable?
- For what period of time can the organisation operate at a reduced capacity before the impact becomes critical?
- How can the plan be tested regularly and effectively, without having a negative impact on ongoing operations?

At the simplest level there are ten key areas that any organisation should address with their BCP:

1. Identify the **chain of command** – normally the directors and senior managers of the organisation.
2. **Risk assessment and response** – conduct a risk assessment to identify the types of risks the organisation could face and devise actions to counteract these.
3. **Core business systems** – identify those systems and data that are so critical that the business would not be able to function without them.
4. **Crisis management group** – nominate a crisis management team to co-ordinate the BCP.
5. **External contacts** – list those contacts outside the organisation who need to be alerted in the event of a serious incident. These can vary according the type of disaster.
6. **Staff contacts** – maintain a current record of all employees' contact information so the organisation can communicate with them in an emergency.
7. **Recording of incidents** – record the details of all major incidents and the actions taken in response.
8. **Train** all staff in their roles and responsibilities in relation to business continuity.
9. **Review and test** – it is essential to regularly review and test the business continuity plan; conduct a comprehensive risk review annually and test the different elements of the plan.
10. **Critical document names and storage** – compile and regularly update a list of the names and locations of key documentation essential for business continuity. Ensure the key people responsible for business continuity can access the list when required.

5.1.3 British Standard (BS) 25999

This British Standard provides a comprehensive set of controls based on BCM best practice and covers the whole BCM lifecycle. It is intended for use by anyone with responsibility for business operations, from board directors and chief executives, through all levels of the organisation. It is relevant to those organisations with a single site and those with a global presence: from sole traders and SMEs to organisations employing thousands of people.

The standard establishes the BCM process, principles and terminology, providing a basis for understanding, developing and implementing business continuity within an organisation and providing confidence in business-to-business and business-to-customer dealings.

5.2 Disaster Recovery Planning (DRP)

Disaster recovery planning (DRP) covers the immediate response to a major event. It ensures that:

- people are made or kept safe
- property is secured, with the most sensitive or highest-value assets receiving the earliest attention
- co-ordination with the emergency services and local government is effectively established and maintained
- customers are assisted in an appropriate and timely fashion.

While a BCP takes a broad approach to dealing with the organisation-wide effects of a disaster, a DRP, which is sometimes regarded as a subset of the BCP, is instead focused on taking the necessary steps to resume normal business operations as quickly as possible.

A DRP is executed immediately after the disaster occurs and details what steps are to be taken in order to recover critical information technology infrastructure. Disaster recovery planning includes establishing a planning group, performing risk assessment, establishing priorities, developing recovery strategies, preparing inventories and documentation of the plan, developing verification criteria and procedure, and lastly implementing the plan.

5.3 The FCA Requirements for Business Continuity and Incident Response

The FCA *Business Continuity Management Practice Guide* aims to help regulated firms in their business continuity planning by identifying and sharing examples of business continuity practice observed in firms that participated in a benchmarking exercise. Examples of observed practice are grouped by topic and organised by theme into modules:

- Corporate Continuity
- Corporate Crisis Management
- Corporate Systems
- Corporate Facilities
- Corporate People.

The Guide can be obtained at www.fsa.gov.uk/pubs/other/bcm_guide.pdf. In effect, it is a checklist of actions and considerations for BCP that could conceivably be used to support planning and design or audit.

Firms are encouraged to take a risk-based approach, adopting a pragmatic and sensible view of which aspects of the Guide are most useful and relevant for them by:

- Mixing and matching standards and best practices in order to deal with their own specific circumstances and risks.
- Exercising common sense when deciding which aspects of the Guide are most relevant to them.
- Adopting more sophisticated arrangements than the examples provided in the Guide, when appropriate.

Therefore, the Guide does not form part of the FCA's formal rules and guidance and is designed to provide a useful basis around which firms and their supervisors can structure their discussions in order to create proportionate responses to the challenge of BCP.

6.   Password Security

Learning Objective

5.6.1   Understand the importance and impact of password security: the role of hashing and the 'reversing' of hashes using online resources; the hacking of password databases; the ease of finding stolen credentials online; dictionary attacks on hashed password tables; longer hashes, Salts, Peppers and encryption: protecting the password management process more effectively; Password Managers and other authentication options that replace or augment password-based solutions

What is the most common password in the world? Some claim it is 'password', others say '1234' or 'qwerty'. It does not really matter who is correct, the point such commentators are trying to make is that it can be easy to guess passwords. The implication is that a lot of financial crimes occur as a result.

But while some crimes might occur for that reason, this is not the main problem with passwords. After all, even if a password could be guessed, it would still require knowing the username and possibly other information about the account holder before hacking into an online account. It might even require using the account holder's device.

The real problem with passwords today is not how users create them; it's how organisations process and store them. The clear majority of password breaches occur because large databases are hacked, and their contents can be read or deciphered. The biggest such hack to date was Yahoo's loss of three billion usernames and passwords, but new examples emerge almost daily, all around the planet.

So, why does it matter if a database is hacked? It is all encrypted and secure, right? Wrong. Surprisingly few large datasets are truly secure. Sometimes, this is down to system administrators not knowing the vulnerabilities in their password management techniques. Take hashing for example.

Most password databases employ hashing; they convert users' passwords to a mathematical expression that describes the unique shape of the password, but conceals the actual password. The hash of the password 'Password1234', using the MD5 hashing algorithm is always going to be ef749ff9a048bad0dd80807fc49e1c0d. You can try this yourself here: tools4noobs.com/online_tools/hash/ (as with any external link, we cannot accept responsibility for any issues you encounter). However, as long as you select MD5, and enter the password exactly as it is presented here, you will get the same hash and that is what will be stored in the database holding your user details.

So, here is the problem. If anyone can calculate the hash of any password, then no password hash is safe. If your database could be seen because someone works on it, or you lost a copy, or it has been hacked and posted online, then the hashes of the most common passwords could be searched to discover if anyone has used them.

Worse, if someone runs out of ideas for common passwords and their hashes, there are websites that have already calculated billions of potential passwords and their hashes. Hashkiller.co.uk holds 829 billion precalculated password hashes. All a hacker needs to do is to paste the hashes from a database into the site and the corresponding passwords, assuming they are on the list of 829 billion, will be displayed. Free of charge, no questions asked.

Either users need to come up with passwords that are not featured on that list of 829 billion possibilities, which can be difficult, or additional security methods are required to hide the hashes from hackers. One option is encryption of the database, as outlined in section 7. Another is to create stronger passwords for users by secretly adding something to them in the database before they are hashed. This is called adding a 'salt', and you can experiment with that here: online-code-generator.com/md5-hash-with-optional-salt.php.

Some companies go farther than this, adding a 'pepper' (essentially a second salt) and using combinations of hashing algorithms to create a greater challenge, but the bottom line is really that the username and password model is now outdated. Multi-factor authentication is required, and even the use of databases to store sensitive customer data is questionable; there are increasingly effective tokenisation solutions on the market that de-risk data storage significantly. These are both optional advanced topics for further reading, although they are outside the scope of this text.

7. Encryption

Learning Objective

5.7.1   Know the fundamentals of encryption: substitution and transposition explained; a short history of encryption, from the Caesar Code to RSA; symmetric encryption explained; prime numbers, semi-primes, the factorisation challenge and asymmetric encryption demystified; ephemeral keys and modern encrypted messaging apps

Encryption is the science of converting plain text, like the text you are reading now, into cipher text and back again via decryption. Here is the encrypted form of the previous sentence using the DES encryption algorithm:

AbzDv7w/dQfnlhXKC8H6+6Dlb++OEBMqMP7bDLWmhvnYM3w3ZQub6Ykk3i15h5OTMQPY2Dr42KU1gA5mcF
guflZxH8cMfOxG3a8nAhqLSdjqwld9AvhwTeZzLyFko8Q9g0wA2F02uREDiEphzQ8Mfll75bSkr0QqBbRnvTODadN
+DVDDlwSWCg==

You can play around with some of the most famous algorithms at tools4noobs.com/online_tools/ encrypt/

Encryption has a long history, going all the way back to Roman times and beyond. The earliest encryption technique is known as the Caesar Cipher. Though simple, it was effective in its day.

The Caesar Cipher involves moving the letters of the alphabet a certain number of places and replacing the letters in a message with the new letters, as shown below:

CDEFGHIJKLMNOPQRSTUVWXYZAB

ABCDEFGHIJKLMNOPQRSTUVWXYZ

Here, the letters have been moved two places to the right, so the encryption KEY is the value 2. If someone wants to send or store the word 'password' using this method, they would have to write it as 'rcuuzqtf'; p=r, a=c etc.

Most forms of historical encryption involved substitution and transposition; substituting one value with another, as above, and then moving the results around to further confuse the picture. However, as modern computers evolved, it became increasingly easy to try all possible moves to reverse the process and come up with readable text.

Enter modern methods such as Data Encryption Standard (DES) and RSA, which is named after its creators, Rivest, Shamir and Adleman. The concept of RSA encryption involves complex algorithms, but at the heart of the system there is a relatively simple concept; very big numbers are hard to factorise.

Although RSA uses prime numbers to produce semi-primes (a semi-prime is the product of two primes), you do not need to be an expert mathematician to grasp the fundamental idea.

If you were told that the secret answer to a question was equivalent to the factors of 15, in whole numbers only, you would probably come up with the response 5x3 or 3x5 quite quickly. No other pair of whole numbers can be multiplied together to produce 15. (By the way, 3 and 5 are prime numbers – they can only be divided by themselves and 1 – so 15 is an example of a semi-prime).

Now, if you were asked the same question in response to the number 15226050279225333360535618378 13263742971806811496138068865790849458012296325895289765400035069200613·9, it might take you a while to work out the answer. In fact, it would take your computer a long time indeed to examine all the possible factors and rule them out. The factors of this large number, known as RSA 100, are:

*   37975227936943673922808872755445627854565536638199, and
*   40094690950920881030683735292761468389214899724061

Without going deeper into how advanced encryption works today, let us just keep this factorisation challenge in mind and remember that this forms a major part of the calculations used to encrypt and decrypt plain and cipher text.

The phrases symmetric and asymmetric encryption are often encountered. Simply put, symmetric encryption occurs when each party, sender and receiver, shares the same secret key for encrypting and decrypting the message. The Caesar Cipher is a symmetric encryption cipher; in the example given, each party uses the secret key '2'.

Asymmetric encryption involves the parties having different keys for encrypting and decrypting messages. RSA is the best known example of this, and it lends itself to being used for authentication in the context of public key infrastructure or PKI; anyone can encrypt messages when they want to log-on to their bank website, for example, but only the bank knows how to decrypt what has been sent. This makes it easier for the bank to manage its customer access, while the fact that they have been able to read and respond authenticates the bank to its users.

'Ephemeral' encryption keys are another important concept widely employed in modern encrypted messaging apps. Keys are stored on a 'key chain' and only used once before being deleted and replaced by the next key in the chain. WhatsApp uses this technique, much to the frustration of law enforcement officers who want to see the messages being sent by known criminals. Each message in a WhatsApp conversation is encrypted with a different key.

We can expect challenges to today's encryption methods once quantum computing comes of age (quantum computers are expected to be able to crack the factorisation challenge), but until then, the use of readily available encryption techniques remains the best way to secure data.

End of Chapter Questions

Think of an answer for each question and refer to the appropriate section for confirmation

1. What is a cyber or information security control?
    Answer reference: Section 1.1

2. What is the purpose of anti-malware applications?
    Answer reference: Section 1.1

3. Where in a typical organisation does ultimate responsibility for governance rest?
    Answer reference: Section 1.2

4. List five common impacts of cyber-security breaches on a firm.
    Answer reference: Section 1.3.4

5. List the five categories of control.
    Answer reference: Section 1.4.1

6. What is the principle of least privilege?
    Answer reference: Section 1.4.3

7. What are the two main steps in an encrypted communications session?
    Answer reference: Section 1.4.7

8. List three of the possible factors of authentication.
    Answer reference: Section 1.4.9

9. What are the main cyber-security issues facing procurement?
    Answer reference: Section 2.3

10. What is volumetric analysis in relation to cyber-security controls?
    Answer reference: Section 3.2.3

11. List three parameters of the desired cyber-security end state.
    Answer reference: Section 3.3.6

12. What is an event in the context of cyber-security incident management?
    Answer reference: Section 4.1.1

Chapter Six
Trends in Economic Crime Compliance

1.	Emerging Threats	227
2.	Ethical Issues	236

This syllabus area will provide approximately 8 of the 50 examination questions

6

We already have the statistics for the future: the growth percentages of pollution, overpopulation, and desertification. The future is already in place. Günter Grass

This chapter examines emerging cyber-security threats, based on past experience of risk, but the learning objectives all relate to existing technologies and services.

1.   Emerging Threats

Learning Objective

6.1.1   Know the key sources of information on emerging vulnerabilities

6.1.2   Know the concept of the internet of things (IOT), the smart home and office, Mirai and related threats/solutions

6.1.3   Understand the evolution and use of big data analytics

6.1.4   Know the specific threats relating to cryptocurrencies such as Bitcoin

6.1.5   Know the specific threats relating to unregulated payment models

6.1.6   Know the specific threats relating to mobile payment devices

6.1.7   Know the specific threats relating to cloud computing

6.1.8   Know the specific risks relating to co-location

6.1.9   Know the purpose and limitations of risk avoidance through cybercrime insurance policies

1.1   The Internet of Things (IoT)

The phrase '**internet of things**' (IoT) refers to the ongoing development of the internet towards a state in which everyday objects are connected online, allowing them to send and receive data and even to make financial payments without human intervention.

The first internet-connected appliance was a Coca-Cola machine installed at Carnegie Mellon University in 1982. It reported statistics, on soft drink stock levels and temperatures, to a management system. By the late 1980s several other classes of connected device were performing similar tasks. One example was a payphone network in which phones that accepted prepaid cards were connected to a centralised management system and were able to report levels of usage and even to provide alerts on faults and errors.

This space is growing at a rapid rate. The author conducted a quick review of his IoT devices at home and came up with the following list:

*   three laptops
*   one PC
*   three mobiles phones
*   one tablet

- one Xbox
- one Smart TV
- one printer
- one CCTV camera
- one ring doorbell
- one security system
- one in-car GPS
- one WiFi router
- one Amazon Echo hub
- one MiFi dongle.

Most of these devices hold some form of sensitive data, including WiFi codes, email addresses and passwords. If the devices are stolen, lost, hacked or simply disposed of carelessly, that data can be exploited by criminals.

The Mirai botnet attacks involved the use of smart devices, including fridges and WiFi cameras, to send out spam and conduct DDoS attacks. Because smart devices are less likely to complain about issues than a user with a slow laptop might be, they represent an increasingly attractive target to hackers of all stripes.

We can see that if there is one thing that can prevent the IoT from transforming the way we live and work, it will be a breakdown in security. The open question remains whether machines will be inherently more secure or less secure than human beings are when active online.

As today's consumers shift towards internet-connected and wearable technology, the need for improved security and a global set of standards in this class of device will become ever more pressing. Not only are traditional data sets, such as personal and financial information already stored on and transmitted by these devices (think mobile phone data being synched with an internet-connected car), but details of current locations and even biometric data such as heart rate and body temperature are collected in bulk, stored and delivered across the internet by these systems. In the modern high-tech world, things move quickly, and innovation often trumps privacy.

An endless multitude of different types of device...

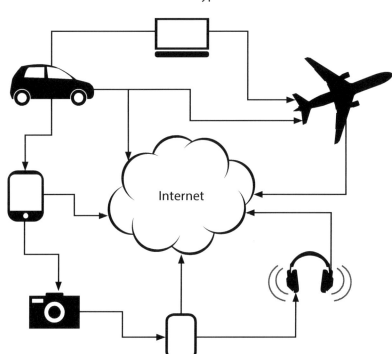

...all interconnected and sharing data online.

Figure 27: The Internet of Things

1.1.1 Diversity of Threats

The IoT already includes a very wide range of devices, including digital home thermostats, smart TVs, car systems (such as navigation, entertainment and engine management computers), networking devices, smart watches, activity trackers and even kettles, toasters and fridges.

The diversity of threats mirrors the diversity of devices and there have already been a number of exploratory attacks on a range of IoT devices. There are even reports of security experts successfully hacking into the engine management and braking systems of interconnected cars, and the communications systems of commercial aircraft in flight via the in-flight entertainment platform. While some of these attacks are admittedly not conducted via the internet, ongoing increases in connectivity suggest that it is only a matter of time before this also happens.

As the market for IoT devices has evolved, it has also become highly fragmented. There is consequently a rich and diverse offering of low-cost hardware platforms and operating systems. Some attacks are already capable of exploiting vulnerabilities in IoT systems and routers and, in one recent case, over 100,000 IoT devices were hacked and used to send out spam emails. If previous trends hold true, we can expect to see attackers focusing on the market leaders, with the most popular devices also being the most popular targets.

1.1.2   Wearable Devices

Wearable fitness and personal health devices will be a $5 billion market by the end of 2016, according to the well-known consulting firm, Gartner. Devices that measure our steps, blood pressure, heart rate and other medical data and then store the results online or locally on the device itself are already available. With more and more devices of this nature coming to market, the security and privacy implications are clear.

In a 2014 Symantec review of 100 health apps in app stores, 20% of the apps were found to transmit user credentials without encrypting them and more than half did not have any privacy policies. On average, each app sends data to five distinct internet domains which serve up a mix of advertising and analytics services. Similarly, security firms have repeatedly demonstrated vulnerabilities in a number of IoT devices, including an internet-connected kettle that could be hacked in order to steal the owner's WiFi password.

Two implications of this trend are the obvious threat to privacy and the potential for insurers to mine this new dataset in order to adjust their premiums, for example, by tracking motor vehicle journeys and speeds. This latter scenario illustrates the relationship between the IoT and the burgeoning **big data** market.

1.1.3   Big Data

Big data refers to large volumes of data that are collected from several sources and then combined and enriched in order to add value. An example is data on millions of consumers' online browsing habits, combined with their geolocation data, to reveal where they are when they purchase specific items.

Few people comprehend just how high the big data mountain has become. When on the internet, users see only the tip of the iceberg. Organisations like Facebook run their own massive data storage repositories at sites around the planet in buildings larger than football stadiums, sucking up vast amounts of power and other resources and holding, in the case of Facebook, a data mountain that is growing by one petabyte every four days. To give the reader some idea of what this means, one petabyte of data is the equivalent of 13.5 years of high definition (HD) video. Google's data store is several times larger.

A significant percentage of mobile apps now collect and then send personally identifiable information to app developers. Consumers are their own worst enemies when it comes to mobile privacy because they actually provide consent for these apps to access their data, even when there is no obvious reason why the application in question needs to know your location, access your photos or extract the details of your contacts. Of the apps examined by Norton Mobile Insight, 22% were found to track users' location information. In fact, according to another Symantec survey, 68% of people will willingly trade their privacy for a free app.

The global community is therefore investing huge sums in storing incredible amounts of digital data, most of which has no economic or business value and much of which will never be accessed even by the people who created it. 2015 was the year in which we started working with zettabytes of data (1ZB equates to 36 million years of HD video!) and it may well be time for the globalisation of data protection laws.

Bulk data collection is not only the domain of corporate firms like Google and Facebook. In 2015, the UK government started the wholesale reform of surveillance law in the guise of the Investigatory Powers Act, which they hoped to see passed by 2017. This covers various kinds of data acquisition and retention.

After two years of intense scrutiny by courts and committees, Britain's legal framework for surveillance had been found wanting and a decision to overhaul surveillance law, rather than simply extend existing powers, indicated that the government was taking heed of some of the criticism it had received.

Other voices contended that the Investigatory Powers Act could well turn out to be the UK government's attempt to correct the technical legal failings of the existing framework, insulating it from criticism by the European Court of Human Rights, while giving it more invasive surveillance powers than it already has. This is a story that continues to unfold, and, in April 2018 the UK High Court handed down a ruling that gave the Government six months to rewrite the Act.

1.1.4   Useful Sources of information on New and Emerging Threats

While there is no single source of reliable information about emerging cyber-security threats, the following sites provide frequent and valuable updates, as well as best practice guidance:

- www.enisa.europa.eu
- www.gov.uk/government/publications/cyber-essentials-scheme-overview
- www.symantec.com/en/uk/security_response/publications/threatreport.jsp
- www.securityweek.com/cybercrime
- www.theregister.co.uk/security

1.2   Cryptocurrency Risks

As we have seen in chapter 1, a cryptocurrency (Bitcoin being the best-known example) is a digital or virtual currency that uses cryptography as a security measure. This use of encryption makes the currency extremely difficult to counterfeit.

This type of currency is not issued or backed by a central authority, such as a central bank, which means it is untouched by the government and is therefore not currently subject to most financial regulation and supervision. There is also no consumer protection provided.

Because of the anonymity granted to users, the cryptocurrency model is widely exploited in money laundering, sanctions breaching and tax-evasion schemes and it is also very popular with organised crime and on black market Darknet sites dealing in illegal items or services.

Bitcoin was the first cryptocurrency to be made available to the public in 2009, but other **cryptocurrencies** are available, including:

- Litecoin
- Namecoin
- PPCoin (also known as Peercoin).

Despite the risks and the widespread use of these payment mechanisms by criminals, cryptocurrency transactions are growing in popularity, partly because of their lower transaction fees.

1.2.1   Cyber-Hawala

Hawala is a traditional payment system that is operated outside the banking system, going back as far as the Middle Ages. It refers to the transfer of money by trusted brokers without any actual movement of funds. Hawaladars, the middlemen who manage the payments, tend to be known to one another. The system is used extensively in Hindu and Islamic cultures.

Cyber-Hawala refers to a money transfer that takes place via the internet, also through a trusted broker. One popular site providing the service is www.webmoney.ru which is reported to have over 15 million users.

Once again, these unregulated and unsecured transactions are not subject to monitoring and can be used for all manner of illegal activities to avoid surveillance and taxation.

1.3   Mobile Payment Risks

Symantec expects the growth in mobile malware to continue, becoming more aggressive in targeting users' financial assets. Already 51% of US adults bank online and 35% use mobile phones to handle transactions. This has created a strong incentive for malware writers to target mobile handsets in order to capture bank details.

There is already malware that can intercept SMS messages containing authentication codes from a bank and forward them to attackers. Fake versions of legitimate banks' mobile applications also exist, designed to trick users into exposing their account details.

1.3.1   Short Message Service (SMS) Mobile Risks

The emergence of cheaper and more accessible technologies and communication channels attracts malicious activity of all sorts. The shift from desktop PCs to mobile devices as the primary computing device is a good example of this trend. As we place greater reliance on our mobile devices, spam, scams and threats are increasingly directed at these devices.

SMS is in fact a mature technology but there has been significant growth in its use as a tool to facilitate transactions and authentication and therefore as a target for attackers. SMS and other mobile messaging technologies are being extensively used to deliver all manner of exploits and unwanted content, ranging from adult content to rogue pharmaceuticals, phishing attacks, banking frauds, and even payday loan spam.

SMS fraudsters offer fictitious items for sale, or jobs and houses for rent, then continue to interact with potential victims by SMS, before switching to email. They then use traditional fraud techniques to extract funds from their victims.

Another variation leads online dating users to websites that charge for a premium adult subscription by sending SMS messages that may be charged at as much as £10.00 per message. All these messages do is to confirm sign up for the supposedly free service.

1.3.2 SMS as a Malware Route

There is also a continually evolving malware landscape in which SMS has been seen as an infection and propagation route for many **Trojans**, worms and another malicious agents. There are cases of malicious apps spreading via SMS to infect new victims by using the contact list on the infected device.

The messages often look legitimate but contain links to download sites for malicious applications. Once again, these infections are monetised by getting users to unwittingly sign up for premium services or by sending them expensive SMS confirmation messages and subscriptions.

Because attackers focus on using dating sites and pornography as a lure, only a very small proportion of those falling victim to such attacks ever lodge a formal complaint with the service provider or with the police. Consequently, this is a hidden crime, the true extent of which is largely unknown. The underlying delivery technology is irrelevant. Scams of this nature feed on human vulnerabilities and ignorance and they will continue to be carried out via whatever future communications technology dominates.

1.4 Cloud Computing Risks

To further complicate an already fragmented picture, we have wide diversity in the way in which information assets are distributed around the planet. Organisations and individuals often store much of their data in the cloud, whether through consumer services like Dropbox or via corporate cloud hosting. The ubiquitous use of mobile devices means that much of our data travels with us rather than remaining in the office where it used to sit. Remote working, along with the outsourcing of many operational functions, means that even if the data does reside on a stationary platform or in a database, that platform or database is far removed from the owner of the data who nevertheless retains responsibility and accountability for its security and reliability.

Although the cloud has now been around for several years, few outside the technical sphere have more than a vague awareness of what it is and how dependent they are on it. The problem is partly in the name, because the very word implies some kind of fuzzy, esoteric and other-worldly environment in which miracles are performed by IT high priests without the benefit of computing hardware, cables or power supply!

An August 2012 survey commissioned by Citrix produced some amusing but also worrying outputs: worrying at least to anyone hoping to engage in informed debate with users about cloud risks and security:

- 95% of respondents who claimed that they never use the cloud actually already do so via various social media and online commerce applications
- 22% admitted that they only pretend to know what the cloud is
- 25% regard the cloud as a good place to keep controversial material, such as pornography, instead of on their hard drives.

In a democratised global computing environment where every single user is his or her own procurement manager, system administrator and security analyst all rolled into one, such a fundamental lack of awareness about a critical technology is dangerous. No doubt, some senior decision-makers have only marginally better levels of understanding and this does not bode well for effective governance and control.

The cloud is simply a collection of computing and storage devices hosted remotely on the internet, usually in vast data centres that have nothing cloudy about them at all. Because these are just computing devices, there is nothing really special about either the risks they are exposed to or the controls that need to be put in place.

The CSA publishes a regular list of the top cloud threats. Table 6.1 shows a summarised version of their listing, ranked in order of severity, which reinforces the point.

Table 6.1 Cloud security risks, as scored by the Cloud Security Alliance, 2016

The Treacherous 12 – Cloud Computing Top Threats in 2016*	
1	Data Breaches
2	Weak Identity, Credential and Access Management
3	Insecure APIs
4	System and Application Vulnerabilities
5	Account Hijacking
6	Malicious Insiders
7	Advanced Persistent Threats (APTs)
8	Data Loss
9	Insufficient Due Diligence
10	Abuse and Nefarious Use of Cloud Services
11	Denial of Service
12	Shared Technology Issues

As perceived by the companies surveyed.

Another information security challenge is that of cloud sprawl. This refers to the often uncontrolled manner in which cloud usage can spread from what was originally intended, as users make their own decisions about when, where and how to use the cloud, often without the knowledge and approval of IT. One survey of business unit leaders and IT decision-makers in 18 countries reported the following statistics related to cloud sprawl:

- 20% of corporate employees have provisioned a cloud service for work purposes without the approval of IT
- 61% stated that self-provisioning was easier than going through IT
- 29% said that there were no ramifications at all and 48% said that they only received a warning.

The likely end-product of such a change is the widespread and undocumented distribution of information assets and the exposure of the data controller to regulatory action, should a data breach occur.

However, merely enforcing policies more rigorously ignores the human factors behind risk, for example the fact that making things easier is a primary concern to users. The starting point for organisational risk control, therefore, is to find out what users and customers want and to balance this with what regulators want and what good governance dictates. If provisioning a cloud service quickly and easily via IT is problematic, then the problem is not the users or the cloud, but rather the IT itself.

1.5   Co-location Risks

Co-location involves a service provider or organisation renting space at a shared data centre facility for computing hardware. Co-location delivers services such as cooling, power, bandwidth and physical security and, in turn, the customer provides servers and storing capabilities.

The space is rented by rack, cabinet, secure cage or even by room. Co-location can offer extra features such as managed services that are in line with the customers' business requirements. A further advantage of having a co-location arrangement is a reduction in capital expenditures because there is no need to establish an in-house computer facility.

There is a potential downside to co-location – the risk of being jointly tenanted with an undesirable third party. For example, ABC bank may not wish to have its servers sitting in the same rack as those belonging to competing XYZ bank. Establishing who the joint tenants might be and excluding undesirable joint tenants is therefore one essential security measure.

1.6   Cybercrime Insurance Policies

Cyber-liability insurance cover (CLIC) has been available for almost a decade, although few security professionals seem to be aware of it and only 10% of UK firms are actually covered. Policies can provide cover to firms in the event of an incident. They may also encourage best practice when insurers offer lower premiums to reflect higher levels of cyber-security.

This type of product has been much more successful in the US, where there is already a mandatory data breach notification requirement in effect in 46 of the 50 states. Data breach notification can be one of the most expensive consequences of a cyber-security breach and this has driven firms to purchase policies to cover them in such an eventuality.

1.6.1   Types of Cover

CLIC is often used to describe a wide range of covers, just as cyber is used to describe a broad range of information security-related tools, processes and services:

- Data breach/privacy crisis management cover for costs related to incident management and investigation, remediation, data subject notification, call management, credit checking for data subjects, legal fees, court attendance and regulatory penalties.
- Multimedia/media liability cover addressing the defacement of websites, as well as intellectual property rights infringements.
- Extortion liability cover for instances of crypto-extortion and any professional fees relating to extortion attack, for example technical services to decrypt the lost data.
- Network security liability to cover third-party costs resulting from denial of service attacks, or costs related to the theft of data stored on third-party systems and cloud servers.

Some elements of a cyber-insurance policy are likely to overlap with cover from other insurance products, specifically those addressing business continuity, third-party supply chain issues and professional indemnity.

1.6.2 Insurance Does Not Cover Everything

Cyber-insurance is not the proverbial silver bullet; it is not a fix for all risk issues. Whether we are protecting ourselves in terms of physical property, general liability or cyber-security risks, neither risk management nor insurance work in isolation, nor does one substitute for the other. Insurance represents just one more line of defence, part of a complex set of layered controls and countermeasures.

Critics of the rapidly growing cyber-insurance market point out that cyber-insurance may not adequately take into account the hidden losses caused by a cyber-attack, particularly intangibles such as brand damage and loss of trust which they say often have the greatest impact. Their argument is that insurance can only ever cover a fraction of the real cost of a major cyber-security incident.

2. Ethical Issues

Cyber-security and cyber-operations in general are not purely technical issues. Fair and ethical practices also play a part in reducing risk and protecting organisations and employees.

Learning Objective

6.2.1 Understand how the use of big data relates to FCA financial promotion rules and treating customers fairly (TCF): consent

6.2.2 Understand the concept of ethical search engine optimisation

6.2.3 Know the concept of a fair usage policy

6.2.4 Know the concept of good online practice

6.2.5 Understand the balance between employee monitoring and employee privacy: the implications of Californian Law A.B. 1844

2.1 Financial Conduct Authority (FCA) Financial Promotion Rules

According to the FCA, financial promotion is *a communication that is an invitation or an inducement to engage in investment activity*. The FCA's financial promotion rules refer to promotions and communications that are directed at consumers in the UK, which are issued by FCA-regulated firms or representatives.

In other words, there is an element of persuasion, the FCA explains. An inducement is an action that is intended to lead ultimately to an agreement to engage in investment activity. So, an advertisement by a firm claiming that customers will make a fortune by investing in securities and that the firm can help them to invest, is an invitation or inducement to engage in investment activity.

Financial promotions of this kind can be communicated through a number of means, such as:

*   product brochures
*   general advertising in magazines, newspapers, radio, TV and websites
*   mailshots
*   written correspondence
*   sales aids.

However, the FCA's financial promotion rules apply across all media, both existing and future. When deciding whether a communication is a financial promotion, the FCA looks at whether it is an *invitation or inducement to engage in investment activity*, not at the media used to communicate it. The rules also extend to cover non-promotional communications. Effectively, therefore, all communications with clients are governed by these rules, including all forms of electronic or online communication.

The focus of the financial promotion rules is misleading advertising and the FCA currently covers the following domains in this regard:

*   savings
*   banking
*   investments
*   insurance
*   mortgage
*   credit cards
*   store cards
*   loans
*   debt management
*   hire purchase
*   credit broking.

Any person or organisation that believes itself to have been the target of misleading advertising in relation to any of the domains listed above may lodge a complaint with the FCA.

2.2   Treating Customers Fairly (TCF)

The FCA has developed the TCF rules in order to ensure that regulated firms provide customers with a full explanation of particular structures, benefits, risks and expenses of any products being purchased. The aim is to decrease the scale of inappropriate products in the wake of many failings over recent years.

The FCA encourages the management teams of regulated firms to consider the following questions in order to ensure that they are in a position to deliver the desired TCF outcomes:

Leadership

- How do you champion the fair treatment of customers to your staff and ensure that it is integral to the way your firm carries out its day-to-day business?
- How do you manage and control your business?
- How do you ensure your recruitment and reward structures complement and support your firm's values?
- How do you educate and train your advisers, sales staff and other customer-facing staff to ensure that your customers achieve a fair deal?
- How do you measure performance and service standards?

Dealing with Customers

- How do you ensure you provide your customers with clear information and/or suitable advice before, during and after sale?
- How do you ensure you deal with complaints fairly and that lessons are learned to ensure you can try to avoid those problems in future?

The FCA describes six desired consumer outcomes from the employment of the TCF principles:

- **Outcome 1** – Consumers can be confident that they are dealing with firms where the fair treatment of customers is central to the corporate culture.
- **Outcome 2** – Products and services marketed and sold in the retail market are designed to meet the needs of identified consumer groups and are targeted accordingly.
- **Outcome 3** – Consumers are provided with clear information and are kept appropriately informed before, during and after the point of sale.
- **Outcome 4** – If consumers receive advice, the advice is suitable and takes account of their circumstances.
- **Outcome 5** – Consumers are provided with products that perform as firms have led them to expect and the associated service is of an acceptable standard and as they have been led to expect.
- **Outcome 6** – Consumers do not face unreasonable post-sale barriers imposed by firms to change product, switch provider, submit a claim or make a complaint.

Firms are expected to make proper use of management information systems in order to monitor the six outcomes in relation to all clients.

Fair treatment of clients of all types must be a priority for firms. The services and products advertised and sold in the retail market should therefore be designed to genuinely match consumers' requirements. Complete and accurate information must also be passed to clients who must be kept informed throughout the whole sale process and advice must be targeted correctly, taking into consideration the consumer's desires.

2.2.1 Consent

Consent is of particular relevance in the big data market and new EU data protection laws stipulate increasingly firm requirements in this regard.

The UK Information Commissioner's Office provides the following interpretation:

The GDPR sets a high standard for consent. Consent means offering people genuine choice and control over how you use their data. When consent is used properly, it helps you build trust and enhance your reputation.

Consent is defined in Article 4(11) of the GDPR as:

Any freely given, specific, informed and unambiguous indication of the data subject's wishes by which he or she, by a statement or by a clear affirmative action, signifies agreement to the processing of personal data relating to him or her.

Article 7 also sets out further 'conditions' for consent, with specific provisions on:

- keeping records to demonstrate consent
- prominence and clarity of consent requests
- the right to withdraw consent easily and at any time, and
- freely given consent if a contract is conditional on consent.

2.3 Californian Law A.B. 1844 and the Implications for Employee Monitoring and Privacy

It has long been common practice in the United States that employers would claim the right to access the social media accounts of candidates for employment. Many employers would insist that candidates surrender their usernames and profiles to them in order that they examine the contents of their social media pages for evidence of dubious activities or connections.

While this continues in many states, in 2012, California introduced a law which prohibits employers from requiring (or requesting) employees or applicants to divulge their social media login information. Other conduct likely to be prohibited under the new law may include requesting that an applicant or employee add the employer as a 'friend', thereby giving the employer access to information not otherwise publicly available.

The law does not explicitly restrict employers from accessing publicly available information. However, employers should still be cautious in conducting online searches. Such searches often uncover information that employers cannot lawfully use to make hiring decisions, such as the candidate's religious denomination or sexual orientation.

While an employer in California may not request or require an applicant or existing employee to divulge his/her personal social media, the law is silent on whether an employer can use private social media information volunteered by an existing employee who is 'friends' with the applicant or employee.

While this law only applies in a distant jurisdiction, one should not forget that California has one of the world's largest economies, larger than most sovereign nations, and that it has long been a trendsetter in terms of many aspects of legislation, economics and culture. Organisations' employee monitoring outside California should take the thinking of this state into consideration when developing their own policies.

2.4   Ethical Search Engine Optimisation (SEO)

Search engine optimisation (SEO) is a commonly used term to refer to enhancements to the marketing power of websites. In general terms, search engines rank sites on the basis of their popularity, normally measured by the number of visits they receive. The higher up the search results page a website appears (its ranking), the more likely it is to receive additional visitors.

Companies for whom sales and marketing through the web are critical components of the business strategy therefore have an extremely strong motivation to optimise their pages in order to improve their ranking. Some of these techniques are regarded as ethical while others are clearly unethical.

2.4.1   Ethical SEO

SEO considers how search engines work, what people search for, the actual search terms or keywords typed into search engines and which search engines are preferred by their targeted audience. Optimising a website may involve editing its content, hypertext markup language (HTML) and associated coding both to increase its relevance to specific keywords and to remove barriers to the indexing activities of search engines. Promoting a site to increase the number of backlinks, or inbound links, is another SEO tactic.

An individual or organisation engaged in ethical SEO will, for example, only include keywords on the page that actually relate to the business of the organisation and information displayed on the webpage.

2.4.2   Unethical SEO

Black hat (or unethical SEO) occurs when those attempting to optimise their website use various dubious techniques to attract visitors who would not otherwise come to the page. A simple example is the inclusion of search terms or keywords in the metadata on the page that are commonly searched for but which have no relevance to the page in question. For example, if a motor vehicle dealer put keywords on his page like 'sexy girls', 'birthday cakes', and 'free flights', while offering none of these services to the public, that would constitute unethical SEO.

Search engines also examine the content of pages and unethical administrators sometimes engage in 'keyword stuffing' (filling their pages with the same keywords repeatedly in order to achieve a higher score).

Another common unethical practice is to initially create a website with very popular content, for example based on providing images and updates about a high-profile celebrity and then changing the content of the page after it has achieved a high ranking with search engines.

2.5   Fair Usage Policies

Fair usage policies were first introduced by telephony providers to provide a contractual basis for responding to excessive use of data by subscribers on fixed-price plans. For example, a subscriber might purchase an all-you-can-eat data package with the provider, who anticipates that the subscriber will have a usage pattern which conforms to norms across the network. However, that subscriber might then engage in downloading videos 24 hours a day, seven days a week, far exceeding their expected level of usage.

240

In the early days of mobile data and of internet in the home, suppliers were often caught by surprise by this type of behaviour which ate into much of the bandwidth of more reasonable users' desired consumption. Unreasonable usage therefore has a serious impact on quality of service.

Many of today's unlimited broadband plans on offer actually have a fair usage or traffic management policy in force, which imposes limits on download volumes or throttles download speeds in order to provide a reasonable level of service to other users nearby.

Common examples of user profiles that exhibit excessive download volumes include:

- users of peer-to-peer networks who upload and download lots of films and music
- online gamers
- people working from home and remotely connecting to the office.

Most broadband connections in the UK have a connection ratio of 50 users to 1 broadband circuit. Restricting or throttling the usage of one person who is using their limited bandwidth excessively is the industry's best effort to provide high-quality service to all.

2.6   Good Online Practices

This workbook contains a great deal about cyber and information security, addressing many of the risks and security practices that corporations should apply. At the end of the day, much of the responsibility for cyber-security rests with the individual user. Here is a top ten list of the things every user can do to improve both personal and organisational cyber-security:

1. If you operate in a username and password environment, make sure that you use cryptic passwords that cannot be easily guessed and that you do not share your passwords or write them down.
2. Beware of phishing scams and potentially malicious links to webpages with which you are unfamiliar.
3. Do not enter personal information online unless you are very sure about the webpage you are using and the security of your connection.
4. Physically secure your work areas and your devices, both in the office and at home.
5. Secure your laptop, tablet and other mobile devices at all times when they are not in use.
6. Always shut down or log off from your devices before leaving them unattended.
7. Make sure that your computer and other devices have reputable and up-to-date anti-malware software installed.
8. Do not keep highly sensitive information on mobile devices or on removable media such as USB drives, unless the device and the information it contains is encrypted.
9. Do not install unsolicited software applications on any device.
10. Make regular backups of all important files or data that you can't afford to lose, unless this is being done for you automatically by your employer or administrator.

End of Chapter Questions

Think of an answer for each question and refer to the appropriate section for confirmation.

1.   What is the common meaning of IoT?
     Answer reference: Section 1.1

2.   What is big data?
     Answer reference: Section 1.1.3

3.   What is a cryptocurrency?
     Answer reference: Section 1.2

4.   What is the cloud?
     Answer reference: Section 1.4

5.   List five cloud risks.
     Answer reference: Section 1.4

6.   List two types of cyber-security insurance cover.
     Answer reference: Section 1.6.1

7.   What is a financial promotion as defined by the FCA?
     Answer reference: Section 2.1

Glossary

Access Control

The process of limiting access to those who are authorised to use facilities, information or systems.

Advanced Persistent Threat (APT)

A form of sophisticated cyber-attack normally directed at businesses and political targets.

Application Program Interfaces (API)

A set of routines, protocols, and tools for building software applications.

Authentication

Processes for validating the identity of a user, employee or visitor to a site, system or information resource.

Authorisation

The granting of authority to a user to access specific tools and information resources.

Bespoke Capabilities

Attack capabilities developed for a specific purpose, for example to attack a particular target.

Big Data

Large volumes of data collected from several sources and then combined and enriched in order to add value.

Bitcoin

A peer-to-peer electronic monetary system based on cryptography.

Black Hat SEO

An unethical search engine optimisation (SEO) technique used to attract people to visit a website they would not otherwise visit.

Blackhole Exploit Kit

One of the most popular and effective cyber-attack toolsets.

Blended Attacks

Combining elements of multiple types of malware or other attack tools.

Botnet

A network of infected computers or mobile devices remotely controlled by an attacker.

Brute Force Attack

An attack designed to obtain a user's login details by trying lists of possible combinations.

Business Continuity

The mechanism by which an organisation continues to operate its critical business units during planned or unplanned disruptions.

Business Impact Assessment (BIA)

A computation intended to quantify risk. (See **Risk Assessment**).

CBEST

Testing framework co-ordinated by the Bank of England to help financial institutions improve their resilience to cyber-attack.

CCTA Risk Analysis and Management Method (CRAMM)

A three stage methodology for risk assessments and analysis.

City of London Police

The UK police force that has responsibility for policing the Square Mile; the original City of London.

Classification

The security category of information, usually on the basis of perceived value or sensitivity.

Cloud Computing

Computing technology and infrastructure hosted on the internet.

Cloud Security Alliance (CSA)

A membership association of organisations that have a stake in cloud security.

Code Injection

The injection of malicious code into a target system in order to produce an unwanted result.

Co-location

A physical site (ie, a data centre) in which individuals or organisations can install their own IT equipment.

Commodity Capabilities

Easy-to-use attack tools and techniques available off-the-shelf.

Community Cloud

A site which shares infrastructure and services between several organisations from a specific community with common concerns.

Critical National Infrastructure

Any infrastructure that is critical to the operations of government, society or the economy.

Cross-Site Scripting

A scenario in which an attacker exploits a vulnerability in a web page to transmit malicious code via it.

Cryptocurrencies

Often unregulated digital payment systems that allow electronic money systems to be decentralised.

Cyber-Enabled Crime

Traditional crimes, for example drug trafficking or money laundering, that have a cyber-component.

Cyber Essentials

A UK government-backed, industry-supported scheme to help organisations protect themselves against common cyber-attacks.

Cyber-Security

A specific term referring to attacks coming via a network such as the internet.

Darknet

A subsection of the **Deep Web** that consists of secret or private networks where connections are made only between trusted peers.

Dark Web

See **Darknet**.

Database

A collection of structured data.

Data Packets

Digital envelopes that stream across a network carrying parts of a message or other content, plus header information that ensures their correct delivery.

Data Segmentation

The principle of storing data with different classifications and uses in separate locations.

Deep Web

The portion of World Wide Web content that is not indexed by standard search engines.

Demilitarised Zone (DMZ)

A secure buffer zone sitting between an internal and external network, such as the internet.

Denial of Service (DoS)

An attack designed to overload critical systems.

Digital Certificates

Issued by a certificate authority to validate the legitimacy of an internet domain.

Disaster Recovery Planning

A subset of business continuity planning focused on taking the necessary steps to resume normal business operations as quickly as possible.

Distributed Denial of Service (DDoS)

An attack that typically floods an organisation's servers with messages or other data, with the result that the organisation loses its ability to communicate online.

Distributed Reflected Denial of Service (DRDoS)

A more sophisticated form of DoS attack where the attack source is more than one, often thousands, of unique IP addresses.

Domain Name Servers (DNS)

Devices that serve up IP addresses to computers using the internet, in exchange for domain names.

Dropbox

A cloud service offering file storage and sharing.

Dropper, Reporter and Wiper

A sophisticated virus with several stages:

- dropper – spreads it around the network
- reporter – sends information about the network back to the attacker
- wiper – erases all or some of the compromised files.

Electronic Money

Digital stores of value that can be used for the purpose of making payment transactions.

Encryption

The encoding of data, using mathematical algorithms, so that it can only be unencrypted and read by someone holding the correct decryption key.

European Union Agency for Network and Information Security (ENISA)

An EU agency that works across all EU institutions and member states.

Europol

The European Police Office, the European Union's federal law enforcement agency.

Fair Usage Policies

Policies that provide a contractual basis for responding to excessive use of services by subscribers.

Financial Conduct Authority (FCA)

A UK statutory body tasked with ensuring that financial markets work well and that consumers get a fair deal.

Firewall

A perimeter security tool that filters traffic in order to detect malicious entities before they can access the internal network and systems.

Format String Vulnerabilities

Exploits that occur when applications incorrectly allow format strings (a part of computer programming language) to be included in user data.

Gateway

Devices that act as a portal between a local network and a public network like the internet.

Geolocation

Identifying the physical location of a person or device on the map.

Hacktivism

Hacking, or breaking into a computer system, for a politically or socially motivated purpose.

Home Office

The UK arm of government responsible for national security, the police services of England and Wales, administration of the justice system and immigration policy and controls.

Hybrid Cloud

A combination of two or more cloud services.

iCloud

A cloud service offering online storage, email, and calendar features.

ICT Risk Management

The application of traditional risk management thinking to information and communications technology infrastructure.

Incident Response

The organisational process of responding to a cyber-security incident.

Information

Data endowed with meaning.

Information Commissioner's Office (ICO)

An independent regulatory body responsible for dealing with the Data Protection Act 1998, and other legislative acts and regulations.

Information Security Control

A countermeasure designed to secure an information or computing asset.

Information Security Governance

A set of responsibilities and practices designed to manage risk through the appropriate use of resources.

Information Security Triangle

The triangle of confidentiality, integrity and availability that is at the heart of information security.

InfoSec

A general term that is used to describe the security of information or data in any form.

Infrastructure as a Service

Infrastructure, such as computing platforms, that is provided remotely on the internet.

Internet

A system of interconnected computer networks that spans the globe.

Internet of Things (IoT)

The ongoing development of the internet towards a state in which everyday objects are connected online.

Internet Society

A professional membership society.

Intrusion Detection System

A security tool that examines events within a network in order to detect evidence of threats that have passed through the firewall.

Keylogger

A device or application that captures all keystrokes entered by a user.

Low Orbit Ion Cannon (LOIC)

A free to download denial of service attack tool.

Malnets

Networks of infected web pages that redirect visitors through a series of legitimate but infected pages towards a central malware server.

Malware

Malicious software such as viruses, worms and trojans.

Man-in-the-Middle Attacks (MITM)

In MITM attacks, an attacker intercepts all communications between two hosts.

Multifactor Authentication (MFA)

A security system using more than one method of authentication from independent sources.

National Crime Agency (NCA)

The UK's lead agency in the fight against organised crime.

National Institute of Standards and Technology (NIST)

The US federal technology agency that works with industry to develop and apply technology, measurements, and standards.

Normalisation

The task of ensuring that each data element appears only once within a database.

Open Source

Publicly available sources of information.

Patch

A software update that corrects an error or a vulnerability in a software application or operating system.

Payload

The particular technique malware employs or the additional piece of malicious code it downloads after it has infected a system.

Penetration Test

A friendly test designed to evaluate realistic technical exploits and risks and describe impacts.

Phishing

Unsolicited electronic messages sent at random that try to entice the reader to respond.

Platform as a Service

Users rent space on remote internet-based computing platforms, either to store data, to run applications, or both.

Policy

An articulation of a well-defined strategy that captures the intent, expectations and direction of management.

Principle of Least Privilege

The requirement that an individual or a programme is not granted greater access privileges than are required.

Private Cloud

Private cloud is cloud infrastructure operated exclusively for a single organisation.

Privilege Management

The assignment, recording and review of specific user rights to individual users. Also known as privilege auditing.

Public Cloud

In a public cloud the services are delivered over a network that is open for public use.

Quality of Service (QoS)

The performance of a computer or telephony network, system or service.

Ransomware

Malware that allows attackers to communicate with victims after encrypting their data or systems.

Recovery Time Objective (RTO)

An expression of the maximum tolerated period during which a device, system, network or application can be unavailable after a cyber-attack, technical failure or disaster.

Relational Database

A relational database is arranged as a collection of related tables.

Risk Assessment

A structured process for determining realistic or viable threats to information security. (See **Business Impact Assessment**).

Robots

Programmes that traverse the World Wide Web automatically indexing webpages and content.

Rootkit

Malware that is able to assume system administrator privileges.

Router

Devices that route data packets between computers on a network.

Scareware

A malicious computer programme created to persuade people to buy unnecessary and potentially dangerous software, such as fake antivirus protection.

Session Hijack

An attack in which a hacker takes control of a user's web session.

Silk Road

Silk Road was an online Darknet black market, best known as a platform for selling illegal drugs

Sniffing

Intruding on traffic as it transits a network.

Software as a Service (SaaS)

Software applications supplied remotely on the internet by a cloud service provider.

Spam

The distribution of unsolicited bulk email and other electronic messages.

Spear Phishing

The targeted version of phishing that takes place when an attacker focuses on specific victims.

Spyware

Malware that is designed to spy on user activities.

Structured Query Language (SQL) Injection

A popular and successful code injection technique.

The Met

The London Metropolitan Police Service (abbreviated to MPS and widely known informally as 'the Met') is the territorial police force responsible for law enforcement in Greater London (excluding the City of London).

Threat Scoring

Exercises that identify threat types by role and measure their severity in detail.

Trojan

Malicious code that hides inside seemingly innocent code.

Username Enumeration

A vulnerability in an application that delivers a response to a failed login attempt indicating whether a username is already on the system or not.

Vetting

The process of screening employees, applicants, contractors, suppliers or others to identify those who may pose a threat.

Virus

A piece of malicious code that requires some kind of user action before it executes.

Voice over Internet Protocol (VoIP)

Technology for the delivery of voice communications and multimedia sessions over the internet.

Vulnerability Management

The cyclical practice of identifying, classifying, remediating and mitigating vulnerabilities in software and firmware.

Watering Hole Attack

An attack that occurs when an attacker monitors the trusted websites regularly visited by his targets.

Wiper

See **Dropper, Reporter and Wiper**

World Wide Web (WWW)

A web of interlinked hypertext documents and applications.

Worm

Malware that is programmed to navigate (or worm) its way around the network searching for a specific kind of device or software application.

Zero Day

An undisclosed and uncorrected computer application vulnerability

Zero Day Exploits

Exploits that have not yet been detected and dealt with by security vendors.

Multiple Choice Questions

The following additional questions have been compiled to reflect as closely as possible the standard that you will experience in your examination. Please note, however, they are not actual CISI examination questions.

1. Which of the following is specifically listed by the US Department of Homeland Security as a critical national infrastructure requiring protection from terrorist attacks?

   A. The space programme

   B. Entertainment

   C. Financial services

   D. Public sports venues

2. What is cryptography?

   A. The act of locking data in a secure safe or vault

   B. The process of concealing data in storage or in transit

   C. The technique of encoding secret data to hide it from spies

   D. Composing messages in ways that make their meaning unclear

3. What is meant by the term the principle of least privilege?

   A. New employees are given the lowest levels of security privileges

   B. An individual or program is not granted greater access privileges than required

   C. Every employee is paid based on their level of security privileges

   D. All security privileges are routinely set to zero before being reviewed

4. When applied to the cryptographic storage of passwords, which of the following best defines the term 'hashing'?

   A. Storing passwords in a strongly encrypted format that fully protects them

   B. Storing passwords in a format that describes the shape of the password and conceals them

   C. The corruption or deletion of stored passwords in a database

   D. A database system that searches for each user's password inefficiently

5. What is meant by user privilege management?

   A. The issue of special privileges to selected employees as a reward for good work

   B. The removal of privileges from selected employees as a punishment

   C. The linking of salary to privilege levels

   D. The assignment, recording and review of specific user rights to individual users

6.   Which of the following correctly defines the functions of a router?

  A.   Defining the routing tables to be used by the internet

  B.   Making the most efficient use of cabling

  C.   Managing the online schedules for a network

  D.   Sending data packets via the best route, based on routing tables

7.   What is social engineering?

  A.   The legal use of population control

  B.   The art of designing cheap housing

  C.   The art of manipulating people

  D.   The process of involving people in urban planning

8.   Which of the following most accurately defines a script kiddie?

  A.   A less-skilled person who executes software scripts or uses programs previously created by expert hackers

  B.   A young person with high levels of skill who writes computer scripts in order to attack computer systems

  C.   A person who searches through corporate rubbish bins in search of computing scripts that might reveal passwords

  D.   A person who posts religious scriptures on social media sites, such as Twitter or Facebook, criticising corporate ethics

9.   What is the primary purpose of FISMA?

  A.   To ensure the security of data stored by corporate firms in the USA

  B.   To ensure the security of data stored anywhere within departments of the federal government

  C.   To ensure the security of personal data relating to US citizens

  D.   To ensure the security of defence and security data stored in US Department of Defense facilities worldwide

10.   Which of the following pairs correctly describes the two classes of cyber-security control?

  A.   General and application controls

  B.   Environmental and organisational controls

  C.   People and technology controls

  D.   Process and technology controls

11.   What is meant by the term authentication?

   A.   The act of verifying a claim of identity

   B.   The act of verifying a claim of authority

   C.   The act of verifying a claim of authenticity

   D.   The act of verifying a claim of authorship

12.   Which of the following best describes the Deep Web?

   A.   Section of the internet that runs on undersea cables

   B.   Part of the internet reserved for academic research and publications

   C.   A hidden part of the internet not accessible to most users

   D.   Part of the internet that is not indexed by standard search engines

13.   What is the Cloud?

   A.   Computing technology and infrastructure hosted on the internet

   B.   Computing technology and infrastructure hosted on satellites

   C.   Computing technology and infrastructure that uses radio signals

   D.   Non-technical marketing terminology describing internet services

14.   Which of the following is an actual UK police force?

   A.   The Airports and Seaports Constabulary

   B.   The Civil Nuclear Constabulary

   C.   The Internet Surveillance Force

   D.   The Special Operations Executive

15.   Which of the following is a motive for DoS attacks?

   A.   Overloading critical systems

   B.   Exposing corporate misdeeds

   C.   Stealing sensitive data

   D.   Insider trading or market abuse

16.   How does the FCA define a financial promotion?

   A.   A communication inducing someone to engage in an investment activity

   B.   A marketing communication raising awareness of an investment opportunity

   C.   When an employee within a firm is promoted to a new role and paid more as a result

   D.   A shareholder report that highlights the financial success of a firm

17. What best describes a Trojan software update?

    A. A DMZ

    B. An update developed to negate packet filtering

    C. An update containing hidden malicious code

    D. An update that facilitates a military attack

18. What is meant by the term Big Data?

    A. Large volumes of data that are processed and stored in the cloud

    B. Very valuable items of personal and corporate data related to financial transactions

    C. Data that are collected from several sources and then combined and enriched

    D. Social media data resources that are exploited for marketing purposes

19. Which of the following is specifically defined as an offence under the CMA?

    A. Unauthorised access with intent to commit or facilitate commission of further offences

    B. Unauthorised access with intent to create a fake social media profile for the purpose of fraud

    C. Unauthorised access with intent to steal a computing device

    D. Unauthorised access with intent to use computer programs for data processing

20. Which of the following most accurately defines the term hacker?

    A. A teenager operating in secret who uses hacking scripts downloaded online to break into corporate and government computer systems

    B. An espionage agent operating in secret who uses advanced tools provided by the state to break into foreign government computers and steal data

    C. A single-issue extremist who gains employment with a corporate firm in order to steal confidential data from computer systems

    D. A person with expert computing skills, who attempts to access a computer system without authorisation, by circumventing or cracking its security

21. What is the main function of a domain name server?

    A. To serve up IP addresses in exchange for domain names

    B. To serve up domain names in exchange for IP addresses

    C. To issue domain names for new websites

    D. To check the accuracy of existing domain names

22. What is the 'Internet of Things'?

    A. The connection of robots and drones online

    B. A future internet on which only computers communicate with each other

    C. A separate network connecting machines in a business

    D. A state in which everyday objects are connected online

23. Which of the following is normally included in the definition of cloud computing?

    A. Software-as-a-Service

    B. BYOD-as-a-Service

    C. Crime-as-a-Service

    D. Computing-as-a-Service

24. Which of the following most accurately defines exploitation in relation to the two stages of a cyber-attack (access followed by exploitation)?

    A. The abuse of children by online paedophiles

    B. The manner in which attackers exploit their access

    C. The exploitation of migrant workers by organised crime gangs

    D. The theft and use of stolen personal data

25. What is a cryptocurrency?

    A. An encrypted financial transaction involving regulated currencies

    B. A digital currency that uses cryptography as a security measure

    C. Game money used by players of World of Warcraft and similar games

    D. A special form of currency used by US espionage agents and Special Forces

26. Which of the following is the primary focus of the NCA?

    A. The fight against terrorism

    B. Crimes committed by UK citizens abroad

    C. The fight against organised crime

    D. Crimes committed by immigrants to the UK

27. What is meant by cloud sprawl?

    A. Large amounts of cloud usage by organisations

    B. Laziness within IT resulting from cloud usage

    C. The uncontrolled spread of cloud usage

    D. Cloud usage that goes beyond national borders

28. What is information security governance?

    A. The duties of the government with respect to data protection

    B. The rules laid out to address information security

    C. The working practices used by staff in order to remain secure

    D. A set of responsibilities and practices designed to manage risk

29. What is spear-phishing?

    A. A hacking attack that targets a specific computer

    B. A social engineering attack that targets a specific organisation

    C. Sending unsolicited electronic messages to targeted individuals

    D. Sending spam messages to random recipients

30. What is meant by the term co-location?

    A. When two computer users are in the same location at the same time

    B. When two security investigators both calculate the same location for a suspect

    C. The online location of a company or other private organisation

    D. Rented space at a shared datacentre facility for computing hardware

31. What is the main social media thrust of Californian Law A.B. 1844 covering employee monitoring and privacy?

    A. Employers cannot demand that employees divulge their social media log-on information

    B. Employees cannot discuss the details of their employment via social media

    C. Employers cannot rule out job applicants based on online search results

    D. Employers can create fake social media profiles in order to secretly befriend employees

32. Which EU treaty established the role of Europol?

    A. The Maastricht Treaty

    B. The Schengen Treaty

    C. The Bonn Treaty

    D. The Versailles Treaty

33. What occurs during the survey phase of a cyber-attack?

    A. Using any means available to find vulnerabilities

    B. Sending questionnaires to users asking about vulnerabilities

    C. Sending engineers to fix vulnerabilities in an organisation

    D. Producing an estimate of cyber-vulnerabilities for insurance purposes

34. Which of the following is a justification for the interception of communications under RIPA?

    A. To prevent or detect crimes

    B. To protect corporate brands or management reputations

    C. To investigate a news story in the public interest

    D. To monitor the internet usage of celebrities

35. Which of the following correctly describes data packets?

    A. A set of data stored on a disk and delivered by the postman

    B. Parts of a larger message sent as a stream of packets, each with its own header

    C. Very large messages bundled up into a single large packet and sent via the internet

    D. A collection of separate unrelated messages all sent at once down a broadband connection

36. How does the NCA define organised crime?

    A. People working together in large numbers to plan, coordinate and conduct crime

    B. People conspiring together in secret to plan, coordinate and conduct crime

    C. People working together in a professional manner to plan, coordinate and conduct crime

    D. People working together on a continuous basis to plan, coordinate and conduct crime

37. The maximum penalty on summary conviction stipulated under the Fraud Act 2006 is:

    A. 12 years

    B. 12 months

    C. 10 years

    D. 6 months

38. What is meant in information security terms by the phrase future desired state?

    A. The geographic location a firm would like to be based in

    B. The required condition of computer equipment after two years' use

    C. A snapshot of all relevant conditions at a point in the future

    D. The awareness level of employees after InfoSec awareness training

39. Which of the following is the correct definition of unstructured data?

    A. Data that cannot be organised and linked without advanced processing

    B. Data that makes no sense to the reader

    C. Data that has been randomly broken up into packets by a computer error

    D. Data that only contains lists of keywords

40. Which of the following is a goal of data segmentation?

    A. Data is broken up into manageable chunks for processing

    B. Data is divided between different systems for efficiency.

    C. Sensitive data is held separately from non-sensitive data.

    D. All data is treated equally in accordance with net neutrality principles.

41. Which of the following is one of the four parallel strands to counter-terrorism promoted by the Hague Programme response of 2004?

    A. Persevere

    B. Promote

    C. Retaliate

    D. Prevent

42. Which of the following is the correct definition of the term internet protocol?

    A. A set of rules describing good manners online

    B. A standardised framework for communications across the internet

    C. A method for converting IP addresses to physical home addresses

    D. The original agreement between nations to setup the internet

43. Which of the following describes the Darknet?

    A. Secret or private networks and pages

    B. Internet cables that are no longer used

    C. A part of the internet only available at night

    D. All internet sites that offer dark, illegal services

44. Which of the following rights of US citizens is protected by the US Privacy Act (1974)?

    A. The right to freedom of association

    B. The right to be forgotten

    C. The right to see records about themselves

    D. The right to absolute personal privacy

45. When you use a search engine like Google, Yahoo or Bing to search the internet, which of the following is true?

    A. You search the entire internet

    B. You search the local internet near you

    C. You search the worldwide indexes of all search engine providers

    D. You search only the indexes of the search engine provider you are using

46. Which of the following best defines the concept of net neutrality?

    A. Providers and governments should treat all data on the internet equally

    B. The internet should not be a target for attack during wartime

    C. All opinions expressed online are considered valid; free speech online

    D. No one government owns the internet; it is a neutral, shared resource

47. Insurance is a common method of:

    A. Eliminating risk

    B. Transferring risk

    C. Avoiding risk

    D. Mitigating risk

48. Which of the following best describes the internet?

    A. Collection of web pages and servers

    B. System of interconnected computer networks

    C. Single centrally managed global network

    D. Collection of web services hosted in the cloud

49. What is the ultimate goal of information security?

    A. Managing risks

    B. Preventing data breaches

    C. Restricting access to information

    D. Catching all cyber-attackers

50. The term 'General Artificial Intelligence ' refers to which of the following concepts?

    A. AI that is designed for use by the military

    B. AI of a general nature, that has no specific function

    C. Advanced AI that can parody human thought and actions

    D. AI systems used for today's FinTech decision-making platforms

Answers to Multiple Choice Questions

1.   **C**   **Chapter 2, Section 3.2.2**

The US Department of Homeland Security defines the 16 critical infrastructure sectors, as follows:

1. chemicals
2. commercial facilities
3. communications
4. critical manufacturing
5. dams
6. defence industrial bases
7. emergency services
8. energy
9. financial services
10. food and agriculture
11. government facilities
12. healthcare and public health
13. information technology
14. nuclear reactors, materials and waste
15. transportation systems
16. water and wastewater systems.

2.   **B**   **Chapter 5, Section 1.1**

Cryptography is frequently employed to encrypt and mask information, either in storage or transit. Tunnelling for example will take data packets and encapsulate them in an encrypted stream to ensure data security during transmission. Encryption can also be employed at file level using encryption to protect information in storage, for example, on a hard drive.

3.   **B**   **Chapter 5, Section 1.4.3**

This requires that an individual (or a program) is not granted greater access privileges than are required to perform the task in question.

4.   **B**   **Chapter 5, Section 6**

Most password databases employ hashing; they convert users' passwords to a mathematical expression that describes the unique shape of the password but conceals the actual password.

5.   **D**   **Chapter 5, Section 1.4.8**

In general terms, privilege management involves the assignment, recording and review of specific user rights to individual users.

6.   **D**   **Chapter 1, Section 1.5.4**

Routers provide a service that is exactly as it sounds – they route data packets between computers on a network. Routers do this by reading the details of the desired address the sender has placed within the packet header and then looking up the location of that address by referring to an external database. Once they know where the packet is supposed to go they send it via an appropriate route, based on routing tables and defined policies.

7.   **C**   **Chapter 4, Section 2.1.8**

Social engineering is the art of manipulating people to:

- perform unplanned actions
- refrain from planned actions.

8.   **A**   **Chapter 4, Section 2.1.2**

Script kiddie is a pejorative term describing supposedly young (although in fact they can be any age) and less skilled persons who execute software scripts, or use programs previously created by expert hackers, to attack computer systems and websites.

9.   **B**   **Chapter 2, Section 3.6**

FISMA assigns responsibilities to various agencies to ensure the security of data stored anywhere within departments of the federal government. The Act requires program officials, and the head of each agency, to conduct annual reviews of information security programs designed to keep risks at or below specified levels in a cost-effective, timely and efficient manner.

10.   **A**   **Chapter 5, Section 1.4.1**

There are essentially two classes of cyber-security control:

- general controls
- application controls.

11.   **A**   **Chapter 5, Section 1.4.9**

Authentication is the act of verifying a claim of identity. There are at least five different types of information that can be used for authentication:

- **Something you know** – things such as a PIN, a password, or your mother's maiden name.
- **Something you have** – a driver's license, a dongle or a magnetic swipe card.
- **Something you are** – biometrics, including palm prints, fingerprints, voice prints and retina (eye) scans.
- **Somewhere you are** – a location or IP address.
- **Somewhere you are not** – a location or IP address.

12.   D   Chapter 1, Section 1.2.1

The Deep Web is also sometimes called the Deepnet, Invisible Web or Hidden Web. It is the portion of World Wide Web content that is not indexed by standard search engines, generally because it sits in large databases that search engines cannot easily reach. The data may be public but registration, username and password access may be required to reach it.

13.   A   Chapter 1, Section 1.3

The cloud is nothing more than computing technology and infrastructure hosted on the internet. For example, if you put pictures into iCloud or Dropbox, you are using the cloud. If you upload videos to YouTube, you are using the cloud. If you post status updates on Facebook to be read by your friends, you are using the cloud.

14.   B   Chapter 3, Section 1.5

See the full reference list of pan-UK departments and police forces in Section 1.5.

15.   A   Chapter 1, Section 4.4.1

All denial of service attacks aim to overload critical systems, such as web services or email, with internet traffic. If the target server cannot handle the volume of malicious traffic, then it is also unable to process legitimate traffic.

16.   A   Chapter 6, Section 2.1

According to the FCA, financial promotion is *'a communication that is an invitation or an inducement to engage in investment activity'*.

17.   C   Chapter 4, Section 1.1.2

Attackers hide their malware inside fake software updates for those legitimate programs, which they publish online and broadcast via spam messages.

18.   C   Chapter 6, Section 1.1.3

Big data refers to large volumes of data that are collected from several sources and then combined and enriched in order to add value. An example is data on millions of consumers' online browsing habits combined with their geolocation data, to reveal where they are when they purchase specific items.

19.   A   Chapter 2, Section 2.1.1

Following its amendment by section 35 of the Police and Justice Act 2006 and Schedule 15 of the Serious Crime Act 2007, the CMA now (2015) defines the following four offences:

- **Section 1 CMA** – unauthorised access to computer material.
- **Section 2 CMA** – unauthorised access with intent to commit or facilitate commission of further offences.
- **Section 3 CMA** – unauthorised acts with intent to impair, or with recklessness as to impairing, operation of computer, etc.
- **Section 3A CMA** – making, supplying or obtaining articles for use in offences under sections 1 or 3.

20.   D   Chapter 4, Section 2.1.1

Hacking is a disputed term that is used to refer to several different types of activity and individual. Perhaps the best description is: *A person with expert computing skills, who attempts to access a computer system without authorisation, by circumventing or cracking its security.*

21.   A   Chapter 1, Section 1.5.5

By entering a text-based name as the address for an email or website, our internet postmen (the routers) need to ask someone or something to translate that name into an IP address. This is the primary function of the domain name servers; they serve up IP addresses in exchange for domain names and then help to execute the necessary routing.

22.   D   Chapter 6, Section 1.1

The internet of things refers to the ongoing development of the internet towards a state in which everyday objects are connected online, allowing them to send and receive data and even to make financial payments without human intervention.

23.   A   Chapter 1, Section 1.4

There are three classes of cloud service:

1. **Software as a Service (SaaS)** – the software applications you use are supplied remotely by the cloud service provider. Users login across the internet and make use of the third-party application without having to own a licence.
2. **Platform as a Service (PaaS)** – users rent space on remote computing platforms, either to store data, to run applications, or both. Some of these services are provided free of charge, as is the case with Dropbox, but the platform is provided in an operational state with the operating system installed and running.
3. **Infrastructure as a Service (IaaS)** – infrastructure such as computing platforms is provided remotely and in a centralised fashion but the user installs and manages the operating system and applications remotely.

24.   B   Chapter 4, Section 2.1

Exploitation: how did the attackers use their access once they had gained it?

25.   B   Chapter 6, Section 1.2

Cryptocurrency (Bitcoin being the best-known example) is a digital or virtual currency that uses cryptography as a security measure. This use of encryption makes the currency extremely difficult to counterfeit.

26.   C   Chapter 3, Section 1.2

The National Crime Agency (NCA) replaced the Serious Organised Crime Agency (SOCA) in late October 2013. The NCA is a national law enforcement agency and is a non-ministerial government department. It is the UK's lead agency in the fight against organised crime, which encompasses people trafficking, drug trafficking, weapons trafficking, cybercrime and economic crimes committed across regional and international borders.

27.   **C**   **Chapter 6, Section 1.4**

Another information security challenge is that of cloud sprawl. This refers to the often uncontrolled manner in which cloud usage can spread from what was originally intended, as users make their own decisions about when, where and how to use the cloud, often without the knowledge and approval of IT.

28.   **D**   **Chapter 5, Section 1.1**

Information security governance is a set of responsibilities and practices designed to manage risk through the appropriate use of resources.

29.   **C**   **Chapter 4, Section 3.1.2**

Spear-phishing: sending unsolicited electronic messages of various types to targeted individuals that either contain an attachment with malicious software embedded within it or a link to a malicious website that serves up malware when visited.

30.   **D**   **Chapter 6, Section 1.5**

Co-location involves a service provider or organisation renting space at a shared datacentre facility for computing hardware. Co-location delivers services such as cooling, power, bandwidth and physical security and in turn the customer provides servers and storing capabilities.

The space is rented by rack, cabinet, secure cage or even by room. Co-location can offer extra features such as managed services that are in line with the customers' business requirements.

31.   **A**   **Chapter 6, Section 2.3**

In 2012 California introduced a law which prohibits employers from requiring (or requesting) employees or applicants to divulge their social media log-on information. Other conduct likely to be prohibited may include requesting that an applicant or employee add the employer as a friend, thereby giving the employer access to information not otherwise publicly available.

32.   **A**   **Chapter 3, Section 1.6**

The establishment of Europol was one of the activities defined in the Maastricht Treaty that came into effect in November 1993.

33.   **A**   **Chapter 4, Section 3.2.1**

Attackers will use any means available to find technical, procedural or physical vulnerabilities which they can attempt to exploit, including the use of open-source information such as LinkedIn and Facebook, other social media sources and domain name management/search services that list the names and contact details of domain name registrants.

Attackers also employ commodity toolkits and techniques, as well as network scanning tools to collect and assess any information about an organisation's computers, security systems and personnel.

34.   **A**   **Chapter 2, Section 2.5.1**

The primary authorised purposes for which the monitoring or interception of communications by authorised firms is permitted to occur, are as follows:

- to prevent or detect crimes
- to prevent public disorder from occurring
- to ensure national security and the safety of the general public
- to investigate or detect any abnormal or illegal use of telecommunication systems.

35.   **B**   **Chapter 1, Section 1.6.3**

When data is passed across a network similar challenges and issues arise. Most networks are shared by many devices and the volumes of data passing through them can be very large. If one device was allowed to dominate the network, to use all its capacity in order to send a large document or file as a continuous stream of bits, none of the other devices on the network would be able to send or receive information until that dominant device had finished. This would not be an efficient way to provide network services.

In order for devices to share the finite capacity of any network, the data they send is broken down into much smaller packets, like digital envelopes, and these packets stream across the network separately, each one sitting between packets going from other devices to different destinations.

Each of these network packets includes a header that contains all the information necessary for the receiving device to do exactly what your publisher was doing in order to reassemble any message or file and present it to a user or application in its complete format.

36.   **D**   **Chapter 3, Section 1.2**

Organised crime encompasses people trafficking, drug trafficking, weapons trafficking, cybercrime and economic crimes committed across regional and international borders on a continuous basis.

37.   **B**   **Chapter 2, Section 2.4.5**

A person guilty of an offence under this section shall be liable:

a. on summary conviction in England and Wales, to imprisonment for a term not exceeding 12 months or to a fine not exceeding the statutory maximum or to both
b. on summary conviction in Scotland, to imprisonment for a term not exceeding six months or to a fine not exceeding the statutory maximum or to both

on conviction on indictment, to imprisonment for a term not exceeding five years or to a fine or to both.

38.   **C**   **Chapter 5, Section 1.3.1**

A snapshot of all relevant conditions at a point in the future (that) describes the principles, policies and frameworks that should apply at that time if the security strategy has been properly implemented and adhered to.

39. **A** **Chapter 1, Section 1.5.1**

Unstructured data is information that is relatively difficult to classify, for example the content of emails, tweets or Facebook posts. While such data is also stored, its elements cannot be organised and linked without advanced processing having taken place, such as deriving sentiment from keywords in an unstructured string of data.

40. **C** **Chapter 5, Section 1.4.7**

Data segmentation refers to the principle of storing data with different classifications and uses in an arrangement that ensures that:

- data can only be accessed, edited, deleted or viewed by those users and systems that have a legitimate need
- sensitive data is captured in a secure manner
- sensitive data is held separately from non-sensitive data
- different classes of data can be protected in different and appropriate ways.

41. **D** **Chapter 3, Section 1.6.5**

Europol also works pro-actively in the development of counter-terrorism goals that adhere to the Hague Programme response of 2004. This promoted four parallel strands:

- prevent
- protect
- pursue
- respond.

42. **B** **Chapter 1, Section 1.5.2**

Internet protocol (TCP/IP) is a standardised framework for communications across the globalised network of networks that is the internet.

43. **A** **Chapter 1, Section 1.2.2**

The Darknet is effectively a subsection of the Deep Web. It consists of secret or private networks where connections are made only between trusted peers, also known as friends. In these dark spaces people who wish to avoid detection or surveillance, or who are engaged in criminal activities such as slavery, offences against children, illegal pornography, drug trafficking and arms dealing, conduct their business with impunity.

44. **C** **Chapter 2, Section 3.5**

The Privacy Act guarantees every US citizen three primary rights:

- The right to see records about themselves, subject to Privacy Act exemptions.
- The right to request the amendment of records that are not accurate, relevant, timely or complete.
- The right to be protected against unwarranted invasions of privacy resulting from the collection, maintenance, use and disclosure of personal information.

45.   D   Chapter 2, Section 1.1.3

When you 'search the internet', you are actually searching the indexes previously built up by the search engine provider you have chosen to use – Google, Yahoo, Bing. This gives search engine providers the power to remove or otherwise conceal any topic, phrase or word of their choosing.

46.   A   Chapter 2, Section 1.1.1

Net neutrality refers to the idea that internet service providers and governments should treat all data on the internet equally, meaning that there should be pricing differentiation by user, type of content, site identity, class of platform, type of application, type of attached equipment or means of communication.

47.   B   Chapter 5, Section 1.3.3

Insurance is a common method of transferring risk from the organisation to the insurer.

48.   B   Chapter 1, Section 1.1.1

The internet is a network of networks: a system of interconnected computer networks that span the globe.

49.   A   Chapter 5, Section 1.2.3

Risk management is the ultimate goal of information security.

50.   C   Chapter 4, Section 3.6.2

General AI – AI that can mimic human thought and communication so effectively that it can pass the Turing Test and fool humans into believing that they are having a conversation with a real person.

Syllabus Learning Map

Syllabus Unit/ Element		Chapter/ Section

Element 1	**The Background and Nature of Information Security and Cybercrime**	Chapter 1
1.1	**Definitions** On completion the candidate should:	
1.1.1	Know the difference between the internet and the World Wide Web	1.1
1.1.2	Know the meaning of: • the Deep Web • the Darknet	1.2
1.1.3	Know the meaning of the term 'cloud computing'	1.3
1.1.4	Understand the meaning of: • Software as a Service (SaaS) • Platform as a Service (PaaS) • Infrastructure as a Service (IaaS)	1.4
1.1.5	Know the meaning of: • database structure • internet protocol (IP) addressing versions 4 and 6 • domain name servers • routers and gateways • data packets	1.5
1.1.6	Know the Financial Conduct Authority (FCA) definition of electronic money	1.6
1.1.7	Understand the definition of information security	1.7
1.2	**Distinctions** On completion the candidate should:	
1.2.1	Know how cyber security is distinct from information security	1.7
1.2.2	Understand the distinction between cybercrime and cyber-enabled crime	2.1
1.3	**Fundamental Issues** On completion the candidate should:	
1.3.1	Understand the fundamentals of cyber-security: • policies and standards • identity and access management • threat and vulnerability management • outside service providers • IT risk management	3.1

Syllabus Unit/ Element		Chapter/ Section
1.4	**Technical Cybercrime Attacks** On completion the candidate should:	
1.4.1	Identify the following types of network-level technical cybercrime attack: • denial of service (DoS) and distributed denial of service (DDoS • distributed reflected denial of service attacks (DRDoS) • man-in-the-middle (MitM) attacks • sniffing attacks • session hijacks • botnets • malnets • spam	4.4
1.4.2	Identify the following types of network-level technical cybercrime attack: • remote code injection • structured query language (SQL) injection • cross-site scripting (XXS) • format string vulnerabilities • user name enumeration	4.7
1.4.3	Identify the most common types of technical cybercrime attack at device level: • device intrusions/hacking • password cracks • physical key loggers • in-built infections at point of manufacture or sale • device-sharing risks • device disposal and maintenance-related data breaches • device theft	4.9
1.4.4	Identify the most common technical cybercrime attack via peripheral devices: • bring your own device (BYOD) risks • removable media risks • printer risks	4.9.5, 4.9.6
1.4.5	Identify the following types of technical cybercrime based on application exploits: • application hacking • password cracks • code injection • malicious websites • drive-by downloads	4.8

Syllabus Unit/ Element		Chapter/ Section
1.4.6	Identify the main types of technical cybercrime arising from malware exploits, including: • viruses • worms • trojans • spyware • rootkits	4.8
1.4.7	Identify the following types of technical cybercrime: • crypto-extortion attacks or ransomware • web attack toolkits and scripts • data leakage and breaches • online frauds and other financially motivated e-crimes	4.5
1.5	**The Human Firewall** On completion, the candidate should:	
1.5.1	Identify the most common types of technical cybercrime stemming from user-level issues: • errors and accidental disclosures • rogue insiders • insider frauds • identity theft • phishing • vishing • pharming • physical intrusions • password sharing and weak passwords • self-provisioning	5.1
1.5.2	Understand social media risk in relation to cybercrime: • social engineering ploys • identity theft • contact network analysis • blackmail • harassment • stalking • grooming • data breaches • reputational harm and brand damage • target acquisition and reconnaissance	5.2

Syllabus Unit/ Element		Chapter/ Section
1.5.3	Know key desktop attack and concealment techniques used in cybercrime: • keylogging • screen-scraping • advanced online searching and reconnaissance • Google and Pastebin • LinkedIn, Facebook and Twitter searches • security and privacy vulnerabilities • image and reverse-image searching methods • mapping and geolocation vulnerabilities	5.3

Element 2	The Legislative Environment	Chapter 2
2.1	**Legal Concepts** On completion the candidate should:	
2.1.1	Understand the key concepts influencing internet law: • net neutrality • free speech on the internet • internet censorship • privacy expectations • intelligence services surveillance • responsibilities of internet service providers (ISPs)	1.1
2.2	**UK Legislation** On completion the candidate should:	
2.2.1	Know the offences created under the Computer Misuse Act (1990): • Offence 1: Unauthorised access to computer material • Offence 2: Unauthorised access with intent to commit or facilitate commission of further offences • Offence 3: Unauthorised Access with Intent to Impair	2.1
2.2.2	• know the maximum penalties applicable to Offence 1	2.1.1
2.2.3	• know the maximum penalties applicable to Offence 2	2.1.1
2.2.4	• know the maximum penalties applicable to Offence 3	2.1.1
2.2.5	Know the amendment to unauthorised access and the two additional offences defined in the Police and Justice Act (2006): • Section 36: unauthorised acts with intent to impair operation of computer • Section 37: making, supplying or obtaining articles for use in computer misuse offences	2.3
2.2.6	Understand how the Fraud Act (2006) relates to cybercrime: • fraud by false representation	2.4
2.2.7	Know the maximum penalty stipulated under the Fraud Act (2006)	2.4.5

Syllabus Unit/ Element		Chapter/ Section
2.2.8	Know how the European Union (EU) General Data Protection Regulation relates to cybercrime	2.2
2.2.9	Understand the core principles of the Regulation of Investigatory Powers Act (RIPA) with respect to communications meta-data and message content	2.4
2.3	**Relevant Foreign Legislation** On completion, the candidate should:	
2.3.1	Know key US regulation and guidance that relates to cybercrime: • Homeland Security Act (2002) • The Department of Homeland Security (DHS) Critical Infrastructure Cyber Community (C-cubed) Voluntary Program • Electronic Communication Privacy Act (1986) • Privacy Act (1974) • Federal Information Security Management Act (2002) • Executive Order 13636, Improving Critical Infrastructure Cyber-Security	3

Element 3	The Public-Private Interface in Combating Cybercrime	Chapter 3
3.1	**Law Enforcement Agencies** On completion, the candidate should:	
3.1.1	Understand the role and activities of the following UK and EU agencies: • the National Crime Agency (NCA) • the Metropolitan Police Service (Met) & SO15 • the City of London Police • regional police forces • Europol	1
3.2	**Standards and Best Practice** On completion, the candidate should:	
3.2.1	Know the purpose and content of the main international standards for information security management	2.1
3.2.2	Know the purpose and content of the UK Government Communication Headquarters (GCHQ) information assurance *Cyber Essentials* scheme	2.6
3.2.3	Understand the purpose and content of the UK Government Communications Headquarters (GCHQ) guidance entitled *10 Steps to Cyber-Security*	2.7
3.2.4	Understand the role of the European Network and Information Security Agency (ENISA)	2.9
3.2.5	Understand the role of the UK National Cyber Security Centre (NCSC)	2.8

Syllabus Unit/ Element		Chapter/ Section
3.3	**Cyber-Security and the Financial Services Industry** On completion, the candidate should:	
3.3.1	Know the role of UK and EU information commissioners in relation to cybercrime	3.2, 3.3.6
3.3.2	Understand the obligations of financial services firms to the information commissioner	3.4
3.3.3	Know the role of the Financial Conduct Authority (FCA) and Prudential Regulation Authority (PRA) in relation to cybercrime	3.5, 3.5.1
3.3.4	Understand the obligations of financial services firms to the FCA and PRA with regard to a cybercrime event	3.5, 3.5.1

Element 4	Cybercrime and the Financial Services Industry	Chapter 4
4.1	**Recognising the Threat** On completion, the candidate should:	
4.1.1	Understand the importance of financial services as a component of critical national infrastructure: • threats and impacts at national level • managing cyber dependencies • national cyber-security culture	1.1.3, 1.1.4, 1.1.5
4.1.2	Understand how financial services firms are exposed to various categories of cybercriminal: • employees and contractors • hacktivists or single-issue extremists • hackers and script kiddies • fraudsters • nation states • organised crime networks • malware developers • software developers • social engineers	2
4.2	**Known Vulnerabilities** On completion, the candidate should:	
4.2.1	Know typical classes of cybercrime vulnerability affecting networks	3.1, 3.2
4.2.2	Know the typical classes of cybercrime vulnerability of connected devices	3.1
4.2.3	Know the typical classes of cybercrime vulnerability of common applications (apps) and browsers	3.1
4.2.4	Know the typical cybercrime vulnerabilities of database systems	3.5

Syllabus Unit/ Element		Chapter/ Section
4.3	**Cybercrime Detection** On completion, the candidate should:	
4.3.1	Know how firewalls are used to detect cyber-attacks and vulnerabilities	4.1
4.3.2	Know how intrusion detection systems (IDS) are used to detect cyber-attacks and vulnerabilities	4.2
4.3.3	Know how anti-malware applications are used to detect cyber-attacks and vulnerabilities	4.3
4.3.4	Know how logging and reporting applications are used to detect cyber-attacks and vulnerabilities	4.4
4.3.5	Know how penetration testing and vulnerability assessment methodologies are employed to detect cyber-attacks	3.6
4.3.6	Know how artificial intelligence is used to detect cyber-attacks and vulnerabilities, its limits and its role in financial services, as well as the resulting cyber security risks	3.6.2
4.3.7	Understand how other common data sources can be utilised to identify evidence of cybercrime, including: • customer complaints • suspicious transactions • internet and website usage patterns • customer device profiles • employee turnover statistics	4.5

Element 5	Combating Cybercrime	Chapter 5
5.1	**Proactive Governance** On completion, the candidate should:	
5.1.1	Understand the goals of information security governance: • scope and charter • organisational and third-party relationships • key cyber-security and information security risk metrics	1.1, 1.2.1, 1.2.2, 1.2.3
5.1.2	Understand the information security framework: • strategy • risk management processes • business impact assessments • policies and procedures • compliance • audit methodologies • testing and validation • training and awareness	1.3

Syllabus Unit/ Element		Chapter/ Section
5.1.3	Know commonly accepted cyber-security control frameworks: • control categories • baseline controls • strengths and methods • components and architecture • inventory management and control (configuration management databases) • user profiles and privileges management and reviews • key metrics • reporting exceptions	1.4
5.1.4	Know effective due diligence techniques for: • customers • employees • service providers	1.5
5.1.5	Understand the impact of culture on cyber-security for international business	1.5.4
5.2	**Risk Management** On completion, the candidate should:	
5.2.1	Know the additional measures financial services firms can take to manage the risk of cybercrime originated or enabled by an employee: • raising awareness • improving the management of privileges for joiners, movers and leavers • classifying and segmenting data • embedding ethical practice in relation to data security • implementing whistleblowing procedures	2
5.2.2	Know the implications of cybercrime for technological procurement: • bespoke software development • standards of software development • supplier due diligence • hardware and software lifecycles, including disposal with respect to corporate social responsibility and the data protection principles	2.3
5.2.3	Know how to manage the risk of cybercrime throughout the employee lifecycle	2.2
5.3	**Stress testing** On completion, the candidate should:	
5.3.1	Understand the application of penetration testing to different types of vulnerabilities	3.3
5.3.2	Understand the correct application of prepared planning and dry-run modelling	3.3.5
5.3.3	Know how firms can measure, or predict, the impact of cyber-attack	3.4

Syllabus Unit/ Element		Chapter/ Section
5.4	**Incident response** On completion, the candidate should:	
5.4.1	Know the role of a computer emergency response team (CERT) or computer security incident response team (CSIRT)	4.1.2
5.4.2	Understand the concept of recovery time objectives (RTO)	4.2
5.4.3	Know the components of an incident management procedure	4.3
5.4.4	Know how to develop an incident management response plan	4.3.1
5.5	**Business continuity** On completion, the candidate should:	
5.5.1	Understand the concept of business recovery and disaster recovery planning (DRP)	5.1, 5.2
5.5.2	Know the purpose of the FCA Business Continuity Management Practice Guide	5.3
5.5.3	Know FCA requirements for business continuity (SYSC 13.8) and incident response	5
5.6	**Password Security** On completion, the candidate should:	
5.6.1	Understand the importance and impact of password security: • the role of hashing and the 'reversing' of hashes using online resources • the hacking of password databases • the ease of finding stolen credentials online • dictionary attacks on hashed password tables • longer hashes, Salts, Peppers and encryption; protecting the password management process more effectively • Password Managers and other authentication options that replace or augment password-based solutions	6
5.7	**Encryption** On completion, the candidate should:	
5.7.1	Know the fundamentals of encryption: • substitution and transposition explained; • a short history of encryption, from the Caesar Code to RSA; • symmetric encryption explained; • prime numbers, semi-primes, the factorisation challenge and asymmetric encryption demystified; • ephemeral keys and modern encrypted messaging apps	7

Syllabus Unit/ Element		Chapter/ Section
Element 6	**Trends in Economic Crime Compliance**	
6.1	**Emerging Threats** On completion, the candidate should:	
6.1.1	Know the key sources of information on emerging vulnerabilities	1
6.1.2	Know the concept of the internet of things (IOT), the smart home and office, Mirai and related threats/solutions	1.1
6.1.3	Understand the evolution and use of big data analytics	1.1.3
6.1.4	Know the specific threats relating to cryptocurrencies such as Bitcoin	1.2
6.1.5	Know the specific threats relating to unregulated payment models	1.2
6.1.6	Know the specific threats relating to mobile payment devices	1.3
6.1.7	Know the specific threats relating to cloud computing	1.4
6.1.8	Know the specific risks relating to co-location	1.5
6.1.9	Know the purpose and limitations of risk avoidance through cybercrime insurance policies	1.6
6.2	**Ethical issues** On completion, the candidate should:	
6.2.1	Understand how the use of big data relates to FCA financial promotion rules and treating customers fairly (TCF): • consent	2.1, 2.2, 2.2.1
6.2.2	Understand the concept of ethical search engine optimisation	2.4
6.2.3	Know the concept of a fair usage policy	2.5
6.2.4	Know the concept of good online practice	2.6
6.2.5	Understand the balance between employee monitoring and employee privacy: • the implications of Californian Law A.B. 1844	2.3

Examination Specification

Each examination paper is constructed from a specification that determines the weightings that will be given to each element. The specification is given below.

It is important to note that the numbers quoted may vary slightly from examination to examination as there is some flexibility to ensure that each examination has a consistent level of difficulty. However, the number of questions tested in each element should not change by more than plus or minus 2.

Element Number	Element	Questions
1	The Background and Nature of Information Security and Cybercrime	12
2	The Legislative Environment	8
3	The Public-Private Interface	5
4	Cybercrime and the Financial Services Industry	7
5	Combating Cybercrime	10
6	Trends in Economic Crime Compliance	8
	Total	**50**

CISI Associate (ACSI) Membership can work for you...

Studying for a CISI qualification is hard work and we're sure you're putting in plenty of hours, but don't lose sight of your goal!

This is just the first step in your career; there is much more to achieve!

The securities and investments sector attracts ambitious and driven individuals. You're probably one yourself and that's great, but on the other hand you're almost certainly surrounded by lots of other people with similar ambitions.

So how can you stay one step ahead during these uncertain times?

Entry Criteria:

Pass in either:

- Investment Operations Certificate (IOC), IFQ, ICWIM, Capital Markets in, eg, Securities, Derivatives, Advanced Certificates; or
- one CISI Diploma/Masters in Wealth Management paper

Joining Fee: £25 or free if applying via prefilled application form   **Annual Subscription (pro rata):** £125

Using your new CISI qualification* to become an Associate (ACSI) member of the Chartered Institute for Securities & Investment could well be the next important career move you make this year, and help you maintain your competence.

Join our global network of over 40,000 financial services professionals and start enjoying both the professional and personal benefits that CISI membership offers. Once you become a member you can use the prestigious ACSI designation after your name and even work towards becoming personally chartered.

* ie, Investment Operations Certificate (IOC), IFQ, ICWIM, Capital Markets

Benefits in Summary...

- Use of the CISI CPD Scheme
- Unlimited free CPD seminars, webcasts, podcasts and online training tools
- Highly recognised designatory letters
- Unlimited free attendance at CISI Professional Forums
- CISI publications including *The Review* and *Change – The Regulatory Update*
- 20% discount on all CISI conferences and training courses
- Invitation to the CISI Annual Lecture
- Select benefits – our exclusive personal benefits portfolio

The ACSI designation will provide you with access to a range of member benefits, including Professional Refresher where there are currently over 100 modules available on subjects including Anti-Money Laundering, Information Security & Data Protection, Integrity & Ethics, and the UK Bribery Act. CISI TV is also available to members, allowing you to catch up on the latest CISI events, whilst earning valuable CPD.

Plus many other networking opportunities which could be invaluable for your career.

Revision Express

You've bought the workbook... now test your knowledge before your exam.

Revision Express is an engaging online study tool to be used in conjunction with most CISI workbooks.

Key Features of Revision Express:
- Examination-focused – the content of Revision Express covers the key points of the syllabus
- Questions throughout to reaffirm understanding of the subject
- Special end-of-module practice exam to reflect as closely as possible the standard you will experience in your exam (please note, however, they are not the CISI exam questions themselves)
- Extensive glossary of terms
- Useful associated website links
- Allows you to study whenever you like, and on any device

IMPORTANT: The questions contained in Revision Express products are designed as aids to revision, and should not be seen in any way as mock exams.

Price per Revision Express module: £35
Price when purchased with the corresponding CISI workbook: £105 (normal price: £116)

To purchase Revision Express:

call our Customer Support Centre on:
+44 20 7645 0777

or visit the CISI's online bookshop at:
cisi.org/bookshop

For more information on our elearning products, contact our Customer Support Centre on +44 20 7645 0777, or visit our website at cisi.org/elearning

Professional Refresher

Self-testing elearning modules to refresh your knowledge, meet regulatory and firm requirements, and earn CPD.

Professional Refresher is a training solution to help you remain up-to-date with industry developments, maintain regulatory compliance and demonstrate continuing learning.

This popular online learning tool allows self-administered refresher testing on a variety of topics, including the latest regulatory changes.

There are currently over 100 modules available which address UK and international issues. Modules are reviewed by practitioners frequently and new topics are added to the suite on a regular basis.

Benefits to firms:
- Learning and testing can form part of business T&C programme
- Learning and testing kept up-to-date and accurate by the CISI
- Relevant and useful – devised by industry practitioners
- Access to individual results available as part of management overview facility, 'Super User'
- Records of staff training can be produced for internal use and external audits
- Cost-effective – no additional charge for CISI members
- Available to non-members

Benefits to individuals:
- Comprehensive selection of topics across sectors
- Modules are regularly reviewed and updated by industry experts
- New topics added regularly
- Free for members
- Successfully passed modules are recorded in your CPD log as active learning
- Counts as structured learning for RDR purposes
- On completion of a module, a certificate can be printed out for your own records

The full suite of Professional Refresher modules is free to CISI members, or £250 for non-members. Modules are also available individually. To view a full list of Professional Refresher modules visit:

cisi.org/refresher

If you or your firm would like to find out more, contact our Client Relationship Management team:

+ 44 20 7645 0670
crm@cisi.org

For more information on our elearning products, contact our Customer Support Centre on +44 20 7645 0777, or visit our website at cisi.org/refresher

er

Professional Refresher

Top 5

SCORM COMPLIANT

Integrity & Ethics
- High-Level View
- Ethical Behaviour
- An Ethical Approach
- Compliance vs Ethics

Anti-Money Laundering
- Introduction to Money Laundering
- UK Legislation and Regulation
- Money Laundering Regulations 2017
- Proceeds of Crime Act 2002
- Terrorist Financing
- Suspicious Activity Reporting
- Money Laundering Reporting Officer
- Sanctions

General Data Protection Regulation (GDPR)
- Understanding the Terminology
- The Six Data Protection Principles
- Data Subject Rights
- Technical and Organisational Measures

Information Security and Data Protection
- Cyber-Security
- The Regulators

UK Bribery Act
- Background to the Act
- The Offences
- What the Offences Cover
- When Has an Offence Been Committed?
- The Defences Against Charges of Bribery
- The Penalties

Latest

Cryptocurrencies
- Bitcoin
- Altcoins
- Central Bank Digital Currency and Cryptofiat
- Trading Cryptocurrencies
- The Impact of Cryptocurrencies

Change Management
- Types of Change
- Change Theories
- The Complexities of Change
- Leading Change
- Key Skills and Competencies

Regulatory Update
- General Regulatory Changes
- Sector Changes

Common Reporting Standard (CRS)
- What is the CRS?
- Implementation and Compliance
- Practical Issues
- The Global Perspective

Cross-Border Investment Services
- The UK System
- Overseas Regulation
- Applicability
- Face-to-Face Meetings
- Distance Communications
- Brexit Implications
- Gifts and Entertainment
- Tax Evasion, Money Laundering, and Terrorist Financing

Operations

Best Execution
- What Is Best Execution?
- Achieving Best Execution
- Order Execution Policies
- Information to Clients & Client Consent
- Monitoring, the Rules, and Instructions
- Best Execution for Specific Types of Firms

Approved Persons Regime
- The Basis of the Regime
- Fitness and Propriety
- The Controlled Functions
- Principles for Approved Persons
- The Code of Practice for Approved Persons

Corporate Actions
- Corporate Structure and Finance
- Life Cycle of an Event
- Mandatory Events
- Voluntary Events

Wealth

Client Assets and Client Money
- Protecting Client Assets and Client Money
- Segregation and Holding
- Due Diligence of Custodians and Banks
- Reconciliations
- Records and Accounts
- CASS Oversight

Investment Principles and Risk
- Diversification
- Factfind and Risk Profiling
- Investment Management
- Modern Portfolio Theory and Investing Styles
- Direct and Indirect Investments
- Socially Responsible Investment
- Collective Investments
- Investment Trusts
- Dealing in Debt Securities and Equities

Banking Standards
- Introduction and Background
- Strengthening Individual Accountability
- Reforming Corporate Governance
- Securing Better Outcomes for Consumers
- Enhancing Financial Stability

Suitability of Client Investments
- Assessing Suitability
- Risk Profiling
- Establishing Risk Appetite
- Obtaining Customer Information
- Suitable Questions and Answers
- Making Suitable Investment Selections
- Guidance, Reports and Record Keeping

International

Foreign Account Tax Compliance Act (FATCA)
- Foreign Financial Institutions
- Due Diligence Requirements
- Reporting
- Compliance

MiFID II
- The Organisations Covered by MiFID II
- The Products Subject to MiFID II
- The Origins of MiFID II
- The Impact of MiFID II
- The Products Covered by MiFID II
- Cross-Border Business Under MiFID II

UCITS
- The Original UCITS Directive
- UCITS III
- UCITS IV
- Non-UCITS Funds
- Latest Developments

cisi.org/refresher

Feedback to the CISI

Have you found this workbook to be a valuable aid to your studies? We would like your views, so please email us at learningresources@cisi.org with any thoughts, ideas or comments.

Accredited Training Partners

Support for exam students studying for the Chartered Institute for Securities & Investment (CISI) qualifications is provided by several Accredited Training Partners (ATPs), including Fitch Learning and BPP. The CISI's ATPs offer a range of face-to-face training courses, distance learning programmes, their own learning resources and study packs which have been accredited by the CISI. The CISI works in close collaboration with its ATPs to ensure they are kept informed of changes to CISI exams so they can build them into their own courses and study packs.

CISI Workbook Specialists Wanted

Workbook Authors

Experienced freelance authors with finance experience, and who have published work in their area of specialism, are sought. Responsibilities include:

- Updating workbooks in line with new syllabuses and any industry developments
- Ensuring that the syllabus is fully covered

Workbook Reviewers

Individuals with a high-level knowledge of the subject area are sought. Responsibilities include:

- Highlighting any inconsistencies against the syllabus
- Assessing the author's interpretation of the workbook

Workbook Technical Reviewers

Technical reviewers to provide a detailed review of the workbook and bring the review comments to the panel. Responsibilities include:

- Cross-checking the workbook against the syllabus
- Ensuring sufficient coverage of each learning objective

Workbook Proofreaders

Proofreaders are needed to proof workbooks both grammatically and also in terms of the format and layout. Responsibilities include:

- Checking for spelling and grammar mistakes
- Checking for formatting inconsistencies

If you are interested in becoming a CISI external specialist call:
+44 20 7645 0609

or email:
externalspecialists@cisi.org

For bookings, orders, membership and general enquiries please contact our Customer Support Centre on +44 20 7645 0777, or visit our website at cisi.org